# Caborn-Welborn

# Caborn-Welborn
## Constructing a New Society after the Angel Chiefdom Collapse

DAVID POLLACK

THE UNIVERSITY OF ALABAMA PRESS

*Tuscaloosa*

Manufactured in the United States of America

*Typeface: AGaramond*

∞
The paper on which this book is printed meets the minimum requirements of American National Standard for Information Science–Permanence of Paper for Printed Library Materials, ANSI Z39.48–1984.

Library of Congress Cataloging-in-Publication Data

Pollack, David, 1951–
Caborn-Welborn : constructing a new society after the Angel Chiefdom Collapse / David Pollack.
p. cm.
Includes bibliographical references (p. ) and index.
ISBN 0-8173-1419-9 (cloth : alk. paper) — ISBN 0-8173-5126-4 (pbk. : alk. paper)
1. Mississippian culture—Ohio River Valley. 2. Mississippian culture—Wabash River Valley. 3. Mississippian pottery—Ohio River Valley. 4. Mississippian pottery—Wabash River Valley. 5. Chiefdoms—Ohio River Valley. 6. Chiefdoms—Wabash River Valley. 7. Excavations (Archaeology)—Ohio River Valley. 8. Excavations (Archaeology)—Wabash River Valley. 9. Ohio River Valley—Antiquities. 10. Wabash River Valley—Antiquities I. Title.
E99.M6815P68 2004
977′.01—dc22

2004000653

# Contents

# Illustrations

# Tables

# Acknowledgments

This book is a revised version of my dissertation, which was completed at the University of Kentucky in Lexington. I would like to thank my dissertation committee (Dr. Richard W. Jefferies, Dr. John Van Willigan, Dr. Kim A. McBride, and Dr. John Watkins) and the outside reader (Dr. Theda Perdue) for their instructive comments and constructive criticisms. I would especially like to thank my dissertation chair, Dr. Tom D. Dillehay, who always took the time to discuss my research, to provide constructive criticism, and to encourage me to examine my data critically and from a variety of perspectives. Over the years, Tom also has been a good friend.

This study was funded, in part, by a Dissertation Improvement Grant from the National Science Foundation. In addition, analysis of the Slack Farm, Caborn, and Hovey Lake ceramics was supported by a grant from the National Endowment for the Humanities. The support of both institutions is greatly appreciated. Ed Winkle of the Laboratory for Archaeological Research at the University of Kentucky deserves a word of thanks for administering both grants.

All successful research projects are dependant upon the active participation and involvement of many individuals, and this study is no exception. I was assisted in the field and laboratory by the following individuals: Dan Davis, Aaron Zibart, Eric Bushee, David McBride, William Lowthert, Don Miller, Chris Bergman, and Ken Duerksen. Dan Davis did most of the artifact illustrations, but John Dean drew the Campbell Punctate jar with 16 handles and the Miscellaneous Incised/Trailed jar (figs. 3.11 and 3.23). David McBride and Dave Fraley took the artifact photographs, and Jennifer Harr assisted on many of the illustrations.

David L. Morgan, director of the Kentucky Heritage Council, deserves a word of thanks for his continued support of my research and of Kentucky archaeology.

I would like to thank Dr. Brian Butler at Southern Illinois University at Carbondale for allowing me to examine their Caborn-Welborn collections and for providing me constructive feedback on my ideas concerning the nature of Caborn-Welborn sociopolitical organization and the late prehistory of the lower Ohio valley. Phil DiBlasi at the University of Louisville, Dr. Jack Schock at Western Kentucky University, Noel Justice at the Glenn A. Black

Laboratory of Archaeology at Indiana University, and Dr. Mary Lucas Powell, former director of the William S. Webb Museum of Anthropology at the University of Kentucky, also graciously made collections available for me to study. Collections also were made available for study by the Smithsonian Institution in Washington, D.C.

Mike Moore also deserves a word of thanks. Not only did he allow me to borrow some of his Caborn-Welborn materials, but Mike freely provided copies of his field notes and other information he had collected on Caborn-Welborn sites. Others who allowed me to examine collections are Charles Mulligan and William Eckman.

I would especially like to thank Cheryl Ann Munson of Indiana University, without whose assistance it would have been difficult to complete this study. Cheryl freely provided me with notes and records she had amassed on several Caborn-Welborn sites. She also made available recently collected materials from Ries-Hasting and collections from Murphy and Ashworth, which she had on loan from the Glenn A. Black Laboratory at Indiana University. Cheryl provided me laboratory space to analyze these materials and a place to spend the night. Most important, she was always willing to listen to my ideas, to discuss and critique them, and at times was willing to agree to disagree.

Over the years I have also benefitted from discussions with other friends and colleagues. Among them are Dr. Jack Rossen, Bill Sharp, the late Dr. Tom Sussenbach, Dr. George Milner, Dr. Wesley Cowan, Dr. Michael Hoffman, and the late Dr. Jimmy Griffin. I would also like to thank the outside reviewers, Dr. Marvin Smith and Dr. Kit Wesler, for their constructive comments and Judith Knight for assisting me in the process of seeing this manuscript transformed into a book.

I would like to thank my parents, Aileen and Sheldon Pollack, for instilling in me an openness to new ideas and a desire to learn more about the world around me. Finally, I would like to thank Gwynn for not only supporting my research endeavors and providing editorial assistance but for also being my best friend.

# Caborn-Welborn

# 1 Introduction

## RESPONSES TO CHIEFDOM COLLAPSE

Understanding how populations reconstruct social, political, and economic relationships after the collapse of a chiefdom has long been of interest to archaeologists (Anderson 1990; Barker and Pauketat 1992; Drennan and Uribe 1987; Earle 1991; Yoffee and Cowgill 1995). Research has shown that societies respond in a variety of ways to the demise of an elite class (Anderson 1990, 1994; Tainter 1988; Welch 1991) and the resulting changes in the social boundaries that serve to distinguish the elite from others (Eisenstadt 1995). Sometimes a society of similar complexity emerges, led by a different faction (Anderson 1990; Brumfiel 1994). Recognizing the important role internal factionalism plays within chiefly societies, archaeologists have referred to this process as the "cycling of political power" (Anderson 1994; Hally 1996). Cycling is often associated with the abandonment of an existing regional center and the establishment of a new center within the same territory. It does not, however, involve the total collapse of a regional chiefdom.

But under certain circumstances, a new elite does not replace the old, and when this happens, the chiefdom usually collapses completely, its center and associated settlements abandoned. In such cases, the regional population may disperse to smaller, more widely scattered settlements within the same general area (Butler 1991; Steponaitis 1991; Welch 1991) or relocate to another region (Anderson 1994; Bareis and Porter 1984; Butler 1991; Muller 1986). Although some characteristics of the earlier sociopolitical organization are probably retained as the social boundaries that distinguished the elite from others are redefined (Knight 1986, 1994), in both situations there is a tendency for political power to become decentralized and extraregional interaction to decline (Tainter 1988).

The creation of political alliances by the remnants of former chiefdoms, taking the form of a confederacy (Galloway 1994; Knight 1994; Swanton 1911, 1946), may represent still another response to the collapse of regional chiefdoms. Confederacies also represent a decentralization of power vis-à-vis former chiefdoms. However, confederacies differ in that under certain circumstances (i.e., in response to external threats), centralized power can return for short periods of time.

Regardless of the type of response, archaeologists have not always been able to find the physical manifestations of chiefdom collapse in the archaeological record. This is owing to the fact that dispersal of regional populations to smaller, widely scattered settlements can result in sites that have low archaeological visibility and are thus difficult to locate. Likewise, it is often difficult to trace population movements or migration in the archaeological record (Anthony 1990).

## THE "VACANT QUARTER"

Up until ca. A.D. 1400, diverse Mississippian polities, including Cahokia, Kincaid, Angel, and Wickliffe, inhabited much of the region in central North America drained by the lower Ohio, Green, the lower and middle Cumberland, lower Tennessee, and central Mississippi rivers. But after the late fourteenth/early fifteenth century, a decline in population density, extraregional interaction, and sociopolitical complexity throughout this region reflects the widespread collapse of these Mississippian polities (see Tainter 1988:193). This region has become known as the "Vacant Quarter" (Bareis and Porter 1984; Butler 1991; Cobb and Butler 2002; Lewis 1990; McNutt 1996; Milner 1990; Morse and Morse 1983; Muller 1986; Williams 1990) (Figure 1.1).

In most cases, researchers working in the Vacant Quarter have been unable to locate post–A.D. 1400 settlements and often refer to their respective regions as having been depopulated or abandoned (Muller 1986). Researchers have hypothesized that late Mississippian settlements throughout the Vacant Quarter likely were small and scattered and therefore are archaeologically difficult to identify (Butler 1991:273).

But every instance of Mississippian chiefdom collapse within the Vacant Quarter did not lead to a decline in population density, the dispersal of the regional population, or the abandonment of the region. Nor was collapse always associated with a decline in intersocietal interaction and access to nonlocal goods. A case in point: the cultural developments that occurred after the ca. A.D. 1400 collapse of the Angel chiefdom near the northern edge of the Vacant Quarter, in the vicinity of the mouths of the Green and Wabash rivers in southwestern Indiana, southeastern Illinois, and northwestern Kentucky during the Caborn-Welborn phase (A.D. 1400–1700) (Figure 1.1) (Green and Munson 1978; Muller 1986; Pollack 1998; Pollack and Munson 2003).

A catastrophic event (e.g., a sudden natural or human disaster) does not appear to have been the cause of the Angel chiefdom's collapse. More than likely, a combination of internal and external factors at work over an extended period of time, such as environmental degradation and the disruption of the local Mississippian prestige goods economy, contributed to its demise. Indeed,

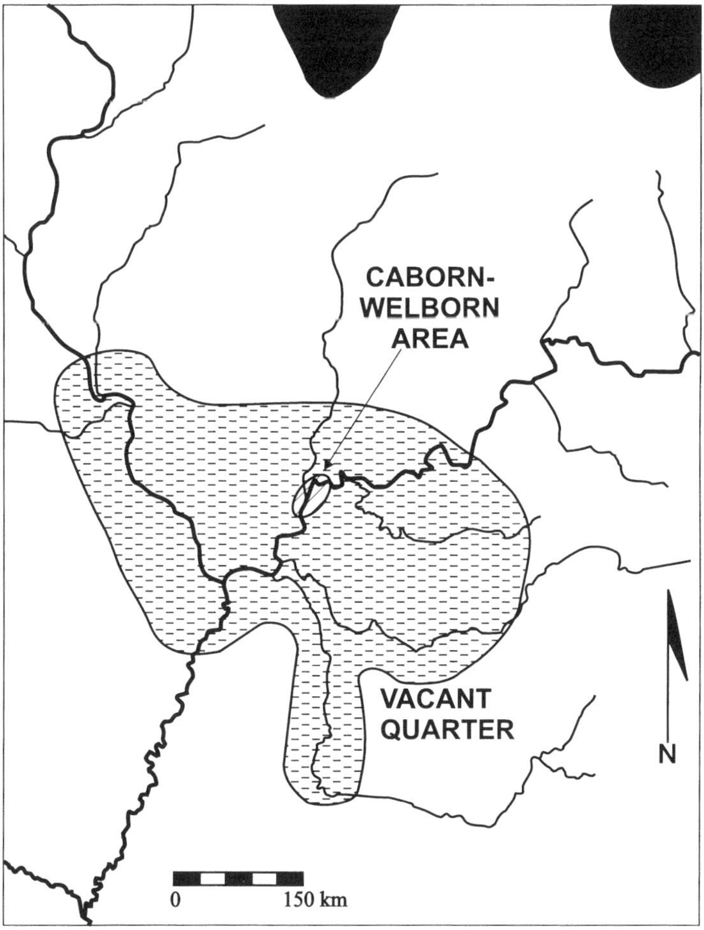


Figure 1.1. The Vacant Quarter (after Williams 1990:174).

the archaeological record in this region suggests that there may have been a period of overlap between the establishment of the first Caborn-Welborn villages and the total abandonment of Angel and its associated settlements (Hilgeman 2000; Pollack 1998).

Regardless of the causes, by ca. A.D. 1400, the power and prestige of the Angel elite had diminished to such an extent that the social and political hierarchy that had been in place for at least two hundred years was no longer able to sustain itself. But instead of abandoning the region or relocating to widely dispersed settlements, this Mississippian population established several small and large villages slightly downstream from Angel (Green and Munson 1978; Pollack and Munson 2003).

## CABORN-WELBORN: A CASE STUDY

While collapse often results in the dispersal of a regional population and a decline in intersocietal interaction, not all cultures respond in this manner. The archaeological visibility of the Caborn-Welborn population and its links to the former Angel chiefdom provide an opportunity to study one population's response to chiefdom collapse. What is of interest here is not the mechanics of collapse but how the Caborn-Welborn population reconstructed social, political, and economic relationships following the collapse of the Angel chiefdom and the demise of neighboring lower Ohio valley Mississippian polities.

The main data sets used to investigate this issue were site ceramic collections and site types. But before regional ceramic and site distribution patterns could be assessed for the information they could provide about the Caborn-Welborn population's social, political, and economic responses to Angel's collapse, a solid descriptive foundation for Caborn-Welborn ceramics had to be laid and an internal regional chronological sequence had to be developed.

Through the analysis of site ceramic assemblages, the salient characteristics of Caborn-Welborn ceramics were identified; ceramic types and attributes that reflected extraregional interaction were noted; and the continuities as well as differences relative to Angel phase ceramic assemblages were identified. Temporally diagnostic ceramic attributes or types, as well as other materials such as historic trade goods, were used to develop an internal Caborn-Welborn chronological sequence. With the temporal trends in Caborn-Welborn material culture identified, it was possible to assess whether observed intersite variation in the distribution of ceramic types and attributes represented chronological developments, intraregional cultural differences, or settlement function.

Ceramic data (as well as nonlocal goods and other artifacts, such as triangular endscrapers and Nodena projectile points) were used to identify and evaluate Caborn-Welborn participation in extraregional exchange and interaction networks. Examination of Caborn-Welborn site types focused on confirming the presence of a settlement hierarchy, identifying the spatial distribution and clustering of settlements and the location of cemeteries, and identifying intersite functional differences as reflected in site ceramic assemblages.

This research indicates that, while Caborn-Welborn social, political, and economic relationships were securely rooted in the traditions of the Angel chiefdom, there were differences that served to distinguish Caborn-Welborn sociopolitical organization from that of the Angel chiefdom. With the establishment of several small and large villages downstream from the Angel site, the Caborn-Welborn population constructed a new social and political order, one that combined elements of old and new.

Caborn-Welborn settlements were centered at the mouth of the Wabash River, 50 km downstream from the mouth of the Green River, which had been the center of the Angel chiefdom (Green 1977; Green and Munson 1978; Pollack and Munson 2003). As had earlier Angel households, Caborn-Welborn households continued to farm the fertile river bottoms, hunt in the uplands, and fish the rich backwater lakes and sloughs. Many continued to reside in large communities, although the regional settlement distribution shrank from a 120 km long area along the Ohio River (the greatest extent of Angel phase settlements) to a 60 km long area (Figure 1.2). To date, more than 80 sites with Caborn-Welborn components have been documented within this area. Of these, ceramics were examined from 50 sites during this research, with most of the intersite comparisons focusing on the 22 site assemblages that contained 30 or more analyzable specimens (rims, decorated sherds, and appendages).

By A.D. 1450, cultural or ethnic differences that distinguished those living upstream from the mouth of the Wabash River from those living downstream from it may have been present in the Caborn-Welborn region. Intraregional variation in Caborn-Welborn Decorated shoulder designs, location of cemeteries, and the types of vessels interred with the dead suggest that although the Caborn-Welborn population was primarily comprised of the descendants of the Angel chiefdom, it also included households that moved to the region after the collapse of polities located farther down the Ohio River.

Caborn-Welborn political organization retained some aspects of Angel's social and political hierarchy. A concentration of settlements within a restricted geographic area and the existence of a settlement hierarchy (with settlements ranging from farmsteads to large villages) point to the presence of Caborn-Welborn leaders who had some degree of power and influence beyond their own village (see Spencer 1993, 1994). It also points to the continuation of some form of formalized social inequality within Caborn-Welborn society. Aspiring Caborn-Welborn elites may have competed with each other to regain control of the entire Caborn-Welborn region, with the goal of centralizing power within one community and reestablishing a regional administrative center. As will be discussed in later chapters, Slack Farm, based on its size and central location, as well as aspects of its material culture, at times may have served some of the functions of a regional center, but there is no evidence to suggest that aspiring Slack Farm elites were ever able to hold onto this power for an extended period of time. While Caborn-Welborn sociopolitical organization does not appear to have been as centralized as that of the earlier

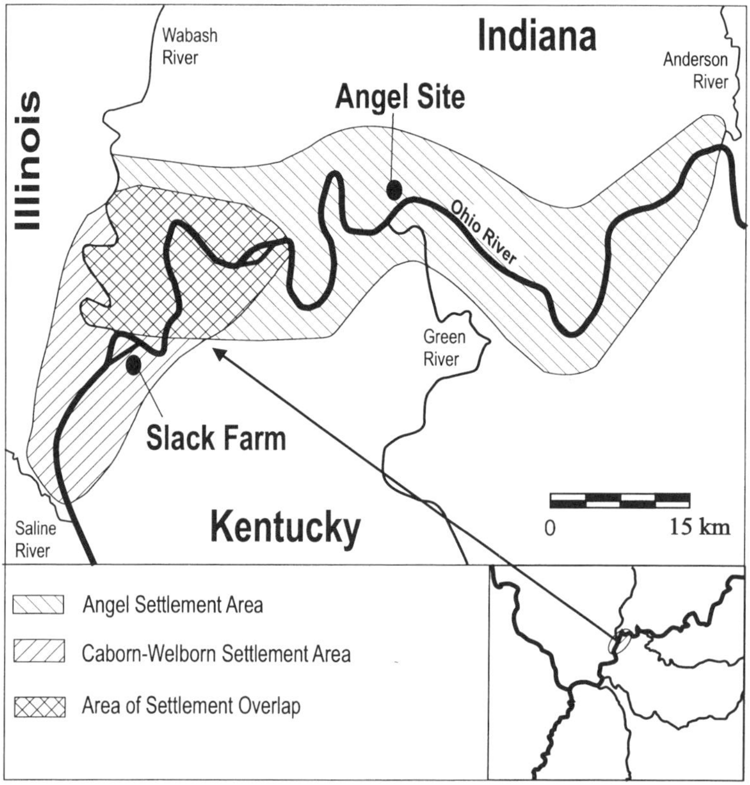


Figure 1.2. Spatial relationship between the Caborn-Welborn region and the Angel region.

Angel chiefdom, since no clearly identifiable regional administrative mound center was ever established and sustained, it does appear to have been more centralized than that of contemporary tribal societies, such as Fort Ancient groups to the east (Pollack and Henderson 1992a) and Oneota groups to the north (Green 1995).

If Caborn-Welborn sociopolitical organization exhibited a greater degree of political centralization than contemporary tribal societies but less centralization than a chiefdom, and considering the existence of cultural or ethnic differences within the region, then Caborn-Welborn may be viewed best as a small riverine confederacy, albeit one that was smaller in scale than the Southeastern confederacies of the Contact period (Galloway 1994; Knight 1994; Swanton 1911, 1946). Some researchers consider that the Creek and Choctaw confederacies developed from segments of former Mississippian chiefdoms that banded together for a common good (Galloway 1994; Knight 1994). These confederacies have been described as having a "scaled hierarchy of potentially impermanent aggregations that developed on a contingent basis in response to crises of greater or lesser importance" (Knight 1994:389). The extent to which confederacies existed prehistorically is not presently known: they may represent a unique response to the external threats imposed by European exploration and settlement of the Southeast. But it is also possible that these kinds of intersocietal alliances predate the Historic period (Blitz 1999; Muller 1997).

If Caborn-Welborn sociopolitical organization did resemble that of a confederacy, it may have been organized somewhat differently than the confederacies of the Contact period. The restricted distribution of Caborn-Welborn sites (in a region about 60 km long) suggests that the various segments of the Caborn-Welborn population enjoyed a greater level of social interaction or integration than may have been the case for the groups that comprised the Historic period confederacies of the Eastern Woodlands. In addition, there is little in the way of archaeological evidence to suggest that Caborn-Welborn settlement patterns represent a response to external threats.

And finally, in terms of Caborn-Welborn economic organization, participation in intersocietal exchange and interaction networks appears to have increased rather than decreased following Angel's collapse (Green and Munson 1978). Aspiring Caborn-Welborn elite maintained old economic ties with Mississippian groups situated to the south of the Ohio valley but also established new economic relationships with Oneota groups living to the north of the Ohio valley (Figure 1.3). This is represented by the presence of nonlocal goods, such as catlinite pipes and marine shell ornaments, and by ceramic types and attributes that reflect extraregional interaction. A reorientation and expansion of extraregional exchange relationships following the widespread collapse of Mississippian chiefdoms throughout the lower Ohio and upper central Mississippi valleys points to increased participation of tribal societies in the Mississippian prestige goods economy.

Through the description of the salient characteristics of Caborn-Welborn ceramics and site types and an examination of their spatial distribution, this study identified intraregional linkages among Caborn-Welborn sites and within subareas of the Caborn-Welborn region. The ceramic type and attribute data, as well as information about the kinds of nonlocal goods recovered from these sites, document the interaction of the Caborn-Welborn population with groups outside the lower Ohio valley. Together, these intra- and extraregional linkages reflect aspects of Caborn-Welborn social, political, and economic relationships, permitting observations to be made concerning the structure of Caborn-Welborn sociopolitical organization, and provide insights into how one population responded to the collapse of a Mississippian chiefdom. How regional Mississippian populations responded to the demise of the elite reflects their unique culture histories as well as some of the variation in

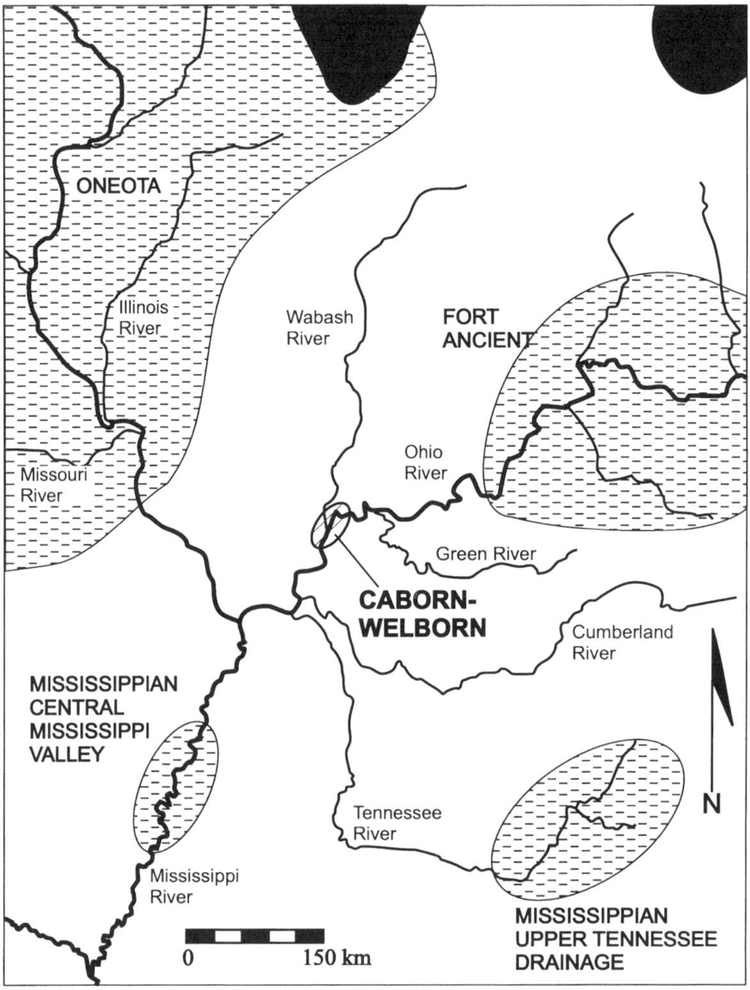


Figure 1.3. Caborn-Welborn and its nearest neighbors ca. A.D. 1500.

the social, economic, and political organization of Mississippian chiefdoms situated throughout the Midwest and Southeast.

The remainder of this book is organized as follows. In chapter 2, basic descriptive information is presented about the Angel and Caborn-Welborn phases in order to provide a context within which to understand what may have occurred following the collapse of the Angel chiefdom. In particular, the sociopolitical organization of the Angel chiefdom is described, and the factors that may have contributed to its collapse and the abandonment of the Angel site and associated farmsteads, hamlets, and small villages are discussed. This is followed by an overview of previous Caborn-Welborn research and Caborn-Welborn subsistence practices.

Ceramic data served as the foundation for much of this research, yet no succinct description of Caborn-Welborn ceramic assemblages was available when this study was initiated. Therefore, chapter 3 presents a description of the types of ceramics found in the Caborn-Welborn region, including information on decoration, rim form, vessel form, and appendages.

In chapter 4, the types of sites (farmsteads, hamlets, small villages, large villages, and blufftop cemeteries) comprising the Caborn-Welborn settlement system are described. Selected sites are discussed for each site type, with information presented on site size, artifact distributional patterns, the history of past research, the nature of intact subsurface deposits, and the presence or absence of cemeteries and a plaza/courtyard at these sites. This chapter concludes with an examination of the spatial distribution of sites within the Caborn-Welborn region.

Angel and Caborn-Welborn ceramics are compared in chapter 5 in order to illustrate the continuities, as well as the differences, in late Angel and early Caborn-Welborn ceramic assemblages. Also, an internal Caborn-Welborn chronology is proposed, based on diachronic trends in ceramic rim form, appendages, and decoration, consisting of early (A.D. 1400–1450), middle (A.D. 1450–1600), and late (A.D. 1600–1700) subdivisions.

Chapter 6 presents intersite ceramic comparisons. Spatial variation in the distribution of Caborn-Welborn ceramic types and attributes is identified, and the composition of ceramic vessel assemblages found at the four Caborn-Welborn habitation site types is compared and contrasted.

With Caborn-Welborn temporal trends identified, it was possible to investigate how the Caborn-Welborn population reconstructed social, political, and economic relationships following the collapse of the Angel chiefdom. The variation in the distribution of some ceramic types and attributes did not represent change over time. These intraregional patterns complement regional differences in cemetery location and types of vessels interred with the dead. Together these patterns point to cultural differences within the Caborn-Welborn region. Regional ceramic patterns also provide information concerning which settlements, by virtue of their location within the Caborn-Welborn region and their function, had more extraregional interaction than others.

Variation in the composition of vessel assemblages associated with the different settlement types suggests that village residents participated in more activities and rituals involved in the preparation, serving, and consumption of food (and, perhaps, the entertaining of guests) than did those living at hamlets and farmsteads. These differences point to linkages between large and small villages and nearby hamlets and farmsteads and identify the dynamics of the Caborn-Welborn settlement hierarchy.

Chapter 7 discusses and interprets the results of this research and considers how the Caborn-Welborn population responded socially, politically, and economically to the collapse of the Angel chiefdom. The first part of this chapter contains an overview of the internal chronology for the Caborn-Welborn phase. This is followed by the identification of earlier Mississippian and contemporary Oneota motifs that were used, and perhaps reinterpreted, by Caborn-Welborn potters. Next, Caborn-Welborn participation in post–A.D. 1400 long-distance exchange networks is examined, as is the role participation in these networks played in sustaining Caborn-Welborn leaders. This is followed by a discussion of why Caborn-Welborn should not be considered a chiefdom, even though it retained some aspects of chiefdom sociopolitical organization. Chapter 7 concludes with a consideration of Caborn-Welborn sociopolitical organization as a small riverine confederacy.

# 2 Pre–A.D. 1400 Mississippian Regional Centers, Angel's Collapse, and Caborn-Welborn Developments in the Lower Ohio River Valley

Like other Mississippian societies in the lower Ohio River valley, and in fact throughout the Midwest and Southeast in general, the Angel chiefdom can be characterized as a cluster of settlements inhabited by a population that was linked socially, politically, and economically and that shared a common ideology (Smith 1978). The Angel site was the center of the Angel chiefdom. It is distinguished from other Angel settlements by virtue of its size and the presence of monumental architecture in the form of numerous platform mounds and stockades, extensive residential areas, a plaza, and large cemeteries (Black 1967; Green and Munson 1978; Hilgeman 2000; Muller 1986). While similar types of locally made objects were used throughout the Angel chiefdom, items made from nonlocal materials, such as Dover and Mill Creek chert and copper or marine shell objects, were used somewhat more frequently at Angel than at nearby farmsteads, hamlets, and small villages (Munson 1983).

Sites like Angel are usually referred to as regional administrative centers or towns. They were home to an elite class, who usually lived on or near a platform mound. The Angel elite would have had some measure of control and influence over households living at the Angel site, as well as those residing in the surrounding countryside. They also would have interacted with elites of neighboring chiefdoms.

The widespread collapse of lower Ohio valley Mississippian polities in the late fourteenth/early fifteenth century included the Angel chiefdom. Along with the Angel site, its associated farmsteads, hamlets, and small villages were abandoned. This was followed by a reorganization of people on the cultural and natural landscape, as social, political, and economic boundaries were redefined during the Caborn-Welborn phase. Researchers have suggested (Munson 2000; Pollack 1998; Pollack and Munson 2003) that the former Angel population relocated slightly downstream in the vicinity of the mouth of the Wabash River after Angel's collapse (Figure 1.2).

In order to begin to understand how the Caborn-Welborn population reconstructed social, political, and economic relationships in the aftermath of the collapse of the Angel chiefdom, it is important to understand how Angel's social, political, and economic institutions were organized and what factors may have contributed to its collapse. These institutions would have provided the foundation, as well as the point of departure, for the Caborn-Welborn population's response to the collapse of the Angel chiefdom. Therefore, the purpose of this chapter is to provide a context within which to consider the nature of the continuities and changes that define Caborn-Welborn vis-à-vis Angel. Pre–A.D. 1400 Mississippian developments in the lower Ohio valley are described first. The sociopolitical organization of the Angel chiefdom is outlined, and the factors that may have contributed to its collapse and the abandonment of the Angel site and its associated farmsteads, hamlets, and small villages are discussed. This is followed by an overview of the Caborn-Welborn phase: its temporal and spatial boundaries, Angel to Caborn-Welborn continuities and differences, and research carried out in the region to date.

## ANGEL AND OTHER LOWER OHIO VALLEY MISSISSIPPIAN REGIONAL CENTERS BEFORE A.D. 1400

In the lower Ohio River valley, pre–A.D. 1400 Mississippian sites are found from the Falls of the Ohio at Louisville, Kentucky, to the confluence of the Ohio and Mississippi rivers. Among the regional centers documented in the lower Ohio valley, Kincaid in southern Illinois (Cole et al. 1951; Muller 1986) and Angel in southwestern Indiana (Black 1967) (Figure 2.1) are distinguished by their size (both are large sites) from several smaller regional centers, such as Tolu, Jonathan Creek, and Tinsley Hill, and by the number of mounds (both contained numerous platform mounds).

The Kincaid site consisted of 19 mounds and several small residential areas encompassing 6 ha, all of which were enclosed by a palisade. Farmsteads and hamlets associated with the Kincaid polity were located primarily on floodplain levees throughout the Black Bottom of southern Illinois and in the vicinity of the Kincaid site. Nearby clusters of hamlets and associated stone box cemeteries have been interpreted as representing dispersed villages (Muller 1978, 1986).

Angel covered more than 40 ha and consisted of 13 mounds, extensive residential areas, associated cemeteries, and stockades (Black 1967). Most of the Angel population appears to have lived at or in close proximity to the Angel site. The remainder lived at farmsteads, hamlets, and small villages on floodplain levees, terraces, and bluff margins adjacent to the Ohio River within a 120 km long area extending from the mouth of the Anderson River in Indiana to the mouth of the Wabash River in Illinois (Figure 1.1) (Green 1977;

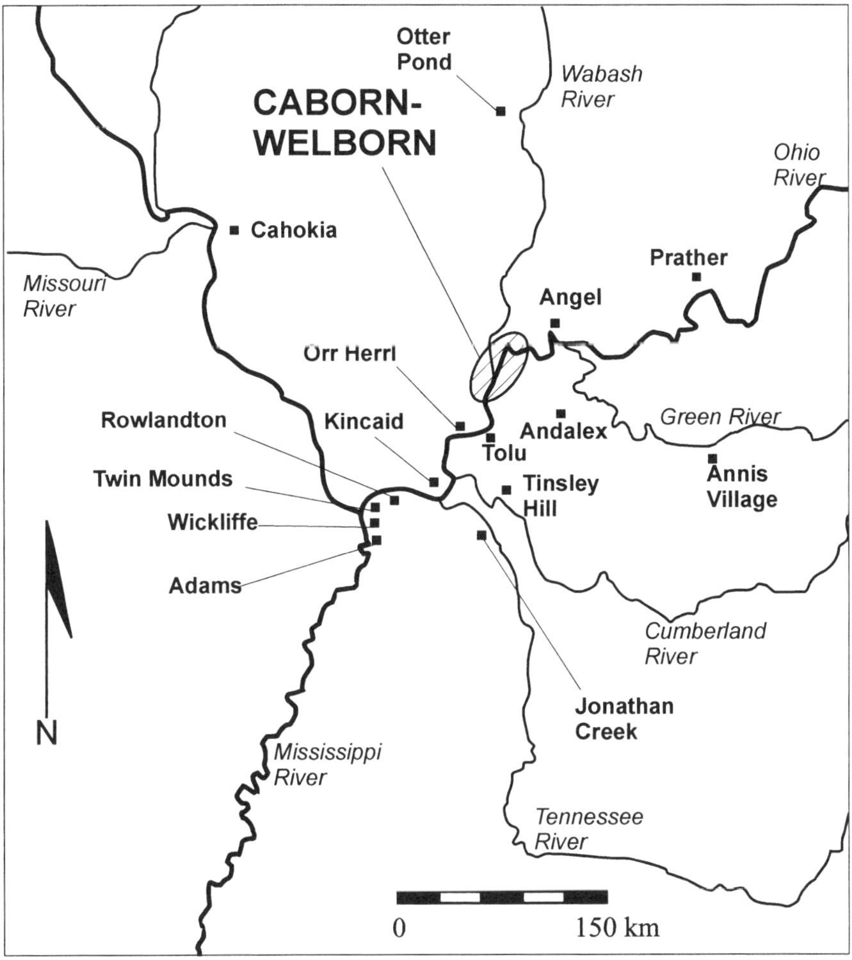


Figure 2.1. Location of pre–A.D. 1400 Mississippian regional centers relative to the Caborn-Welborn region.

Green and Munson 1978; Munson 1983). The presence of a large number of burials (n = 310) at Angel (Schurr 1992) and the absence of burials at small villages, such as Southwind (Munson 1994), suggest that most members of Angel society were interred at the Angel site (Pollack and Munson 2003).

Of the few Mississippian sites that have been recorded east of the Angel site, the best known is the poorly documented Prather site, which is situated in the vicinity of Louisville and is reported to have three mounds (Griffin 1978:551; Guernsey 1939). The closest Mississippian center to the north of Angel, situated along the Wabash River, is Otter Pond in Illinois, which may have had as many as 12 platform mounds (Muller 1986:248), while the closest centers to the south along the Green River in Kentucky are single-mound centers, such as Annis Village (Lewis 1990) and Andalex Village (Niquette 1991).

Two small mound centers have been identified in the region located midway between Angel and Kincaid: Tolu (Webb and Funkhouser 1931), with three mounds, and Orr Herrl, with one mound (Butler et al. 1979). The Jonathan Creek site (Loughridge 1883; Schroeder 2003; Webb 1952), with its seven mounds and extensive residential areas (over 70 structures were identified), and Tinsley Hill (Clay 1963a, 1963b, 1997; Lane 1993; Schwartz 1961), which consists of a village, cemetery, and platform mound, are located to the south of Kincaid along the lower Tennessee and Cumberland rivers, respectively. Rowlandton, which had at least one mound, and Twin Mounds, which had two mounds, are located along the Ohio River downstream from Kincaid (Kreisa 1988, 1995).

Muller (1986:187, 206) notes that some of the smaller mound centers located near Kincaid were related in some manner to this large regional center, but he avoids tackling the issue of how they may have been linked or how they may have interacted with one another in the lower Ohio valley region. Kreisa (1995:173) has argued that mound centers such as Tolu, Twin Mounds, and Rowlandton, which date from A.D. 1200–1400, represent an expansion of the Kincaid chiefdom during the thirteenth century, rather than the in situ development of smaller regional polities. He bases his interpretation on the absence of earlier Mississippian components at these sites and similarities in material culture (Kreisa 1990, 1995:173). Unfortunately, Kreisa's evidence for the lack of early Mississippian occupation in this portion of the Ohio River valley is derived from very limited archaeological data. While the sites that he examined lack early Mississippian components, the absence of such a component at a particular site cannot be equated with the lack of habitation in an entire portion of the valley, unless it can be shown that other sites in the region also lack early Mississippian components.

The abandonment of the lower Ohio valley and the collapse of the region's Mississippian chiefdoms may have begun sometime in the fourteenth century, with Kincaid's decline as an important regional center after around A.D. 1300. But Kincaid's decline and eventual abandonment may not have been abrupt and could have taken place over several decades (Butler and Cobb 1996:12). Chiefdoms along the Ohio River downstream from the mouth of the Saline River, as well as other small polities, may have emerged (or reemerged). The timing of this cycling of chiefdoms within the lower Ohio valley has yet to be worked out. Most of the small mound centers mentioned by Kreisa appear to have been occupied when the influence of the Kincaid chiefdom was on the decline (Butler and Cobb 1996). As such, these centers may not have been subordinate to Kincaid and may have enjoyed local autonomy (Butler and Cobb 1996:9).

Irrespective of these polities' relationship to Kincaid or to the other still-functioning regional polities, by A.D. 1400 or 1450 at the latest, all of the Mississippian chiefdoms in the lower Ohio River valley had collapsed (Figure 2.1). Their collapse led to the abandonment of the regional mound centers and their associated villages, hamlets, and farmsteads.

With the exception of the Caborn-Welborn region, evidence of post–A.D. 1450 Mississippian settlements is lacking throughout the lower Ohio valley and much of the upper-central Mississippi valley (hence the Vacant Quarter; see Cobb and Butler 2002; Muller 1986; Williams 1990) (Figure 1.2). It is not currently known what happened to the other Mississippian populations of the lower Ohio and upper-central Mississippi valleys, but scholars presume that they relocated to other regions or moved to more dispersed settlements (Matternas 1995).

## ANGEL SOCIOPOLITICAL ORGANIZATION

At the top of the Angel settlement hierarchy was the Angel site. This large regional administrative center was located east of Evansville, Indiana, and slightly downstream from the mouth of the Green River. Occupied for most, if not all, of the Angel phase (A.D. 1000–1400), the site was the focus of social, political, and economic life for the Angel population. Calibrated radiocarbon dates from the Angel phase site have midpoints that range from the mid-twelfth to the early-fifteenth century (table 2.1). These dates yield a calibrated mean date of A.D. 1300(1309,1355,1384)1400.

The bulk of the Angel population appears to have lived at or in close proximity to the Angel site, with the remainder living at farmsteads, hamlets, and small villages. None of the smaller villages contained platform mounds or cemeteries, but at the Southwind site (Munson 1994), houses were organized around a central plaza and the village was enclosed by a stockade. A large number of burials (n = 310) have been documented at Angel (Schurr 1992). This, coupled with the absence of burials or cemeteries at associated farmsteads, hamlets, and villages, suggests that Angel served as the primary burial locale for the whole chiefdom.

The Angel polity appears to have been a nucleated, simple (two-tier) chiefdom (Hilgeman 1992; Schurr 1992). Nucleated simple chiefdoms are characterized by a concentration of population at a regional center (Blitz 1993a), with the remainder living at smaller nearby settlements. In general, simple chiefdoms exhibit only one level of political hierarchy above the local community, a system of graduated ranking, and a population in the low thou-

Table 2.1. Radiocarbon Dates from Angel and Caborn-Welborn Phase Sites.

| Site Sample No. | Age BP | Calibrated date | Material |
|---|---|---|---|
| **Angel Phase**[a] | | | |
| Angel | | | |
| Beta-39235 | 950±80* | 970(1041,1150)1270 | Wood |
| Beta-39232 | 840±80* | 1020(1222)1300 | Wood |
| M-7 | 760±100 | 1040(1280)1405 | Wood |
| Beta-39234 | 750±80 | 1160(1282)1400 | Wood |
| DIC-2357 | 680±50 | 1270(1298)1400 | Wood |
| Beta-44768 | 660±60 | 1270(1302)1410 | Wood |
| Beta-44769 | 640±60 | 1280(1307,1360,1379)1420 | Wood |
| DIC-2358 | 630±45 | 1290(1310,1353,1385)1410 | Wood |
| Beta-39233 | 590±60 | 1290(1398)1440 | Wood |
| M-5 | 580±100 | 1270(1400)1483 | Wood |
| Beta-44771 | 570±50* | 1300(1403)1440 | Wood |
| Beta-44770 | 530±50 | 1310(1415)1450 | Wood |
| M-4 | 530±100 | 1280(1415)1630 | Wood |
| DIC-1024 | 510±50/40 | 1320(1426)1470 | Wood |
| *Average* | *632±17* | *1300(1309,1355,1384)1400* | |
| Ellerbush | | | |
| DIC-238 | 900±50/60 | 1020(1165)1280 | Wood |
| Southwind | | | |
| UGa-4715 | 805±125 | 890(1168)1390 | Corn |
| Stephan-Steinkamp | | | |
| Beta-22087 | 670±90 | 1220(1300)1430 | Wood |
| Beta-22088 | 640±100 | 1220(1307,1360,1379)1450 | Wood |
| **Caborn-Welborn Phase** | | | |
| Slack Farm[c] | | | |
| ISGS-2849 | 640±70* | 1270(1307,1360,1379)1430 | Corn |
| Beta-62688 | 630±60* | 1280(1310,1353,1385)1430 | Wood |
| Beta-62695 | 600±50* | 1290(1328,1333,1395)1430 | Wood |
| ISGS-2851 | 570±70* | 1290(1403)1450 | Corn |
| Beta-62689 | 570±50* | 1300(1403)1440 | Corn |
| Beta-62690 | 550±50* | 1300(1408)1440 | Corn |
| ISGS-2850 | 470±70* | 1320(1438)1630 | Corn |
| Beta-62694 | 420±50* | 1420(1454)1640 | Corn |
| ISGS-2853 | 390±70* | 1410(1478)1650 | Corn |
| *Average* | *541±19* | *1400(1410)1430* | |

Table 2.1. *Continued*

| Site Sample No. | Age BP | Calibrated date | Material |
|---|---|---|---|
| <u>Hovey Lake</u> | | | |
| Beta-140948[e] | 650±50* | 1280(1305,1367,1373)1410 | Corn |
| ISGS-2852[f] | 560±70* | 1290(1405)1460 | Corn |
| Beta 119392[b] | 540±50* | 1310(1410)1450 | Soot |
| Beta 102580[b] | 550±40* | 1310(1410)1440 | Wood |
| DIC-2360[b] | 250±60 | 1490(1657)1950 | Wood |
| <u>Caborn</u> | | | |
| Beta-39278[c] | 580±40* | 1310(1330,1347,1393)1411 | Nut |
| Beta-38381[c] | 570±50* | 1300(1403)1440 | Wood |
| ISGS-2851[e] | 400±70* | 1410(1473)1650 | Grass |
| Beta-38382[c] | 380±50* | 1440(1483)1650 | Wood |
| <u>Leonard</u> | | | |
| RL-82[d] | 460±125 | 1290(1441)1950 | Wood? |
| RL-83[d] | 345±190 | 1287(1518,1580,1624)1955 | Wood? |
| <u>Murphy</u> | | | |
| Beta-119795[e] | 650±40* | 1290(1305,1367,1373)1400 | Corn |
| Beta-119796[e] | 640±40* | 1290(1307,1360,1379)1410 | Corn |
| Beta-141110[e] | 600±30* | 1300(1325,1345,1395)1410 | Soot |
| Beta-119391[e] | 470±40* | 1410(1438)1480 | Corn |
| Beta-119794[e] | 340±40* | 1450(1520,1569,1627)1650 | Soot |
| <u>Bone Bank</u> | | | |
| Beta-140947a[e] | 650±40* | 1290(1305,1367,1373)1400 | Corn |
| Beta-140947b[e] | 640±30* | 1290(1307,1360,1379)1400 | Corn |
| Beta-140950[e] | 540±40* | 1310(1410)1440 | Corn |

Calibrated for 2 Sigma from CALIB computer program following Stuiver and Pearson 1993.
* Corrected for isotopic fractionation C-12/C-13.
[a] *Angel phase dates:*
Hilgeman 1992 and Munson 1994 (only acceptable dates presented).
*Caborn-Welborn phase dates:*
[b] Munson 1997
[c] Munson and Jones 1991
[d] Green and Munson 1978
[e] Munson 2000; Pollack and Munson 1998a

sands (Blitz 1993a; Earle 1991; Johnson and Earle 1987; Steponaitis 1978, 1991; Wright 1984). They are represented archaeologically by an administrative center with one or more platform mounds and by associated farmsteads, hamlets, and villages.

Considered in a different way, the Angel polity also can be viewed as a group-oriented chiefdom (Feinman 1995:264; Renfrew 1974:74–79) or one in which the elite employed a corporate strategy to maintain their positions within Angel society (Blanton et al. 1996; King 2003). At the Angel site, there is little evidence of differential access to personal wealth (Kellar 1967). Grave goods, which primarily consisted of chipped stone tools, bone awls, undecorated pottery vessels, pottery ear plugs, and bone hairpins, were found with slightly less than 10 percent of the Angel site burials. Objects manufactured from nonlocal materials interred with the dead included conch shell columella, shell beads, pendants and gorgets, a sheet-copper crescent, other copper artifacts, and galena cubes (Kellar 1967; Schurr 1992:307). Within Angel society, greater importance appears to have been placed on the elite's ability to organize communal activities and group rituals that served to link the polity's various settlements than on individual displays of wealth. Monumental public architecture, however, is very evident at Angel. It takes the form of platform mounds and stockades (Black 1967).

According to Hilgeman (1992, 2000) the most extensive and intensive occupation of the Angel site occurred during the fourteenth century (Angel 3: A.D. 1325–1450). As households were attracted to this regional center, one would expect that the elite's status would have been enhanced. However, Clay (1997) has suggested that by Angel 3, the power and prestige of the Angel elite had actually declined to such a point that they had little influence beyond their own community. As evidence for this decline, he argues that the Angel 3 occupation at the Angel site postdated the construction of new platform mounds, although he does acknowledge that some of the existing mounds continued to be added to and maintained during this time. If the construction of platform mounds is associated with the rise to prominence of elites (Hally 1996), then a period of new mound construction within a regional center, such as Angel, could reflect changes in elite status or ongoing elite competition (Anderson 1990). On the other hand, a period characterized by a lack of new mound construction but having continued additions to existing mounds could reflect political stability, as a ruling elite solidified and maintained its position within society (Hally 1996). Therefore, an absence of new mound construction at Angel, coupled with the maintenance of existing mounds, does not necessarily point to a decline in the prestige of the elite as suggested by Clay (1997). Rather it reflects the stability of the ruling Angel elite.

Based on the evidence at hand, Angel is probably best viewed as a nucleated, simple (two-tier) or group-oriented chiefdom that shows evidence of elite competition in the form of numerous platform mounds (Feinman 1995:264; Hilgeman 1992, 2000; Renfrew 1974:74–79; Schurr 1992). It remained relatively stable until its collapse ca. A.D. 1400.

## COLLAPSE OF THE ANGEL CHIEFDOM

By ca. A.D. 1400, but not later than A.D. 1450, the Angel chiefdom had collapsed. Platform mounds were no longer maintained; the elite had lost their power to command; and the regional center at Angel, as well as the surrounding villages, hamlets, and farmsteads, was abandoned. Identifying the factors that contributed to the collapse of the Angel chiefdom can help explain how the Caborn-Welborn population reconstructed social, political, and economic relationships following its demise. But identifying these factors is not easy. With the exception of Angel (Black 1967; Hilgeman 1992) and Southwind (Munson 1994), few Angel phase sites have been intensively or extensively investigated, and most remain poorly dated. Therefore, it is not possible to determine whether Angel farmsteads, hamlets, and small villages were abandoned prior to or at the same time as the Angel site.

Based on available archaeological evidence from the lower Ohio and central Mississippi river valleys, researchers (Green and Munson 1978; Hall 1991; Muller 1986; Rindos and Johannessen 1991; Williams 1990) have identified a variety of factors that may have contributed to the collapse of regional Mississippian polities within the area encompassed by the Vacant Quarter (Williams 1990) (Figure 1.2). By extension, these explanations can be applied to the Angel chiefdom.

Most explanations for the collapse of these chiefdoms focus on changes in agricultural yields and the concomitant undermining of elite influence. Following this line of thought, changes in climate patterns (prolonged drought or cold, e.g., the Little Ice Age), or the local environment (degradation, drought, resource depletion, or soil exhaustion) led to a decline in agricultural yields. This decline would have put a great deal of stress on the Mississippian political system and the ability of the elite to mobilize tribute, because household faith in the ability of the elite to govern would have been undermined by the falling yields (Anderson 1994; Green and Munson 1978; Muller 1986; Rindos and Johannessen 1991; Williams 1990). The political instability created by this environmental stress would have led households to abandon the elite, thus contributing to the chiefdom's collapse.

Others (Hall 1991; Muller 1986) have suggested that elite influence could have been undermined by the introduction of new varieties of corn and beans. If one of the major roles of the elite was to manage subsistence risks (Muller and Stephens 1991), then a reduction in these risks associated with improved yields following the introduction of these new varieties could have allowed households greater autonomy and undermined the power of the elite (Hall 1991; Muller 1986), again, leading households to abandon the elite and contributing to the chiefdom's collapse.

Following the collapse of the Angel chiefdom, the short downstream settlement shift of Mississippian households to an area that may not have been intensively or extensively utilized (Green and Munson 1978; Muller 1986) suggests that local environmental factors, such as the depletion of local resources or soil exhaustion, might have contributed to the abandonment of the Angel site and its associated settlements. But whether changes in local environmental conditions led to the collapse of Angel society remains to be determined.

A drawback to explanations that rely on local environmental change to explain the collapse of a particular regional chiefdom and the dispersal of the population that comprised it is that such explanations do little to explain the processes involved in the widespread and contemporary collapse of regional Mississippian polities throughout the area encompassed by the Vacant Quarter (Williams 1990). Similarly, explanations that rely on degradation of the local environment do not provide insights into why the collapse of neighboring Mississippian chiefdoms also did not lead those regional populations to shift their settlements short distances, as has been documented in the Wabash-Ohio River confluence area.

Another explanation for the collapse of Mississippian chiefdoms in the Vacant Quarter focuses on how changes in external relationships may have affected the regional elites' power and prestige. It cites the disruption of the Mississippian prestige goods economy/interaction sphere as a causal factor in the collapse of regional Mississippian chiefdoms.

Mississippian chiefdoms in the lower Ohio valley, or elsewhere for that matter, did not develop or exist in isolation from their neighbors. Mississippian societies appear to have developed over a very broad area at about the same time, which points to some level of extraregional interaction among regional Mississippian chiefdoms (B. Smith 1990). The elite of neighboring Mississippian polities would have been linked to each other economically, through exchange and interaction networks, and possibly socially and politically, through alliances and marriage. Participation in the Mississippian prestige goods economy/interaction sphere may have played an important role in the development and maintenance of regional elites (Brown et al. 1990; Steponaitis 1991; Welch 1991), providing them access not only to nonlocal goods but also with information and esoteric knowledge about the world that they could use to validate their positions within society (Hall 1991; Helms 1979; Knight 1986; Schortman and Urban 1992; Welch 1991). Within such an economy, the elites would have controlled and regulated access to nonlocal goods obtained through exchange relationships (Brown et al. 1990; Frankenstein and Rowlands 1978; Peregrine 1992; Smith 1986; Steponaitis 1986; Welch 1991), and these goods also would have assumed meaning as social valuables within Mississippian societies (McGuire 1989:49). Disruption of the exchange of these nonlocal goods and/or information would have had the potential to undermine the power and prestige of the elites, which over time would have contributed to the collapse of regional chiefdoms.

At first glance, citing the impact that disruption of the Mississippian prestige goods economy/interaction sphere may have had on local elites may seem like an appropriate explanation for only a few of the larger Mississippian polities, such as Moundville (Welch 1991) or Cahokia (Kelly 1991). This is because a great deal of variation has been documented in the amount of nonlocal goods found at Mississippian centers, with the smaller polities often yielding significantly fewer nonlocal goods than the larger ones. Identification of interregional differences in access to nonlocal goods led Steponaitis (1991) to suggest that in some areas, the more powerful chiefdoms may have prevented their smaller neighboring polities from acquiring these materials.

However, it is also possible that the elite of smaller chiefdoms did not need large quantities of prestige goods to validate and maintain their positions within their respective societies. This may have been the case for the Mississippian polities in the lower Ohio valley and some parts of the central Mississippi valley, where evidence for long-distance exchange, sumptuary goods, or storage of tribute is meager (Edging 1995:208; see also Kreisa 1990:142).

The same may have been true for the Angel chiefdom. Evidence for the involvement of the Angel elite in the wider Mississippian exchange of prestige goods and ritual knowledge comes from the recovery of small quantities of marine or copper artifacts and the recovery of ceramic vessels of certain forms or ones that display Southeastern Ceremonial Complex motifs. The overall paucity of objects recovered from Angel that were manufactured from nonlocal materials (i.e., only 63 shell beads, pendants, and gorgets and only 104 copper artifacts) (Kellar 1967:462–463) suggests that the Angel elite were not actively involved in the acquisition of large quantities of nonlocal prestige goods. However, the residents of Angel did have greater access to nonlocal goods than households living at subsidiary settlements, as reflected in the larger quantities of Dover and Mill Creek chert found at Angel than at smaller Angel phase settlements (Munson 1983). And just the rarity alone of marine shell and copper objects within the Angel polity would have made them prestigious items, enhancing their value and the mystery surrounding them (Schortman and Urban 1992).

Some of the best evidence of the Angel elite's involvement in the wider Mississippian prestige goods economy/interaction sphere comes from ceramic vessels. The occurrence of Ramey Incised ceramics at Angel and other sites throughout the Midwest has been interpreted as representing an ideology that involved the elite's interpretation of the cosmos and the communication of their interpretation to other households (Pauketat and Emerson 1991:935). Angel Negative Painted vessels display Southeastern Ceremonial Complex motifs (Waring and Holder 1945; Hilgeman 1992, 2000), including sun circles, cross-in-circles, bilobed arrows, and bird heads (Hilgeman 1991, 1992:232; Kellar 1967:474, Figure 540). While these ceramics were probably produced locally, the designs depicted on them are similar to those found at Mississippian sites throughout the Southeast. The recovery of Ramey Incised–like vessels and Angel Negative Painted vessels from Angel reflect the Angel elite's participation in Mississippian religion and cosmology through the exchange of information and esoteric knowledge.

It is the opinion of this author that the disruption of the Mississippian prestige goods economy/interaction sphere may have had as much impact on the Angel elite's ability to govern as local environmental degradation or changes in climate. Although difficult, at present, to demonstrate based on the available archeological record, it is quite possible that the widespread late-fourteenth/early-fifteenth-century collapse of Mississippian chiefdoms throughout the lower Ohio valley undermined the Angel elite's ability to acquire the nonlocal goods and the information they needed to validate their positions within Angel society.

In response to the demise of nearby polities, the Angel elite may have sought to establish new exchange relationships. With the expansion of long-distance exchange networks, the status of aspiring elites may have risen, especially if those in power could no longer control or regulate who had access to nonlocal goods and information. As the prestige of aspiring elites rose, intersocietal factionalism may have increased. Such a situation certainly would have undermined the Angel elite's ability to retain the allegiance of the local populace, contributing to a decentralization of power and the eventual collapse of the Angel chiefdom.

Some researchers working in the lower Ohio valley have suggested that the disruption of the Mississippian prestige goods economy/interaction sphere had little impact on the Angel elite's ability to lead, citing evidence that Angel continued to be a viable regional center following the decline and collapse of the Kincaid polity in the early to mid-1300s (Hilgeman 1992). But Angel was not the only polity in the lower Ohio valley that appears to have postdated Kincaid. As previously noted, other regional centers situated along the lower Ohio River and its tributaries were occupied until at least A.D. 1400. They include Twin Mounds (Kreisa 1995) and perhaps Tolu (Webb and Funkhouser 1931) in the lower Ohio valley; Tinsley Hill in the lower Cumberland (Clay 1963a, 1963b, 1997; Lane 1993; Schwartz 1961); and Annis Village (Lewis 1990) along the Green River. As Butler and Cobb (1996:9) have noted, with the decline of Kincaid as a regional center after A.D. 1300, a series of other small polities may have emerged (or reemerged) along the Ohio River south of its confluence with the Saline River.

Thus, the collapse of the Kincaid chiefdom would not have deprived the Angel elite of access to nonlocal goods and information, since other regional centers in the lower Ohio valley continued to be occupied. However, a completely different set of circumstances would have presented themselves ca. A.D. 1400, when all of these small regional polities were in decline. Then the Angel elite would have been deprived of access to the nonlocal goods and information so vital to their ability to lead. If they could not find another source for these goods and information, they may have faced a challenge from aspiring elites, which could have led to the cycling of chiefly power within the Angel homeland or the collapse of this regional chiefdom (Anderson 1994; Hally 1996).

Like neighboring chiefdoms, a new cycle of chiefdom formation did not follow the collapse of the Angel polity. But unlike its neighbors, the local Angel population did not disperse or relocate completely to another region upon the chiefdom's collapse. Rather, the bulk of the population moved 50 km downstream to the vicinity of the mouth of the Wabash, where they constructed a new social and political order and initiated new economic relationships during the subsequent Caborn-Welborn phase. At present, it is not known if the entire Angel population relocated to the Caborn-Welborn region, or if some households moved to other regions, or if some simply established more dispersed settlements in the uplands away from the Ohio River. To date, archaeological surveys conducted in other portions of the lower Ohio River floodplain and in the uplands north and south of the Ohio River have generated little or no information about settlements in the lower Ohio valley after A.D. 1400 (Butler 1991; Lewis 1990; Muller 1986).

The general absence of earlier Mississippian settlements on the broad floodplain ridges in the vicinity of the mouth of the Wabash River has led some archaeologists to suggest that what was to become the heart of the Caborn-Welborn region may have functioned as a buffer zone between the Angel and Kincaid polities (Green and Munson 1978; Muller 1986). If this was the case, then at least initially, families may have been attracted to this area because it was not directly under the influence of Angel or any other Mississippian chiefdom. Groups also may have relocated to this area because, being uninhabited, or relatively so, it had not suffered as much environmental degradation as other portions of the Ohio River floodplain (that is, if local environmental degradation was indeed a factor in the collapse of the Angel chiefdom). As such, the features that made this location so attractive, its good agricultural soils and the variety of other natural resources available within the nearby sloughs and swamps, would have been the same as those that had made their former home so attractive.

Whether a decline in agricultural yields, the disruption of the Mississippian prestige goods economy/interaction sphere, or some other as-yet-identified factor(s) undermined the prestige and power of the Angel elite, the fact remains that by ca. A.D. 1400, the Angel chiefdom had collapsed. Although the status of the former Angel leaders had changed, many aspects of the earlier Angel religion, economy, and politics may have been retained as the regional population reconstructed social, political, and economic relationships during the subsequent Caborn-Welborn phase.

## CABORN-WELBORN

### Temporal and Spatial Boundaries

Caborn-Welborn was defined by Munson and Green (1973; Green and Munson 1978) as the late Mississippian cultural manifestation situated in the vicinity of the confluence of the Wabash and Ohio rivers. It is characterized by a concentration of settlements established after the collapse of the Angel chiefdom and the abandonment of the Angel site (Black 1967) and its associated settlements ca. A.D. 1400 (Green and Munson 1978) that continued until ca. A.D. 1700. Calibrated radiocarbon dates from Caborn-Welborn sites tend to cluster in the late fourteenth and fifteenth centuries (Table 2.1). In general, they are later than Angel phase dates, but there is some overlap in the radiocarbon date ranges for both phases. Such overlap is to be expected, since Caborn-Welborn is derived from the earlier Angel phase.

Caborn-Welborn sites are located on the floodplain, terraces, and bluff margins adjacent to the Ohio River from near Geneva, Kentucky, downstream to the mouth of the Saline River in Illinois. This encompasses an area that is about 60 km long (northeast/southwest) but which parallels almost 100 km of the Ohio River (Figure 1.3). The distribution of Caborn-Welborn settlements reflects, in part, the levee, swale, and slough system of the Ohio River floodplain. Within the Caborn-Welborn region, these types of environments are present on both sides of the Ohio River.

A constriction of the floodplain on both sides of the Ohio River marks the western edge of the Caborn-Welborn region. Although no Caborn-Welborn sites have been found downstream from the mouth of the Saline River, this area does appear to have supported earlier Mississippian populations, as evidenced by small regional centers such as Tolu (Webb and Funkhouser 1931) and Orr Herrl (Butler et al. 1979) (Figure 2.1). Thus, even though the spatial extent of floodplain levees and swales is much more restricted downstream from the mouth of the Saline River than upstream, there were still sufficient agricultural soils and other resources to support Caborn-Welborn households, had they chosen to settle in this area.

Cypress Bottoms near Geneva, Kentucky, marks the eastern edge of the Caborn-Welborn region. Upstream from this locale, the floodplain and terraces remain relatively broad throughout the area encompassed by earlier Angel settlements. Angel phase sites are found as far east as the mouth of the Anderson River in southern Indiana (Figure 1.2). At this point, the floodplain again becomes much more constricted (Munson 1994:2). Given the presence of extensive ridge and swale floodplain deposits upstream from the Caborn-Welborn area, there is little evidence to suggest that environmental conditions limited or constrained the distribution of Caborn-Welborn settlements here.

The eastern and western boundaries of the Caborn-Welborn region do not appear to be a product of sampling biases. Large-scale intensive surveys conducted just upstream from this region documented hundreds of sites, none of which contained diagnostic late Mississippian Caborn-Welborn materials (i.e., triangular endscrapers or Caborn-Welborn Decorated pottery) (Robinson 1982). Likewise, surveys conducted downstream from the Caborn-Welborn region also have not documented any late Mississippian settlements (Ahler et al. 1980; Butler et al. 1979).

Caborn-Welborn sites tend to be located on the highest floodplain ridges, especially those situated near sloughs and swampy areas (Figure 2.2), and they are primarily associated with Nolin or Huntington silt loam soils. These soils are well drained and high in natural fertility (Converse and Cox 1967:17; Jacobs 1981:32). Gaps in the distribution of Caborn-Welborn settlements tend to correspond to the location of historic communities, industrial development, and low-lying and poorly drained areas that are the first to be flooded.

The floodplain of the Ohio River in this region is characterized by an extensive system of ridges or levees separated by swales or sloughs. These long, low ridges extend either parallel or perpendicular to the Ohio River, often for several hundred meters. The flat areas between the ridges range in width from 6 to 15 m (Converse and Cox 1967:2). Unlike swales, which hold water only after flooding, sloughs hold water year-round. Within the Caborn-Welborn region, sloughs range in size from mudholes to lakes covering more than 10,000 ha. During historic times, many of the sloughs were breached and ditches were dug to drain swamps and backwater lakes. The placement of tile drainage systems in fields allowed farmers to cultivate additional floodplain acreage (McWilliams 1979; Works Projects Administration 1941).

Above the floodplain are two systems of terraces. The first system is situated about 3 m above the floodplain and 3 m below the second terrace. It is low and flat and made up of alluvial deposits that are Middle-Late Woodfordian in age. In the Wabash drainage, it is known as the "Maumee Terrace"

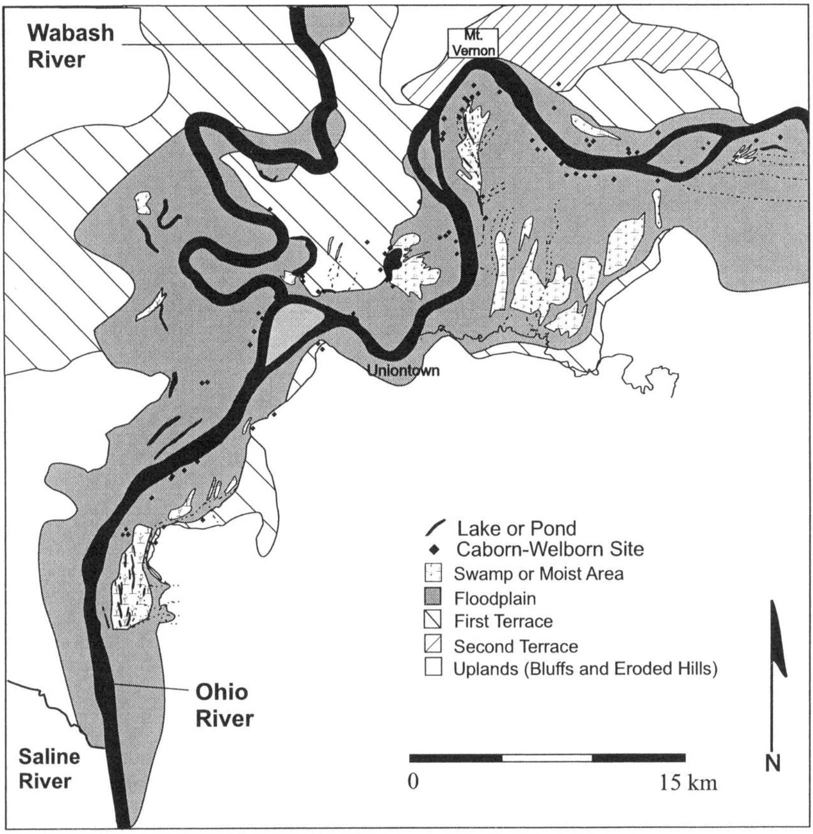


Figure 2.2. Distribution of Caborn-Welborn sites relative to the natural environment.

(Fidlar 1942) and in the Ohio valley as the "Cary Terrace" (Ray 1965). It has relic bars and swales but only limited stream development. Unlike the floodplain, few aquatic food resources are associated with the first terrace.

The second terrace, which is known as the "Shelbyville Terrace" in the Wabash valley (Fidlar 1942) and the "Tazewell Terrace" in the Ohio valley (Ray 1965), dates to the Middle Woodfordian period. It is flat and is situated at an elevation that rarely, if ever, floods. In the southern Wabash valley, it is associated with slackwater deposits that filled small stream valleys. Broad expanses of this second terrace are found on the Indiana and Illinois side of the Ohio River, associated with loess and low dune formations. Throughout most of the Caborn-Welborn region, the floodplain and its associated low terraces along the Ohio and Wabash rivers range in width from 2 to 15 km but tend to average about 5 km wide.

The uplands within the Caborn-Welborn area, which range in distance from .5 to 10 km from the Ohio River, are generally located about 3 km from the river. Blufftops, cliffs, or sharp escarpments rarely occur on the north side of the Ohio River, being more common to the south. As with the second terrace, loess deposits are common in the uplands.

## Angel to Caborn-Welborn Continuities and Differences

Population continuity from the Angel to the Caborn-Welborn phase is reflected in similarities in settlement patterns, settlement systems, subsistence patterns, and material culture (Green 1977; Green and Munson 1978; Munson 1983; Pollack and Munson 1996; Rossen 1995). During both phases, settlements tended to be associated with floodplain levees situated near the Ohio River. Small villages, hamlets, and farmsteads are associated with both phases, reflecting the continuation of a settlement hierarchy throughout the Caborn-Welborn phase.

However, some Caborn-Welborn site types differ from those documented for the Angel phase. They include large villages (3 to 14 ha) but no regional centers, and, unlike the preceding phase, cemeteries are associated with all Caborn-Welborn habitation types. While some Caborn-Welborn villages are larger than others, even the largest lack platform mounds or other signs of corporate architecture (Munson 1983), and no single community appears to have dominated the region, as Angel did during the Angel phase. As will be discussed later, based on its size, central location, and length of occupation, Slack Farm may have, at times, assumed some of the administrative roles of a regional center.

The floodplain location of Caborn-Welborn settlements and a reliance on maize supplemented with other food resources points to a continuation of the riverine floodplain orientation of the earlier Mississippian population (Green 1977; Green and Munson 1978; Muller 1978, 1986; Muller and Stephens 1991; Munson 1995; Smith 1978). Caborn-Welborn farmers would have cultivated the floodplain levees and procured wild plants, fish, reptiles, and other animals from backwater sloughs and marshes situated near their settlements. They also would have exploited migratory waterfowl and large mammals (Smith 1978).

Like the earlier Angel population, Caborn-Welborn farmers grew a variety of plants including corn, squash, tobacco, and starchy-oily seeded plants, such as maygrass, chenopod, sunflower, and marshelder (Rossen 1994, 1995). In addition to these plants, beans were grown in Caborn-Welborn fields. Caborn-Welborn households also relied on nuts for part of their diet, primarily hickory and black walnut, but they consumed as well small amounts of butternut, pecan, acorn, and beechnut. A variety of fleshy fruits and berries including grape, persimmon, pawpaw, and plum would have been collected in the vicinity of Caborn-Welborn communities.

Although corn was a staple of both the Angel and Caborn-Welborn diets, carbon isotope data indicate that Caborn-Welborn groups may have slightly reduced their households' maize consumption (Powell et al. 1996; Schurr 1992, 1994). For instance, the Slack Farm population yielded a mean carbon isotope value of –10.9, which is somewhat lower than the mean value of –9.1 obtained from Angel as well as other pre–A.D. 1400 Mississippian regional centers in the lower Ohio valley, such as Wickliffe (mean = –9.6) and Tinsley Hill (mean = –8.7). However, it should be noted that while Caborn-Welborn households may have consumed less corn than earlier Angel households, the C12/C13 ratios, as well as the paleobotanical remains (Rossen 1994, 1995), indicate that corn still constituted a significant part of their diet.

While Caborn-Welborn groups appear to have slightly reduced their corn consumption and added beans to their diet, relative to the Angel phase population, the animal subsistence patterns and the amount of meat consumed by Caborn-Welborn households apparently continued unchanged from the preceding Angel phase. Nitrogen values obtained from Angel (mean = 8.9) and Caborn-Welborn (mean = 9.1) skeletal remains indicate that both populations consumed similar amounts of aquatic foods, animal protein, and legumes (Powell et al. 1996).

A variety of animal resources would have been present in the vicinity of Caborn-Welborn sites. As it was for most Mississippian populations in the lower Ohio and central Mississippi valleys (Smith 1978), deer appears to have been an important source of meat for the residents of Caborn-Welborn communities (Garmiewicz 2000; Terry Martin, personnel communication 1997). The presence of deer and bison bones in site assemblages indicates that these animals were components of the Caborn-Welborn diet, as were small mammals, such as raccoons, beavers, opossum, squirrels, and rabbits. Turtles also appear to have been taken in quantity. Birds (ducks and turkey) and fish (gar, catfish, buffalo, bass, and drum) may not have been as important to the diet of Caborn-Welborn people (Garmiewicz 2000; Terry Martin, personnel communication 1997) as they were to Mississippian groups living in the central Mississippi River valley (Smith 1978).

With respect to material culture, continuity is best reflected by ceramics (discussed in more detail in chapter 5), particularly vessel forms (e.g., utilitarian jars, bowls, pans, and bottles) and appendage forms (e.g., strap handles and bifurcated lugs), and by nonvessel ceramic objects (e.g., pestles, disks, ear plugs, and owl effigy pendants). Certain ceramic trends initiated during the Angel phase continued into the Caborn-Welborn phase. They include widening and thinning of jar handles, an increase in the number of hemispherical bowls with notched or beaded rim strips, and an increase in the number of shallow bowls with outslanting walls (deep rim plates, cf. Hilgeman 2000) (see chapter 5). Continuity is also reflected in the designs placed on ceramic vessels. Although there is a shift from a preference for negative painted to trailed, incised, and/or punctated designs, the primary motif found on both Angel Negative Painted and Caborn-Welborn Decorated ceramic vessels consists of a series of line-filled triangles (see chapters 3 and 5) that may represent a sun symbol.

Contrary to the scenario of continuity between Angel and Caborn-Welborn presented above, Hilgeman (2000:236–241) feels that the archaeological record of the lower Ohio valley does not reflect population, settlement, or ceramic continuity from the Angel to Caborn-Welborn phase. Rather, she argues for the presence of an as-yet-unidentified earlier (pre–A.D. 1400) Mississippian group living in the vicinity of the mouth of the Wabash who are not related to Angel but who are the ancestors of the Caborn-Welborn population. She also raises the possibility that the Caborn-Welborn population may have been derived from Oneota or other Mississippian groups from the lower Mississippi valley who relocated to the area, although she provides no evidence to support this suggestion (see also Muller 1986). In her discussion, she also does not identify where the Angel population went, if they did not relocate to the mouth of the Wabash after the collapse of the Angel chiefdom.

In arguing for the presence of an earlier, as-yet-unidentified pre–A.D. 1400 Mississippian population in the vicinity of the mouth of the Wabash, Hilgeman does not identify which sites in this area contain evidence for this Mississippian occupation. She also does not identify a regional mound center or large village that would have been associated with this Mississippian population. The Angel site is the closest regional center upstream from the mouth of the Wabash River, but Hilgeman does not extend Angel's influence to the mouth of the Wabash River. Orr Herrl, a single mound site located about 60 km from the mouth of the Wabash, is the closest downstream regional center. However, this site does not appear to be of sufficient size or importance to have exerted influence over settlements located near the mouth of the Wabash River. Without a regional mound center, or a range of identified settlement types, one is left with an as-yet-unidentified earlier Mississippian presence at the mouth of the Wabash that lacks a clearly defined settlement hierarchy.

Hilgeman does suggest that some Caborn-Welborn phase sites may contain more than one Mississippian component, and this is to be expected in the area where settlements of the two phases overlap (Figure 1.2). However, Hilgeman based this statement on the presence of late Angel diagnostics in Caborn-Welborn site ceramic collections. She argues (2000:240) that several minor decorated types recovered from Hovey Lake, such as Old Town Red, Manly Punctate, O'Byam Incised, Beckwith Incised, and Parkin Punctate, indicate that it contains a Mississippian component that is contemporary with Angel 3 (A.D. 1325–1450). However, there is nothing in the archaeological record (i.e., distribution of artifacts, houses, and features) to suggest that Hovey

Lake contains more than one Mississippian component. These ceramics could just as easily represent the continued use of earlier decorated types, especially at early Caborn-Welborn phase sites such as Hovey Lake, whose initial period of occupation may have overlapped with the terminal decades of the Angel phase.

While Hilgeman (2000) acknowledges that line-filled triangular designs on Angel Negative Painted vessels are similar to those on Caborn-Welborn Decorated jars, she argues that, based on their context of recovery and design execution, these two types are not related. With respect to context of recovery, she seems to feel that unlike Angel Negative Painted, which is primarily known from domestic contexts, Caborn-Welborn Decorated jars are primarily associated with mortuary contexts. This is simply not the case. Though some Caborn-Welborn Decorated vessels have been recovered from mortuary contexts (see chapter 6), Caborn-Welborn Decorated is well represented within surface collections at sites from which no human remains have been identified. Where human remains have been recovered, there does not appear to be a correlation between cemetery areas and the distribution of Caborn-Welborn Decorated sherds. In addition, at some sites, large amounts of Caborn-Welborn Decorated ceramics have been recovered from pit features. At Slack Farm, Caborn-Welborn Decorated accounts for 53.4 percent of the analyzed ceramics from large pits, and at Caborn this type accounts for 67.0 percent of the analyzed ceramics from pit features (Pollack and Munson 1996).

Hilgeman is correct in noting that different techniques were used to decorate Angel Negative Painted plates and Caborn-Welborn Decorated jars and that the use of line-filled triangular designs is associated with other ceramic types, such as Barton Incised, O'Byam Incised, and Wells Incised. While all of these types reflect the widespread use of this motif, only Angel Negative Painted and Caborn-Welborn Decorated are considered to be good diagnostics for their respective lower Ohio valley phases. In addition to the use of lines to lay out triangles and to fill these triangular areas, both types are characterized by the use of dots or punctation to fill the triangular areas. Given the close geographical proximity of Angel and Caborn-Welborn sites to each other and the overlap in their distribution, and the similarities in the dominant motifs placed on ceramic vessels during these two phases, it seems reasonable to assume that there is a relationship between the common motifs placed on Angel Negative Painted vessels and on Caborn-Welborn Decorated vessels. By the later half of Angel 3, negative painting was on the decline (Hilgeman 2000:223–224), and it is quite possible that this decline continued into the Caborn-Welborn phase, where negative painting was replaced by incised/trailed or punctated designs that were intended to convey similar messages (see chapter 5). The alternative explanation is that by accident, two unrelated groups living in the same area but at different times chose to use the same motif to decorate their ceramic vessels. To this author, such an explanation does not appear to be plausible. For all of the reasons outlined above, the Caborn-Welborn population is considered to have been derived, at least in part, from the earlier Angel population.

## Previous Archaeological Investigations

Lyon (1871) was the first to conduct investigations in the Caborn-Welborn region. He tested several sites, including Grundy Hill and Slack Farm. However, it is difficult to determine from his field records which sites he investigated or where particular artifacts were found. For example, he recovered Caborn-Welborn Decorated ceramics from a site he called the Lindsey Mounds. The location of this site has yet to be determined.

In 1898, Clifford Anderson, who was working for Warren K. Moorehead (1906; Adams 1949), conducted fieldwork at the Murphy site in southeastern Indiana. During the course of his investigations, he documented the presence of at least three cemeteries and recovered a large number of ceramic vessels, marine shell objects, pipes, and copper artifacts.

Sometime in the late 1800s or early 1900s, a large number of ceramic vessels were obtained from private collectors by the Museum of the American Indian (Munson 1997). These vessels reportedly came from Bone Bank in southwestern Indiana. Unfortunately, additional provenience information does not exist for any of these materials.

It was not until the mid- to late 1960s that Hoffman (1966), during a survey for the Newburgh Lock and Dam, recorded several Caborn-Welborn sites: Hart, Site 15He40, Site 15He37, Site 15He38, Site 15He43, Site 15He51, Site 15He52, and Gough. The presence of cemeteries was noted at two of these sites (Site 15He51 and Gough). Many of Hoffman's sites were revisited by archaeologists from the University of Louisville in the late 1970s and early 1980s. In the late 1960s, limited excavations were conducted at the Leonard site in Indiana (Henn 1971) and in the late 1970s, additional Caborn-Welborn sites were recorded in southeastern Illinois as part of an archeological survey for the proposed Smithland Lock and Dam (Butler et al. 1979).

As part of his research on Mississippian settlement patterns in southwestern Indiana, Green (1977) compared and contrasted the distribution of Angel and Caborn-Welborn phase sites. He also assigned habitation sites to specific site types (see also Green and Munson 1978), based primarily on settlement size, and noted that, while the Caborn-Welborn phase lacked a regional center with platform mounds, it was characterized by an increase in village size relative to Angel phase small villages. Although Angel phase sites are found over a larger area than Caborn-Welborn phase sites (Figure 1.2), Green (1977:177–178; see also Green and Munson 1978) characterized the Angel population as being more nucleated than the Caborn-Welborn population. He argued that since most of the Angel population lived at or in the vicinity of the Angel site, this represented population aggregation and a concern for defense. During the subsequent Caborn-Welborn phase, most of the population, rather than being concentrated at one community, lived at one of several small or large villages. Green interpreted this more dispersed settlement pattern as reflecting a reduction in external threats and a greater concern with economic issues. He went on to suggest that a more dispersed settlement pattern was associated with a reduction in the amount of labor needed to obtain the necessary quantities of subsistence goods and natural resources.

Since the late 1970s, Cheryl Ann Munson has conducted limited investigations at Hovey Lake (Munson 1980) and Caborn (Munson et al. 1987, 1989) in southern Indiana. Together, Munson and this author carried out more extensive investigations at the Slack Farm site in Kentucky (Pollack and Munson 1996, 1998) (see chapter 4 for more detailed information on these investigations). Recently, Munson (1995, 1997, 2000) has conducted additional investigations at Hovey Lake, Murphy, and Bone Bank and has undertaken additional surveys in the Caborn-Welborn region. This work has generated new information on the organization of Caborn-Welborn villages as well as on Caborn-Welborn material cultural and subsistence patterns.

These investigations have shown that Caborn-Welborn villages are characterized by high artifact densities, thick midden deposits, large storage pits, and plazas. They also contain multiple cemeteries. Within each cemetery, burials usually were laid out in parallel rows, often head to head or toe to toe. While within-village cemeteries are the norm in the central and eastern portions of the Caborn-Welborn region, as will be discussed in chapters 4 and 6, in the western section of the region, individuals were primarily interred in blufftop cemeteries. Blufftop cemetery burial distinguishes Caborn-Welborn mortuary patterns from those of the earlier Angel phase but is consistent with the mortuary practices of other pre–A.D. 1400 Mississippian societies of the lower Ohio valley. Caborn-Welborn mortuary practices also are distinguished from those of the preceding Angel phase by an increase in the number of individuals accompanied by grave goods. At both within-village and blufftop cemeteries, whole ceramic vessels often were placed with the dead. Other types of grave goods included copper or brass beads, tubes or bracelets, marine shell beads and pendants, and limestone or catlinite disk pipes (Adams 1949; Green and Munson 1978; Moorehead 1906).

## SUMMARY

The Angel chiefdom has been characterized as a nucleated, simple (two-tier) or group-oriented chiefdom consisting of a regional administrative center, the Angel site, and associated small villages, hamlets, and farmsteads. Located across from the mouth of the Green River, the Angel site was the center for religious, social, and political life for nearby settlements. The bulk of the Angel population is believed to have lived at or near the Angel site, and cemeteries are associated only with this regional center.

By the early fifteenth century, the Angel chiefdom, as well as its contemporaries in the lower Ohio and upper-central Mississippi valleys, had collapsed. The collapse of these regional chiefdoms led to the abandonment not only of the regional centers but of their associated villages, hamlets, and farmsteads as well. The collapse of these chiefdoms may have been a result of environmental degradation as well as disruption of the local Mississippian prestige goods economy/interaction sphere, which undermined elite authority within regional Mississippian polities. Throughout most of this region, there is little or no archaeological evidence of post–fourteenth century Mississippian settlements.

In the mouth of the Wabash region, cultural developments stand in sharp contrast to those of nearby regions. Although the collapse of the Angel chiefdom is associated with the abandonment of all Angel settlements, the Angel population does not appear to have relocated to another region. Nor is the collapse of the Angel chiefdom associated with a settlement shift to smaller, more dispersed settlements that have low archaeological visibility. Rather, it resulted in short (ca 50 km) downstream shift in settlements. Where before settlements were centered near the mouth of the Green River, during the Caborn-Welborn phase they were centered at the mouth of the Wabash River.

Continuity from the Angel to Caborn-Welborn phase is reflected in subsistence and settlements patterns and material culture. Both Angel and Caborn-Welborn subsistence patterns were geared toward the levee and swale system of the Ohio River floodplain (Green 1977; Green and Munson 1978). For both, maize accounted for a substantial portion of the diet, and faunal exploitation patterns were geared to the hunting of deer, small mammals, and birds, supplemented by fish and reptiles. Settlements tended to be located on floodplain levees or nearby terraces and a settlement hierarchy is clearly in evidence during both phases. Continuity in material culture is primarily represented by ceramic vessel and appendage forms, nonvessel ceramic objects, and design motifs placed on ceramic vessels.

The demise of the Angel chiefdom did bring with it some important changes, however. Beans were added to the Caborn-Welborn diet. Ceramic designs were no longer made using the negative painting technique. Cemeteries were associated with all Caborn-Welborn domestic sites, not just the largest ones. And missing from the Caborn-Welborn settlement system is a clearly identifiable regional center with platform mounds. Platform mounds signified the presence of an elite class at Angel. The absence of platform mounds at any Caborn-Welborn site suggests that, along with the downstream shift in settlements, the transition from Angel to Caborn-Welborn was marked by changes in the social and political boundaries that defined the status and responsibilities of Caborn-Welborn leaders.

Caborn-Welborn developed in the aftermath of the demise of Angel as well as other regional Mississippian chiefdoms situated throughout the lower Ohio and upper-central Mississippi valleys. As households reconstructed social, political, and economic relationships, they also created a new cultural expression—one that had ties to the past, but one in which leadership may have been decentralized and one that was involved to a greater extent in extraregional exchange networks and interaction spheres. Subsequent chapters will discuss the changes in political centralization, social boundaries of the elite, and increased involvement in intersocietal exchange networks that distinguished the response of Caborn-Welborn populations to the collapse of a regional Mississippian chiefdom from that of their neighbors.

# 3 Ceramic Descriptions

Ceramics, triangular endscrapers, and small quantities of Euro-American trade goods are the three main material culture attributes that archaeologists use to identify Caborn-Welborn components. Of the three, ceramics are by far the most numerous and the most temporally and functionally sensitive artifact class. For these reasons, the interpretations arrived at during this research were built mainly upon patterns identified within regional Caborn-Welborn ceramic data. But before these interpretations can be discussed, descriptions must be provided for each ceramic type and ceramic group found in the Caborn-Welborn region. It should be noted that only a subset of these types is present at most sites, but each has been recovered from at least one Caborn-Welborn site. Interpretations of the spatial distribution of ceramic types and attributes within the Caborn-Welborn region are provided in chapter 6.

## DEFINITIONS AND ANALYTICAL METHODS

During the course of this study, 19,264 sherds and whole or reconstructable vessels were analyzed. The focus of the analysis was rims greater than 4 $cm^2$, appendages, and decorated sherds. Excluded from this study were plain rims less than 4 $cm^2$ and all plain, fabric-impressed, and cordmarked body sherds (with the exception of sherds with fabric impression on their interior surfaces) regardless of size. These exclusions were made so that the size of the analyzed sample would be more manageable and because analysis of the small plain rims and body sherds would have contributed little to the identification and interpretation of intraregional spatial patterns and extraregional interaction. Using these criteria, the size of the study sample was reduced from more than 400,000 sherds to slightly more than 19,000. Nonvessel ceramic objects such as pestles, disks, ear plugs, and pendants also were excluded, because they have a low frequency of occurrence in most site assemblages.

Whenever possible, each sherd or ceramic vessel was assigned to a previously defined ceramic type (Table 3.1). For the most part, the ceramic typology developed by Phillips et al. (1951) and later refined by Phillips (1970) was employed to classify these specimens. This typology, which is based primarily on surface treatment and decoration, has been used with some modification by other researchers working in the lower Ohio and central Mississippi valleys (Clay 1963a, 1979; Kreisa 1988; Lewis 1986; O'Brien and Fox 1994; Pollack 1998; Pollack and Munson 1998a; Pollack and Railey 1987; Wesler 1992). Although Phillips et al. (1951) and Phillips (1970) used a type/variety classificatory scheme, no attempt was made to assign any of the Caborn-Welborn ceramics to a specific variety. Use of the type/variety system has proven to be extremely unwieldy and has resulted in a plethora of varieties that are site-specific and difficult to use and replicate.

Most plain Caborn-Welborn jars are tempered with coarse fragments of shell and have temper and paste characteristics that are consistent with Mississippi Plain (Phillips 1970). On the other hand, most plain bowls, bottles, and plates are tempered with much finer fragments of shell and are similar to Bell Plain (Phillips 1970). Pans with fabric-impressed exterior surfaces were classified as Kimmswick Fabric Impressed, and those with net-impressed exterior surfaces were assigned to Kimmswick Net Impressed. Pans with plain exterior surfaces were classified as Kimmswick Plain (Phillips 1970). In contrast to Kimmswick Fabric Impressed pans, some bowls have fabric-impressed interior surfaces. These specimens were classified as Tolu Fabric Impressed (Clay 1963a; Webb and Funkhouser 1931). Cordmarked pans and jars were classified as Shell Tempered Cordmarked.

Sometimes a slip was applied to the exterior and/or interior surface of a vessel, and such sherds were classified as Old Town Red. Although technically a surface treatment, slipping was considered a decoration in the discussion that follows. Other forms of decoration included incised, trailed, engraved, punctated, or negative painted designs placed on the exterior surfaces of jars, bowls, and bottles. Some of these decorative attributes also were placed on the interior surface of a rim or vessel. Whenever possible, these decorative attributes were used to assign specimens to previously defined types.

While most sherds could be assigned to a previously defined type, several incised and trailed sherds could not be classified. These sherds were classified as "Miscellaneous Incised/Trailed." Also, no attempt was made to assign the Oneota-like sherds to a previously defined type. Because the source area of these ceramics or the people who made them has yet to be determined, it was felt that assigning them to a specific type or to several types would imply that they were derived from a particular area.

In the remainder of this chapter, Caborn-Welborn ceramic types and ceramic groups of the Caborn-Welborn phase (plain and decorated) are described. These are followed by descriptions of nonlocal decorated ceramic types and groups (Oneota-derived and central Mississippi valley–derived) and the miscellaneous decorated ceramic group. For each type, where applicable, information is provided on vessel and rim form, orifice diameter, decoration,

Table 3.1. Ceramic Types Found in the Caborn-Welborn Region.

| Ceramic Type | Frequency | Percentage |
|---|---|---|
| Kimmswick Plain | 971 | 5.0 |
| Kimmswick Fabric Impressed | 1,038 | 5.4 |
| Mississippi Plain | 6,402 | 33.2 |
| Bell Plain | 3,754 | 19.5 |
| Kimmswick Net Impressed | 8 | 0.0 |
| Shell Tempered Cordmarked | 26 | 0.1 |
| Tolu Fabric Impressed | 43 | 0.2 |
| Parkin Punctate | 42 | 0.2 |
| Caborn-Welborn Decorated | 6,087 | 31.6 |
| Manly Punctate | 219 | 1.1 |
| Matthews Incised | 47 | 0.2 |
| Old Town Red | 123 | 0.6 |
| Angel/Kincaid Negative Painted | 8 | 0.0 |
| Walls Incised/Engraved | 30 | 0.2 |
| O'Byam Incised | 15 | 0.1 |
| Oneota-Like | 211 | 1.1 |
| Fortune Noded | 2 | 0.0 |
| Beckwith Incised | 17 | 0.1 |
| Miscellaneous Incised or Trailed | 58 | 0.3 |
| Barton Incised | 4 | 0.0 |
| Mound Place Incised | 57 | 0.3 |
| Kent Incised–Like | 6 | 0.0 |
| Campbell Punctate | 64 | 0.3 |
| Campbell Applique | 19 | 0.1 |
| Campbell Incised | 11 | 0.1 |
| Vernon Paul Applique | 1 | 0.0 |
| Ranch Incised–Like | 1 | 0.0 |
| Total | 19,264 | 100.0 |

line width, handle type, ratio of handle width to thickness, lip treatment, and appendage type.

## CABORN-WELBORN UNDECORATED TYPES AND GROUPS

### Mississippi Plain

In general, Mississippi Plain vessels were tempered with larger shell fragments and have a coarser paste than Bell Plain vessels. They also tend not to have been as highly burnished. Mississippi Plain vessel forms include jars, bowls, bottles, and funnels. Both the jar and bowl categories include pinch pot vessels, which are small, crudely made, hand-modeled vessels distinct from the smallest vessels manufactured by coiling.

### *Jars*

Mississippi Plain jars have globular to subglobular bodies with direct, slightly outflaring, or recurved rims (Figure 3.1). Most jars have a rounded rim/neck juncture, but some exhibit an angled rim/neck juncture. Jar orifice diameters range from 4 to 44 cm.

Jar handles are primarily wide, thin, parallel-sided or triangular straps (Figure 3.1c–e) (mean width to thickness ratio of greater than 3.0) attached to the rim at the lip and extending to below the base of the neck. Thick straps (mean width to thickness ratio of 2.0 to 3.0), intermediate loop/strap (mean width to thickness ratio of 1.5–2.0), and loop (mean width to thickness ratio of less than 1.5) handles are also present. Mississippi Plain handles have a mean width to thickness ratio of 3.0 to 1.0.

Decoration on Mississippi Plain jars consists primarily of lugs, nodes, and horizontal strips, but sometimes punctations are present on jar lips. Lugs, which are tabular in form and wider than they are thick, tend to be attached to the rim at the lip and include single, paired or multiple (more than two), bifurcated, and notched examples (Figures 3.1a,b,g,h and 3.2). Sometimes the lugs encircle the entire vessel. Most are flat and oval in shape, but some have a triangular or rectangular appearance. When not attached at the lip, paired or bifurcated lugs were placed about 1 cm below the lip. These specimens tend to have a more rounded appearance than lugs attached at the lip.

In contrast to lugs, nodes have a conical or subconical form (Figure 3.2c). In general, they are also smaller than lugs. Nodes were attached at the lip or were placed from .5 to 1.5 cm below the lip. They occur by themselves, in pairs, or as a linear arrangement of three or more nodes. Sometimes the nodes encircle the entire vessel. A few specimens have a small depression in the center of the node. This gives them the appearance of a dimple or they may be U-shaped. These nodes are usually found on jar shoulders. Single plain nodes also were sometimes placed on vessel shoulders.

Notched or plain horizontal strips tend to be found .5 to 1.0 cm below the lip (Figure 3.2b). These strips were often placed on opposing sides of a vessel, but some vessels have four strips. The latter rarely have handles. On some jars, the applied strip encircles the entire vessel.

When handles are present, they usually occur in even numbers, with most having two opposing handles. Some have four handles; still others have as

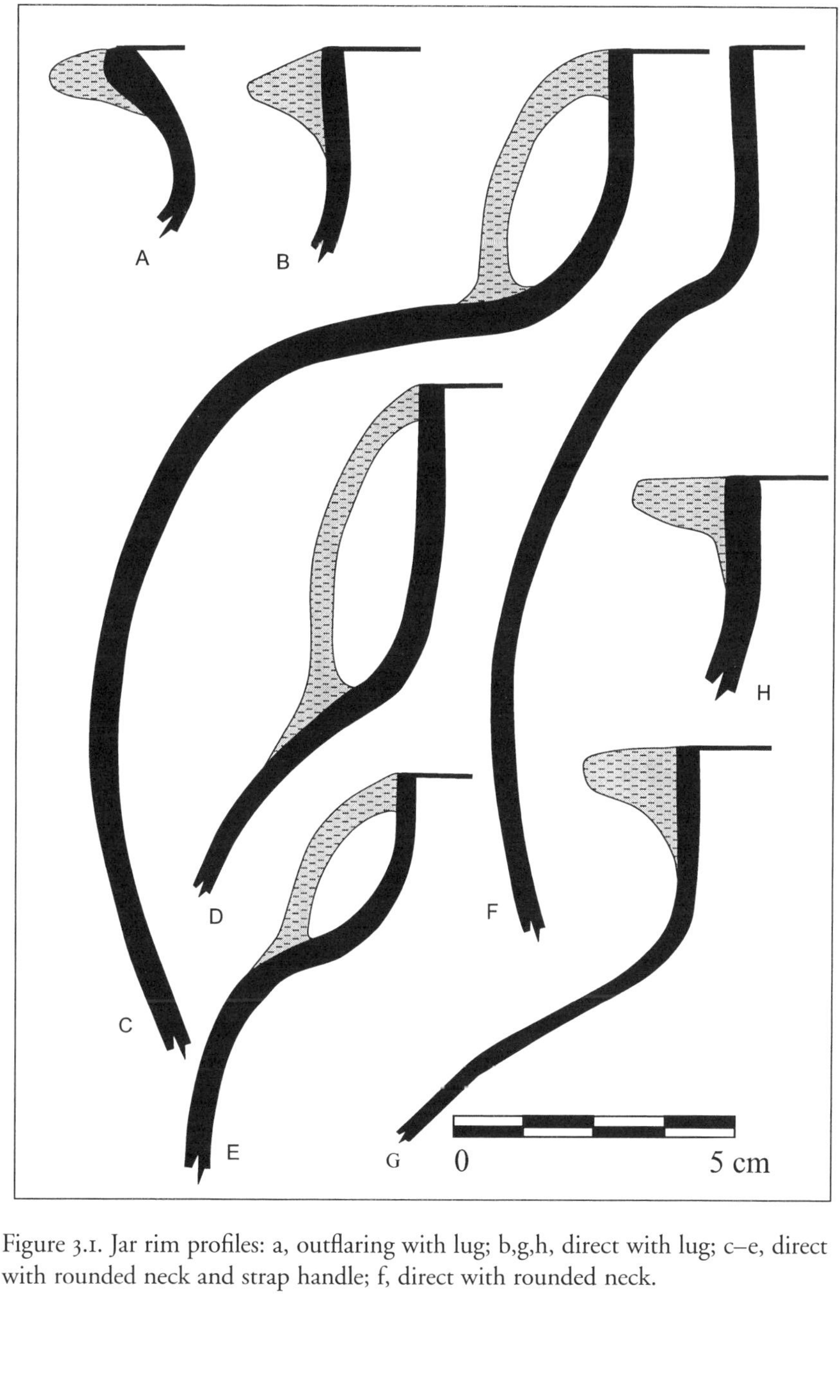


Figure 3.1. Jar rim profiles: a, outflaring with lug; b,g,h, direct with lug; c–e, direct with rounded neck and strap handle; f, direct with rounded neck.

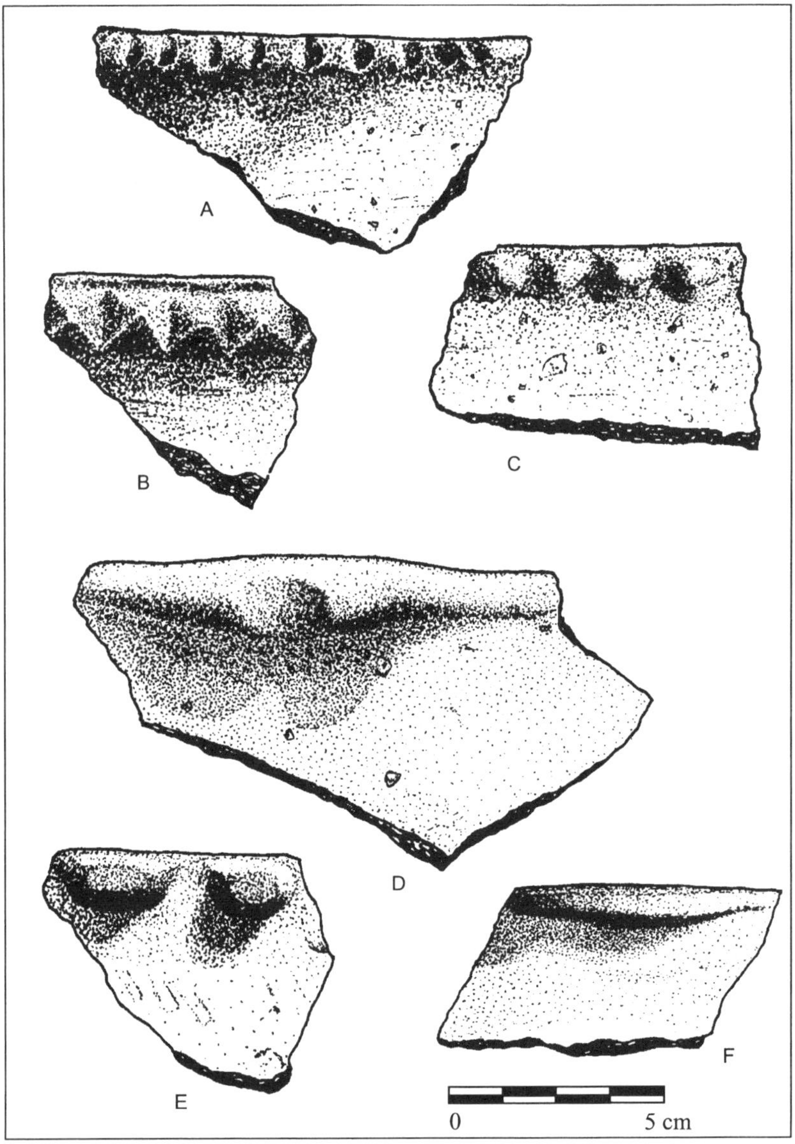


Figure 3.2. Jar appendages: a, notched oval lug; b, notched horizontal strip; c, nodes; d, bifurcated lug; e, paired oval lug; f, single oval lug.

many as eight. Though Mississippi Plain jars with more than four handles do occur, they are rare in Caborn-Welborn assemblages.

Several rims have pairs of drilled holes. These holes do not appear to have been used to mend vessel walls. Other rims have highly polished lips. A few Mississippi Plain jar lips are decorated with punctations or notches. Oblong and circular punctations are primarily restricted to the lip. Occasionally, these punctations extend across the tops of jar handles. Vertical notches were sometimes placed on the lip or on the exterior edge of the lip, directly above a thin strap handle.

### *Bowls*

Most Mississippi Plain bowls are shallow vessels with outslanting rims and flat bottoms (Figure 3.3a–g), but some are hemispherical bowls with direct (Figure 3.3h–k) or slightly incurving rims. Mississippi Plain bowl orifice diameters range from 8 to 26 cm. Appendages associated with Mississippi Plain bowls include notched horizontal strips (Figure 3.4a,b), notched flat lugs, and dual plain fish fins. None of the Mississippi Plain bowl lips were decorated.

### *Bottles*

Most of the Mississippi Plain bottle rims are from wide-mouthed bottles with direct rims and rounded necks (Figure 3.5f–i). However, some wide-mouthed bottles have sharply angled rim/neck junctures, and others have a slight bulge or flange on the interior of the rim/neck juncture (Figure 3.5f,g). A few of the bottle rims lack well-defined necks (Figure 3.5d,e), and some are from hooded water bottles. Most of the bottles have subglobular shapes. Caborn-Welborn bottles range in orifice diameter from 4 to 12 cm.

### *Funnels*

These thick-walled vessels have direct rims and sides that taper to a smaller opening at the bottom of the vessel. All have plain exterior surfaces. Orifice diameters at the top range from 8 to 20 cm and at the bottom from 2 to 6 cm.

## Bell Plain

As with Mississippi Plain, Bell Plain jars, bowls, plates, and bottles can be present in Caborn-Welborn collections. General characteristics of each vessel form are presented below.

### *Jars*

Bell Plain jars tend to have direct rims and rounded necks, while a few have recurved rims (Figure 3.1). In general, these vessels, which range in orifice diameter from 4 to 16 cm, are smaller than their Mississippi Plain counter-

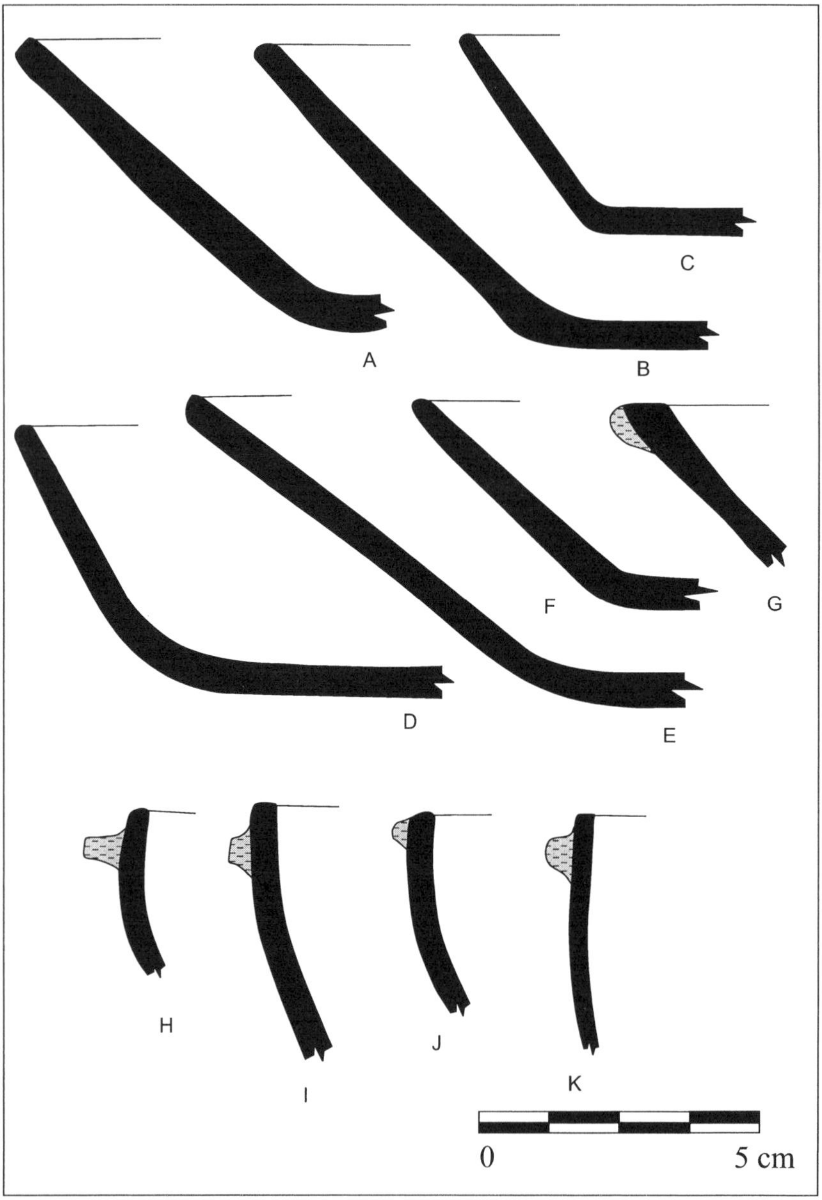


Figure 3.3. Bowl rim profiles: a–f, outslanting with flat bottom; g, outslanting with node; h–j, direct, with applied horizontal strip; k, direct with nodes.

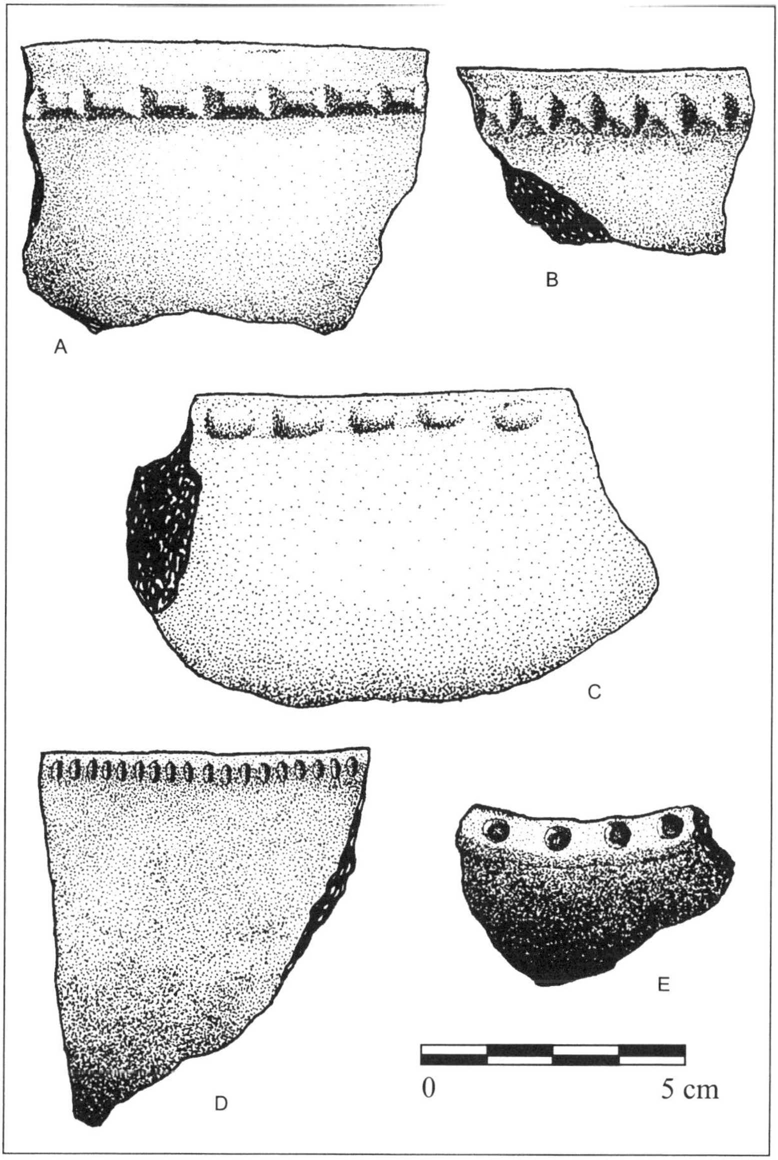


Figure 3.4. Bowl appendages and lip decoration: a,b, applied horizontal strip; c, nodes; d, exterior lip notching; e, punctated lip.

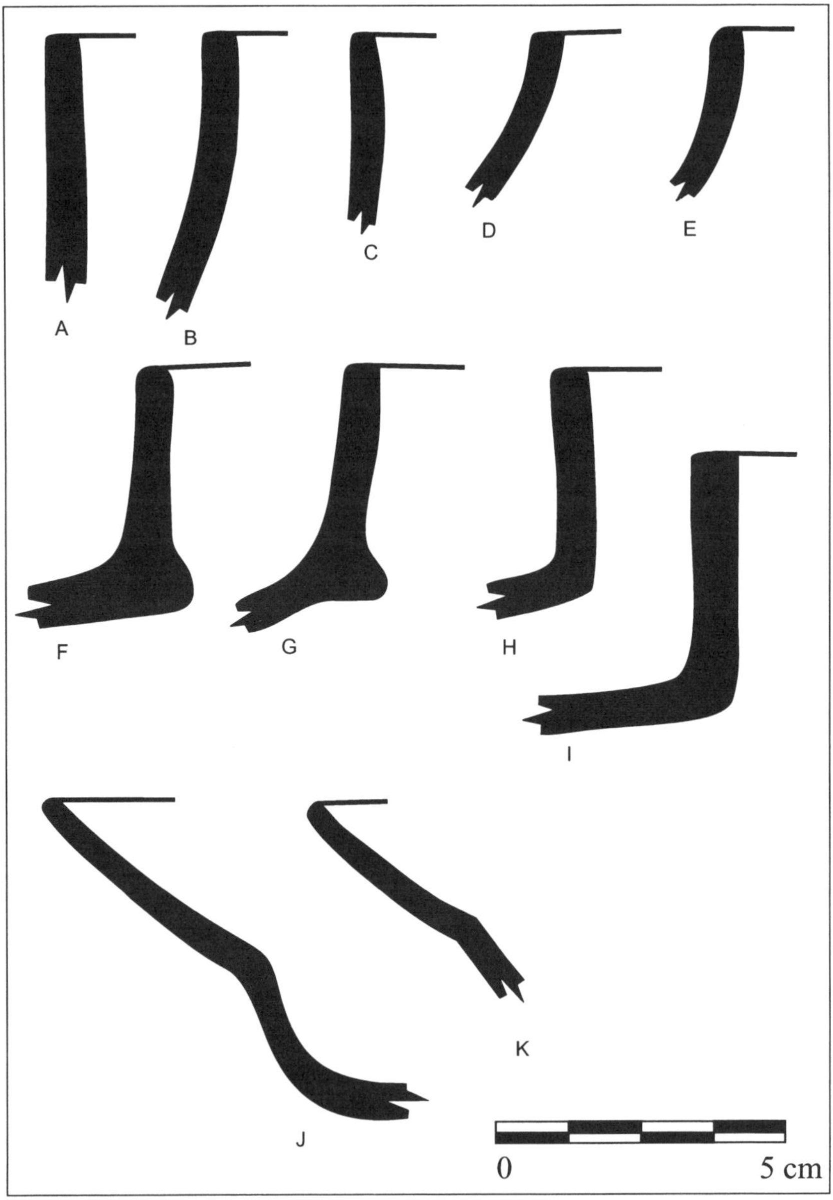


Figure 3.5. Bottle and plate rim profiles: a–c, long-necked bottles; d,e, inslanting (almost neckless) bottles; f,g, wide-mouthed bottles with interior protrusion; h,i, wide mouthed bottles with sharp rim/neck juncture; j,k, plates.

parts. The only appendage associated with Bell Plain jar rims are parts (head and fins) of fish effigy vessels.

### *Bowls*

Bell Plain bowls include both simple hemispheres with direct and incurving rims (Figure 3.3h–k), and shallow open vessels with outslanting walls and flat bottoms (Figure 3.3a–g). The latter have been referred to by some researchers (Hilgeman 2000) as "deep rim plates." Many of the shallow bowls have castellated rims (Figure 3.6). Other rims are portions of conch shell bowls. Some animal effigy bowls have a modeled head (e.g., ducks, humans, and other unknown animals) and sometimes a tail attached to the rim (Figure 3.7). Others (e.g., fish and humans in supine positions) were shaped by modeling the vessel wall to depict a head and other major features, such as legs or a tail, and by adding small lugs to indicate minor features, such as ventral fins.

Bell Plain bowl orifice diameters range from 4 to 34 cm. Not surprisingly, shallow bowls with outslanting walls tend to have larger orifices than hemispherical bowls.

Bowl appendages include notched or plain horizontal strips (Figure 3.4a,b), paired or multiple nodes (Figure 3.4c), and plain, notched, bifurcated, and incised/engraved lugs. Appendages are primarily associated with hemispherical bowls. As with jars, nodes tend to be found below the lip and occur in groups of two or three, but sometimes they encircle the entire vessel. Applied strips, which are usually notched, also are located below the rim and encircle the vessel. Both the encircling nodes and applied strips give the appearance of a string of beads and have been referred to as "beaded bowls." Lugs are usually flat and oval and are attached to the rim at the lip. Most are undecorated. As with plain lugs, incised/engraved lugs tend to be oval and flat. Some of these may represent tails or fins associated with effigy rim riders.

In general, lip decoration is more common on bowls than on jars. Lip decoration consists primarily of vertical or diagonal notches (Figure 3.4d). About two-thirds of the vertical notches are found on the exterior edge of the lip (Figure 3.4d). In comparison, slightly more than 50 percent of diagonal notches are located on the top of the lip. Oblong, circular, reed, triangular, and crescent-shaped punctations also were used to decorate lips (Figure 3.4e), and diagonal dashes were observed on a few rims. Punctations tend to be located on top of the lip, much like diagonal notching. Similar techniques were used to decorate the lips of both hemispherical and shallow bowls.

### *Plates*

Plates are a variety of bowls, and sometimes it is difficult to distinguish them from shallow bowls with outslanting walls. In this study, outslanting rims

Figure 3.6. Shallow bowls: top, with outslanting walls and flat bottom; bottom, with outslanting walls, flat bottom, and castellated rim.

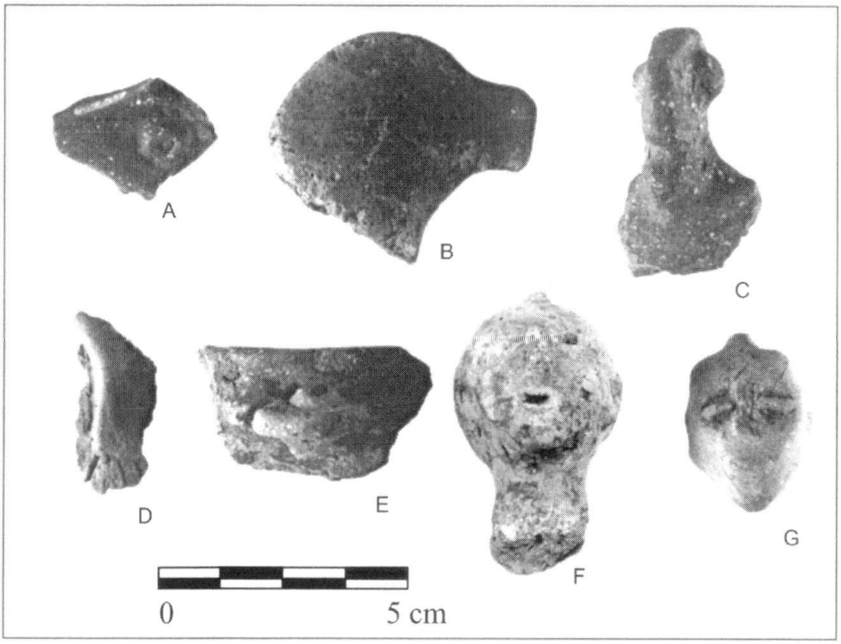


Figure 3.7. Bowl effigy attachments: a,e, fish; b, duck; c, bird(?); d, arm or leg; f,g, human.

associated with a distinct well were classified as plates (Figure 3.5j,k). Undoubtedly, some of the rims assigned to the shallow bowl category represent portions of plates lacking this distinctive well. Bell Plain plate rims range in orifice diameter from 16 to 28 cm.

### *Bottles*

Long-necked, hooded, wide-mouthed, and neckless bottles can be present in Caborn-Welborn collections. Long-necked (Figure 3.5a–c) and hooded bottles tend to have narrower openings and to be smaller than wide-mouthed bottles. As with the Mississippi Plain bottles, most of the wide-mouthed Bell Plain bottles have rounded necks, but some have a sharply angled rim/neck juncture (Figure 3.5h,i), while others have a slight thickening or flange on the interior of the rim/neck juncture (Figure 3.5f,g). Bottles have vessel orifice diameters ranging from 4 to 10 cm.

The only appendages associated with Bell Plain bottles are a single node attached just below the lip of the bottle and a few thin strap handles attached at the lip and the base of the rim. The one measurable handle has a width to thickness ratio of 3.6 to 1. A couple of bottles have opposing pairs of drilled holes located just below the rim.

### *Other*

Detached portions of animal and human effigies could not be assigned to a specific vessel form. Animal and human effigies include portions of applied arms, hands, and feet and a variety of effigy heads (fish, plain and incised bird [primarily duck], and human) (Figure 3.7a–g).

### Kimmswick Fabric Impressed

The only vessel form associated with this type is that of a very shallow bowl or pan that was coarsely tempered with large shell particles. Rims with fabric-impressed exterior surfaces tend to thicken toward a rounded lip, which often protrudes outward from the body of the vessel (Figure 3.8a–c). A few rims thicken slightly toward the lip (Figure 3.8d,e), and some exhibit no evidence of thickening (Figure 3.8h–k). Fabric-marked rims range in orifice diameter from 14 to 94 cm.

The textile impressions on the exterior surface of pan rims and body sherds indicate that these fabrics were manufactured by twining (Drooker 1992). The main textile structure represented is plain twining. Other major textile structures include alternate-pair twining and plain twining with transposed interlinked warps. The latter, along with grouping of weft rows in pairs or triplets, and crossing warps, were often used to create geometric patterns in these fabrics (Henderson 1999, 2003; Henderson et al. 1996).

### Kimmswick Plain

As with Kimmswick Fabric Impressed, the only vessel form associated with Kimmswick Plain is a shallow bowl or pan. About one-third of the plain pans have rims that thicken toward the lip (Figure 3.8d,e), which often protrudes outward from the body of the vessel (Figure 3.8a–c).

Unlike Kimmswick Fabric Impressed pans, many plain pan rims exhibit no thickening or only minor thickening of the lip (Figure 3.8h–k), and some have lips that are thinner than the body of the vessel (Figure 3.8f,g). Exterior surfaces of many of these vessels exhibit wipe or smoothing marks, and they tend to have somewhat thinner walls than pans with exterior protrusions. Kimmswick Plain pans range in orifice diameter from 12 to 68 cm.

### Kimmswick Net Impressed

Except for their exterior surfaces, Kimmswick Net Impressed specimens are pan rims that are very similar to those classified as Kimmswick Fabric Impressed. Kimmswick Net Impressed vessel orifice diameters range from 36 to 52 cm.

### Shell Tempered Cordmarked

Both jars and pans can have cordmarked exterior surfaces.

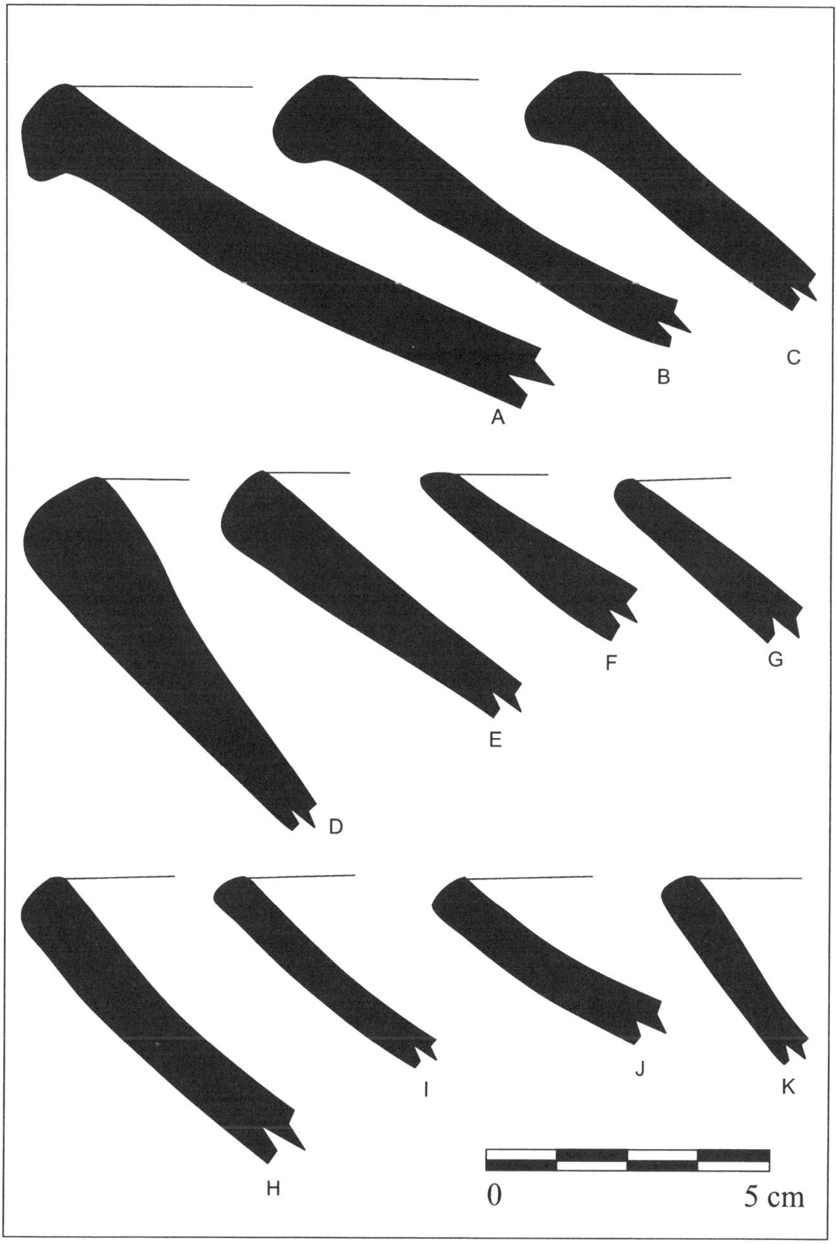


Figure 3.8. Pan rim profiles: a–c, with exterior lip protrusions; d,e, thickens toward lip; f,g, thins toward lip; h–k, no thickening of lip.

### *Jars*

These vessels have cordmarked bodies and plain necks. They are similar in shape to Mississippi Plain jars. These globular jars have direct, slightly outslanting, or recurved rims. A somewhat higher percentage of cordmarked rims have a sharply angled rim/neck juncture than do Mississippi Plain jars. Cordmarked jars range in orifice diameter from 16 to 30 cm. The only appendages associated with these jars are a plain triangular lug and a pair of nodes.

### *Pans*

Cordmarked pans are similar in size and shape to Kimmswick Fabric Impressed specimens. All have the exterior protrusion that is so common on Caborn-Welborn Kimmswick Fabric Impressed vessels. These pans range in vessel orifice diameter from 28 to 42 cm.

## Tolu Fabric Impressed

Tolu Fabric Impressed is distinguished from Kimmswick Fabric Impressed by the presence of interior fabric impressions. While this type was defined by Clay (1963a) as being associated with vessels that have paste and temper attributes consistent with Mississippi Plain, many of the Tolu Fabric Impressed sherds from Caborn-Welborn sites, as well as from the Tolu site (Webb and Funkhouser 1931) itself, are portions of finely tempered and well-fired bowls that have paste and temper characteristics consistent with those of Bell Plain. An examination of Tolu Fabric Impressed vessels from Tinsley Hill indicates that only the lower half of these bowls had been impressed with fabric, and the remainder of the interior wall was plain. Thus, unless one had a large vessel section, rims from Tolu Fabric Impressed vessels would have been classified as Mississippi or Bell Plain. The textile structure represented on Tolu Fabric Impressed is generally plain twining with extra weft twists that form a "bird's-eye" motif.

# CABORN-WELBORN DECORATED TYPES AND GROUPS

## Angel/Kincaid Negative Painted

The negative painted ceramics recovered from Caborn-Welborn sites resemble Angel Negative Painted (Figure 3.9b) and its companion type, Kincaid Negative Painted (Hilgeman 1992). The former is associated with plates (Figure 3.9b) and the latter with bottles. Within Caborn-Welborn collections, these types are not as common as Old Town Red. Sherds assigned to these types have paste and temper characteristics that are consistent with a Bell Plain paste.

Both brown-on-buff, and red-on-black negative painted sherds have been found at Caborn-Welborn sites. They are either part of line-filled triangles (Figure 3.9b) or are portions of some type of circular design.

## Beckwith Incised

Some jar sherds exhibit incised designs that extend from just below the rim to slightly below the neck. The only recognizable motif is that of a rectilinear guilloche (Figure 3.9a), which is the defining characteristic of the type Beckwith Incised (Clay 1963a; Cole et al. 1951; Lewis 1986, 1990; Phillips 1970; Pollack and Railey 1987). It should be noted that O'Brien and Fox (1994:162) assign a similar motif to Barton Incised. In this analysis, assignment of sherds to Barton Incised was restricted to specimens having line-filled triangular areas that are located between the lip and the neck.

Beckwith Incised vessels are primarily jars with direct rims, but some are outflaring or recurved. Vessel orifice diameters range from 4 to 16 cm. Handles were not associated with any of the Beckwith Incised rims, but several other types of appendages, including single or bifurcated lugs attached to the lip and a node attached below the lip, were associated with this type.

## Caborn-Welborn Decorated

Caborn-Welborn Decorated (Munson 1984) jars are characterized by trailed, incised, and/or punctated designs located between the neck and shoulder (Figures 3.10–3.15). All of the Caborn-Welborn Decorated rims are portions of globular jars that are similar in shape to those classified as Mississippi Plain (Figure 3.1). Most of these vessels have direct rims with rounded necks. Outflaring rims with rounded necks and vessels with recurved rims are also well represented.

A few Caborn-Welborn Decorated rims have direct or outflaring rims associated with sharply angled rim/neck junctures. These rims lack the interior lip modification and notched loop handles that characterize Oneota-like ceramics. Most have plain lips, but some have oblong punctations or dashes on top of the lip (Figure 3.11a).

Caborn-Welborn Decorated jar orifice diameters range from 4 to 34 cm. Handles on Caborn-Welborn Decorated vessels have a mean width to thickness ratio of 3.2 to 1. In general, thin strap handles are associated with larger jars (mean orifice diameter of 16.1 cm) than thick strap (mean orifice diameter of 8.5 cm), intermediate loop/straps (mean orifice diameter of 9.6 cm), or loop handles (mean orifice diameter of 9.0 cm). Jars usually have two handles, but some have four thin straps.

Many of the handles assigned to this type are decorated with trailed, incised (Figure 3.10a), and/or punctated designs (Figure 3.12b) or have central grooves, notched edges, drilled holes, applied nodes, or an applied strip. Trailing or incising occurs as a series of vertical or horizontal lines or nested chev-

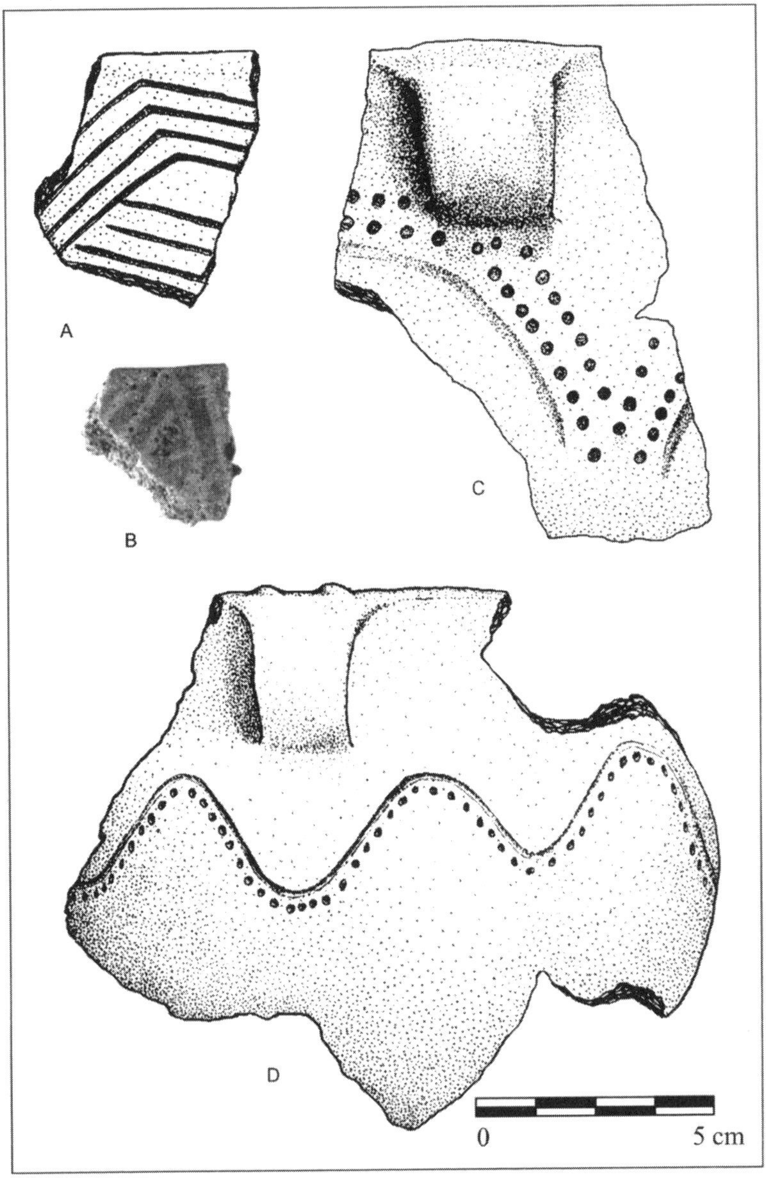


Figure 3.9. Lower Ohio valley decorated ceramic types: a, Beckwith Incised; b, Angel Negative Painted; c,d, Manly Punctate with thin strap handles.

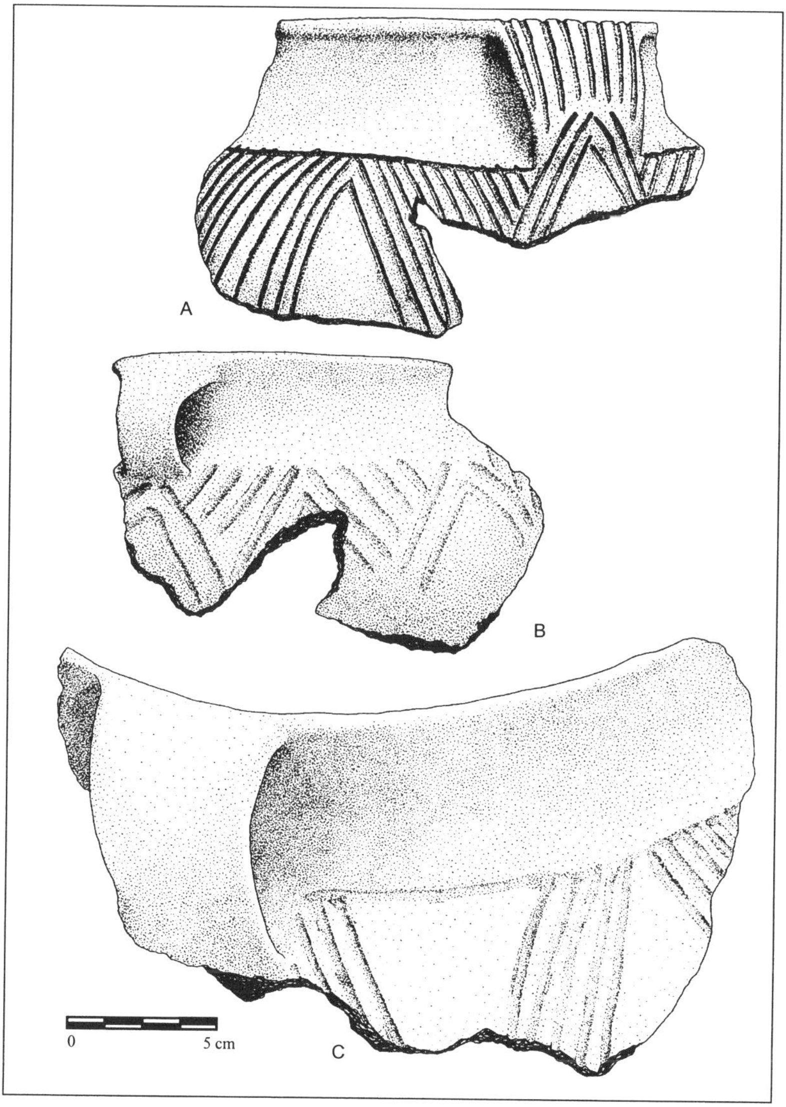


Figure 3.10. Caborn-Welborn Decorated with lines used as fill: a, line-filled triangles and incised thin strap handle; b, line-filled triangles and thin strap handle; c, unfilled triangles and thin strap handle.

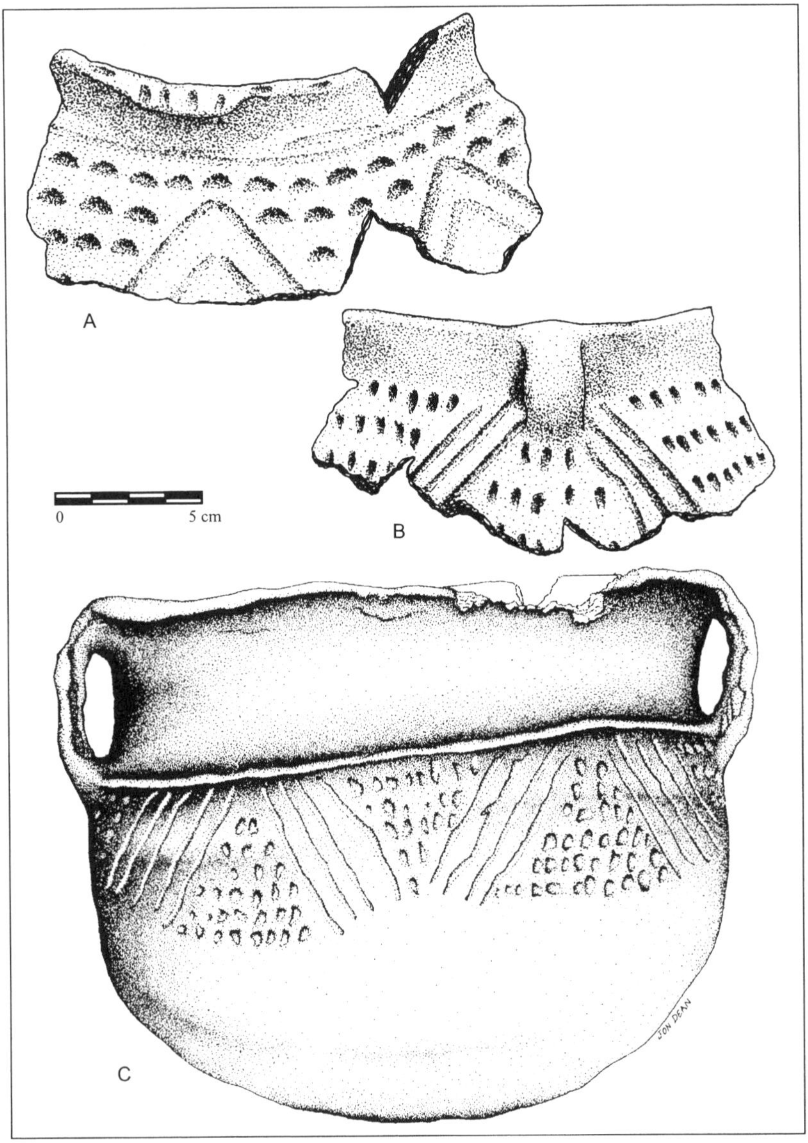


Figure 3.11. Caborn-Welborn Decorated with punctation used as fill: a, oblong punctations on lip and rectangular lug; b, thick strap handle; c, opposing thin strap handles.

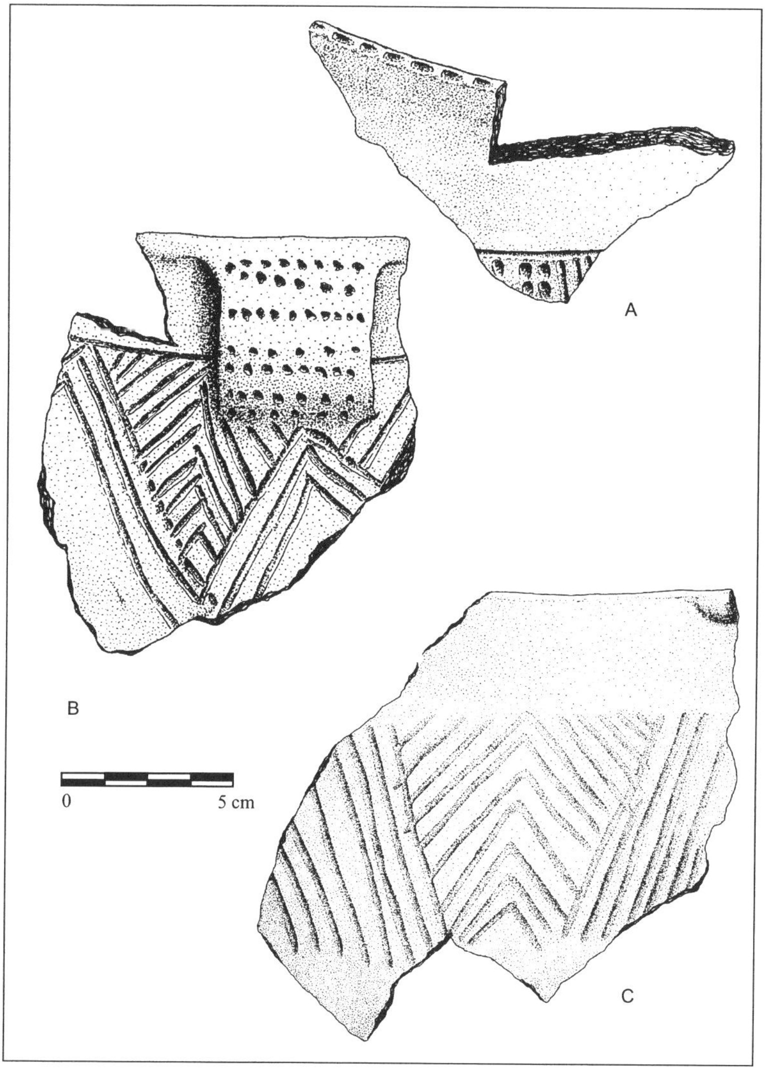


Figure 3.12. Caborn-Welborn Decorated: a, punctations on lip; b, line-filled triangles and punctations on thin strap handle; c, rising chevrons and lug fragment.

rons. Punctations cover the entire handle or occur as a single row placed down the center of the handle. Alternating rows of lines and punctations are present on some handles. One handle has a series of horizontal notches extending across its exterior surface. In Caborn-Welborn collections, this handle form tends to be associated with Oneota-like vessels that have sharply angled rim/neck junctures and interior lip notching or trailing. This handle, however, is

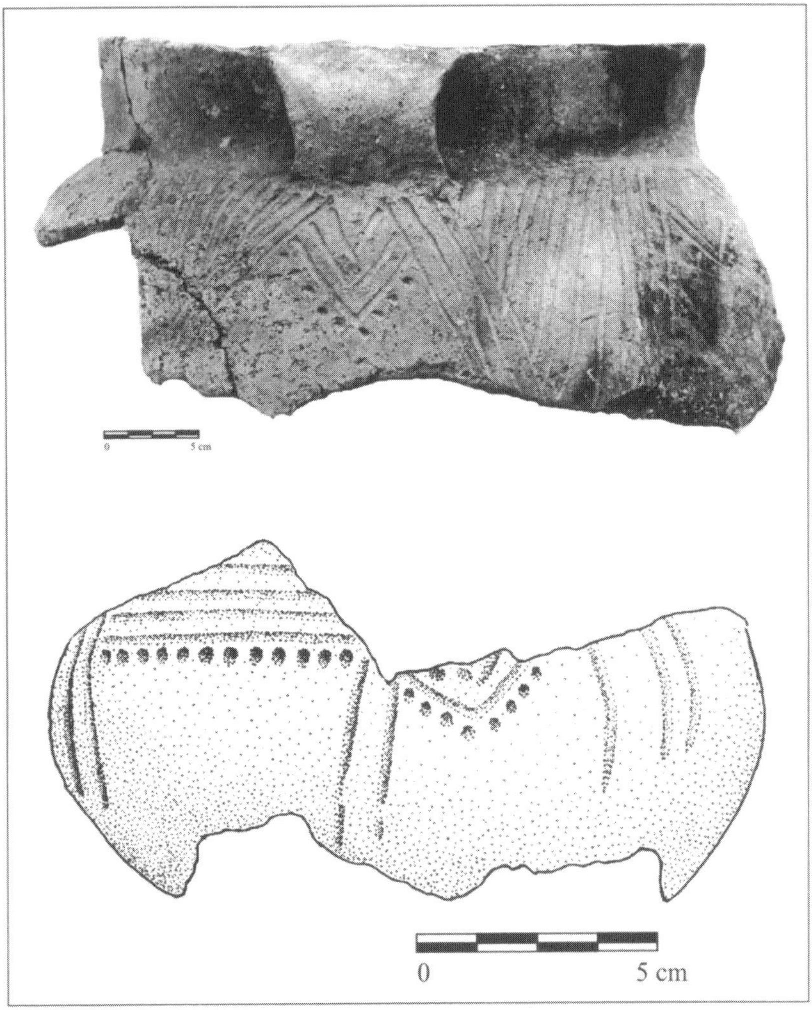


Figure 3.13. Caborn-Welborn Decorated: top, line-filled triangles and descending chevrons bordered by punctations (Oneota hawk motif) and thin strap handles; bottom, example of Oneota design on a Caborn-Welborn Decorated jar showing punctations bordering descending chevrons and horizontal lines, with panels demarcated by vertical lines.

associated with a compound vessel that has a rounded neck and lacks interior lip decoration.

A variety of other appendages are associated with Caborn-Welborn Decorated jars. They include single, bifurcated, or notched lugs; single, paired/multiple, or dimpled nodes; and notched horizontal or vertical strips and plain vertical strips. Most were attached at the lip or just below the lip. Some, how-

Figure 3.14. Range of variation in Caborn-Welborn Decorated jar shoulder design (note: a and q are the most common).

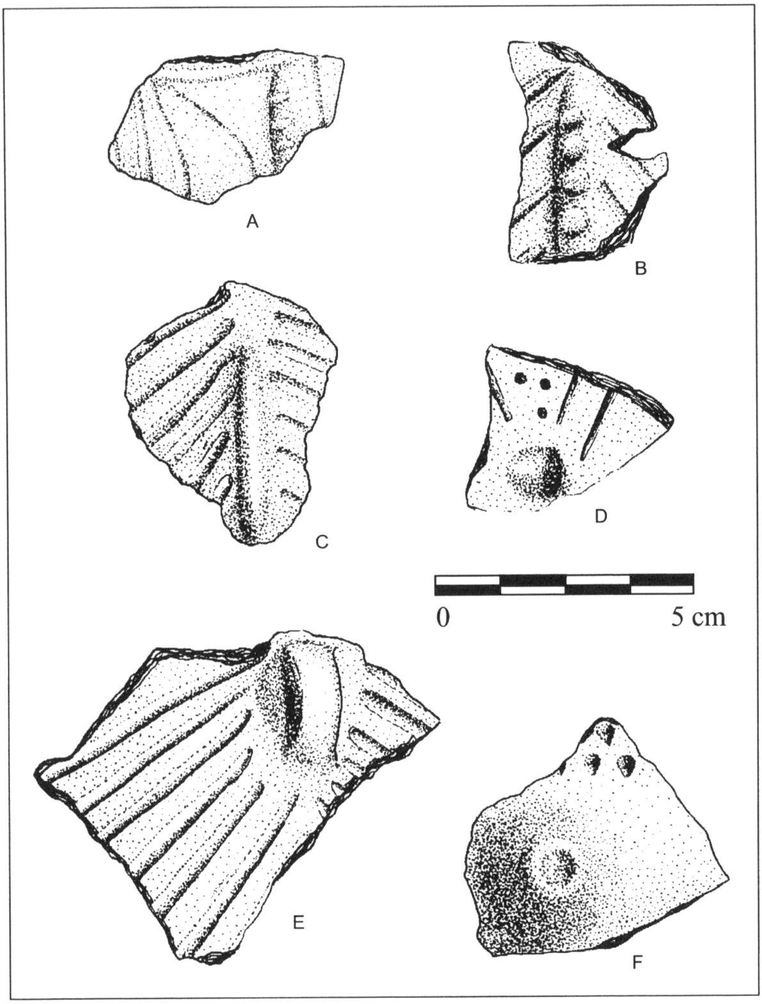


Figure 3.15. Caborn Welborn Decorated: a,b, notched vertical strip; c, plain vertical strip; d, node; e, lug; f, dimpled node.

ever, including notched vertical strips and plain or dimpled nodes, are located below the neck and were incorporated within Caborn-Welborn designs (Figure 3.15).

Decoration on lips consists primarily of oblong punctations on top of the lip (Figures 3.11a and 3.12a). A few rims are associated with circular or triangular punctations. Still other jar lips were decorated with diagonal dashes or vertical notches. Sometimes vertical notches and occasionally triangular punctations were placed on the exterior of jar lips.

The most distinctive decorative treatment associated with Caborn-Welborn

Decorated sherds are trailed, incised, and/or punctated designs on vessel shoulders. These designs consist primarily of triangular areas demarcated by incised or trailed lines that form an opposing series of triangles (Figures 3.10 and 3.11). Alternating rows of lines and punctations or just punctations also were used to lay out the triangular areas (Figure 3.14t,ee). Often a line was used to form an upper border for the design (Figure 3.10a,c), and sometimes a line also was placed directly below the design to create a lower border (Figure 3.14j). In addition to incising, trailing, or punctation, the exterior or interior surface of a few Caborn-Welborn Decorated jars also have a red slip.

Descending triangles were usually filled with parallel, incised, or trailed lines (Figure 3.10a,b) or with a series of punctations (Figure 3.11), but sometimes they were left plain (Figures 3.10c and 3.14e). The parallel lines used to fill triangular areas tend to be oriented obliquely, but they can occur as vertical and horizontal lines. As will be discussed in chapters 5 and 6, the use of lines and punctations as fill varies temporally and spatially in the Caborn-Welborn region.

In some instances, rising triangles on Caborn-Welborn jars also were filled with parallel lines or rows of punctations (Figures 3.11b,c and 3.14j,k,r,t,v), but these areas usually were left plain (Figure 3.10c). Sometimes 3–4 horizontal lines or descending chevrons (Figures 3.13 and 3.14t–y) were used to fill part of the triangular space. Most of the groups of horizontal lines and descending chevrons were bordered by a row of punctations (Figures 3.13 and 3.14x,y). These designs are similar to elements of the thunderbird or hawk motif noted on Oneota ceramics (Benn 1989; Hall 1991). Nested rising chevrons, which rarely are bordered by punctation, also were used to fill triangular areas (Figures 3.12c and 3.14c,d). In addition to being used to fill triangular areas and as an outer border, punctations were used to fill areas between diagonal or vertical lines (Figure 3.14cc,dd) and as an inner border (Figure 3.14bb).

Punctations on Caborn-Welborn Decorated vessel shoulders can be associated with trailed or incised lines. Usually punctations were used to fill triangular areas (Figure 3.11), but they were also used as a border (Figure 3.13). Most of the punctations are oblong in shape, but some are circular (most appear to have been made with a pointed object, but some were made with a hollow reed) and others are triangular or crescent-shaped. Still others resemble a dash more than a punctation.

In several respects, Caborn-Welborn Decorated designs are similar to those described for Barton Incised (O'Brien and Fox 1994; Phillips 1970; Phillips et al. 1951): both are characterized by triangular areas filled with parallel lines. However, on Barton Incised vessels, such designs are usually restricted to the area between the rim and neck (Figure 3.21d), while on Caborn-Welborn Decorated jars they are located below the neck and tend to be associated with vessels that have shorter necks and more pronounced shoulders. The use of multiple lines to lay out the design field also serves to distinguish Caborn-Welborn Decorated from Barton Incised, and in particular Barton Incised var. *Arcola,* which, like Caborn-Welborn Decorated, is characterized by line-filled triangular motifs located below jar necks.

Decoration on some Oneota jars also consists of alternating panels of lines and punctations (e.g., Boszhardt 1994; Gibbon 1973). However, the layout lines on Oneota jars tend to be oriented vertically and rarely intersect each other (see Figures 3.13 and 3.14z for examples of Oneota designs on Caborn-Welborn Decorated jars). Rather than creating triangular areas, the net result is a series of panels or trapezoidal spaces that encircle the vessel. Thus, in general, the orientation of the Caborn-Welborn layout lines and the use of opposing triangular space tend to distinguish Caborn-Welborn designs from Oneota designs.

As mentioned and to be discussed further in chapter 5, some of the designs on Caborn-Welborn Decorated jars are similar to those on Angel/Kincaid Negative Painted plates. The most common design associated with both types consists of layout lines that were used to create opposing descending and rising triangles. These triangular areas were usually filled with lines or, in the case of Caborn-Welborn Decorated, punctations, and in the case of Angel/Kincaid Negative Painted, dots.

## Manly Punctate

Manly Punctate (Phillips 1970) is characterized by undulating rows of punctations, which often parallel an incised or trailed line (Figure 3.9c,d). The undulations form a series of arches around the neck of jars, extending from the maximum point of constriction to the shoulder. On lobed vessels this design tends to follow the upper edges of the lobes, while on nonlobed specimens it extends to the neck.

Manly Punctate rims are primarily from globular jars with direct rims and rounded necks. Vessels with direct rims and angled necks, outflaring rims and rounded necks, and recurved rims also are present in some Caborn-Welborn collections. Manly Punctate vessels range in orifice diameter from 4 to 18 cm.

Within Caborn-Welborn collections, Manly Punctate is characterized by a great deal of variability with respect to the number of rows of punctation and lines. Most Manly Punctate vessels have two or three rows of punctations or a combination of rows of punctations and lines (Figure 3.9c). Others have one row of punctations, and a few have a combination of four or more rows of punctations and lines. Lip decoration consists of circular punctations on the lip or vertical notches on the exterior of the lip.

Unlike Parkin Punctate or Campbell Punctate vessels, which sometimes have a large number of handles at Caborn-Welborn sites, Manly Punctate jars primarily have only two opposing handles attached at the rim. Handles are usually thin, parallel-sided straps (Figure 3.9c,d) having a mean width to thickness ratio of 3.8 to 1, but a few are intermediate loop/strap handles. The only other type of appendage associated with Manly Punctate vessels is paired or multiple nodes.

## Matthews Incised

Sherds lacking punctations but exhibiting from one to three parallel curved lines that form an undulating design similar to that of Manly Punctate were classified as Matthews Incised (Phillips 1970). Within Caborn-Welborn collections, this type is usually characterized by one curved line (Figure 3.16c,d). As with Manly Punctate, this design on lobed vessels tends to follow the upper edges of the lobes (Figure 3.16d), and on nonlobed specimens it extends from the neck to the shoulder of the jar.

Matthews Incised jars usually have direct rims and rounded necks, and vessel orifice diameters range from 4 to 18 cm. Handles on Matthews Incised jars are usually thin, parallel-sided straps attached at the rim and have a mean width to thickness ratio of 3.9 to 1. The only other type of appendages associated with these vessels are bifurcated lugs and dimpled nodes (Figure 3.16c). Some jars have opposing pairs of strap handles and bifurcated lugs (Figure 3.16b). Lip decoration consists of crescent-shaped punctations on the lip.

## Mound Place Incised

Decoration on Mound Place Incised (Phillips et al. 1951:127–129) consists of two or more parallel horizontal lines located just below the lip of Mississippi or Bell Plain bowls (Figure 3.16a). From three to five lines are present on each rim, and these lines have a mean width of 1.0 mm, ranging in width from 0.8 to 1.1 mm. On some vessels, these lines dip to avoid intersecting a node or an effigy rim rider. All of the Mound Place Incised sherds in Caborn-Welborn collections have paste characteristics that are consistent with Bell Plain. Mound Place Incised bowl rims have an orifice diameter of 12 cm.

## O'Byam Incised/Engraved

All of the O'Byam rims (Figure 3.16b) exhibit a Bell Plain paste and all are derived from shallow bowls with outslanting walls, with some specimens having a castellated rim. It is possible that some of the rims are portions of plates, but all lacked the distinctive well diagnostic of plates. Orifice diameters range from 6 to 34 cm.

Most of the line-filled triangles on O'Byam rims from Caborn-Welborn sites are filled with diagonal lines, but some are horizontal. Some of these rims also exhibit diagonal lip notching. In general, the designs on O'Byam rims from Caborn-Welborn sites are rather poorly executed (Figure 3.16b), in comparison to O'Byam vessels recovered from Mississippian sites in the lower

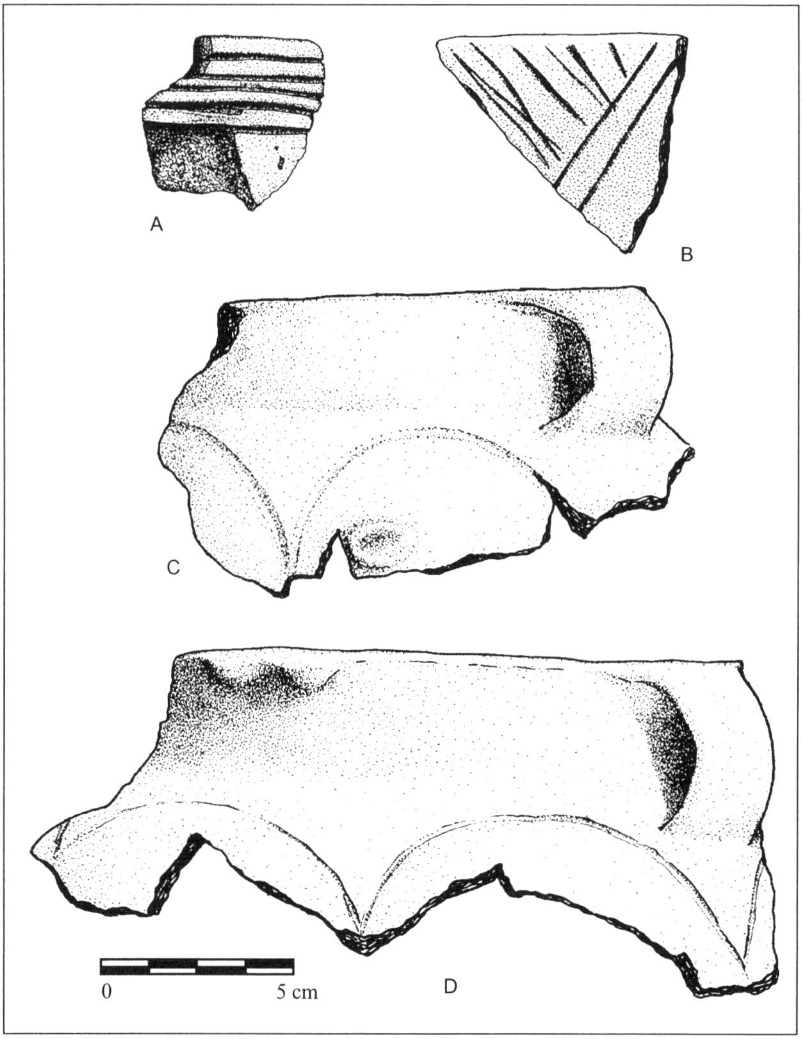


Figure 3.16. Lower Ohio valley decorated ceramic types: a, Mound Place Incised; b, O'Byam Incised/Engraved; c, Matthews Incised with dimpled node and thin strap handle; d, Matthews Incised with bifurcated lug and thin strap handle.

Tennessee-Cumberland and Mississippi River valleys (Clay 1963a; Lewis 1986; Pollack and Railey 1987).

## Old Town Red

All of the slipped sherds, regardless of color, were included within this type (Phillips 1970). Though most of the sherds are red-slipped, a few orange- or brown-slipped specimens are also present. Most of the Old Town specimens have a Bell Plain paste, but some exhibit a Mississippi Plain paste. Both bowls and bottles are represented.

*Bowls*

Slightly more than half of the Old Town bowl rims are from shallow bowls with flat bottoms and outslanting walls. Many of these rims are associated with castellations. Bowl orifice diameters range from 6 to 18 cm. Only the interior surfaces of some bowls were slipped, while a slip was applied to only the exterior surface of others. A few were slipped on both surfaces. A few rims exhibit vertical or diagonal lip notching.

*Bottles*

Most Old Town Red bottle rims are from long-necked bottles. These vessels range in orifice diameter from 4 to 6 cm.

## CERAMIC TYPES AND GROUPS THAT REFLECT EXTRAREGIONAL INTERACTION

### Oneota-Like

The frequent co-occurrence of sherds with a sharply angled rim/neck juncture, notched rectangular loop handle, and interior lip notches, dashes, and trailing (Figures 3.17–3.20) led to the recognition that Caborn-Welborn ceramic collections contain Oneota-like ceramics. All jar rims with interior lip decoration and all notched loop handles were assigned to this type.

While most Oneota-like jars have globular bodies, direct rims, and a sharply angled rim/neck juncture (Figure 3.17), some have slightly outflaring rims and a sharply angled rim/neck juncture. Vessels with direct rims and rounded necks, or recurved rims, are also present. As a group, these vessels range in orifice diameter from 4 to 38 cm.

Handles associated with Oneota-like rims tend to be either loops (Figure 3.18e) that are rectangular in cross-section or intermediate loop/straps (Figures 3.17 and 3.18). They have a combined width to thickness ratio of 1.6 to 1. A few rims are associated with thick or thin straps (Figure 3.19d,h). Most of the loop and intermediate loop/strap handles are notched, and many are attached to the rim below the lip, extending to just below the rim/neck juncture (Figures 3.18e,f and 3.19b,h). A few handles have incised or trailed vertical or diagonal lines. No other appendage types (i.e., lugs, nodes, or strips) are associated with Oneota-like vessels.

Oneota-like vessels exhibit a great deal of variability in lip decoration. On about three-quarters of the rims, decoration is restricted to the interior of the lip (Figures 3.18a,c; 3.19a,c,f,g; and 3.20a), and on about one-quarter of the rims, it is restricted to the top of the lip (Figure 3.20c,d). Interior lip decora-

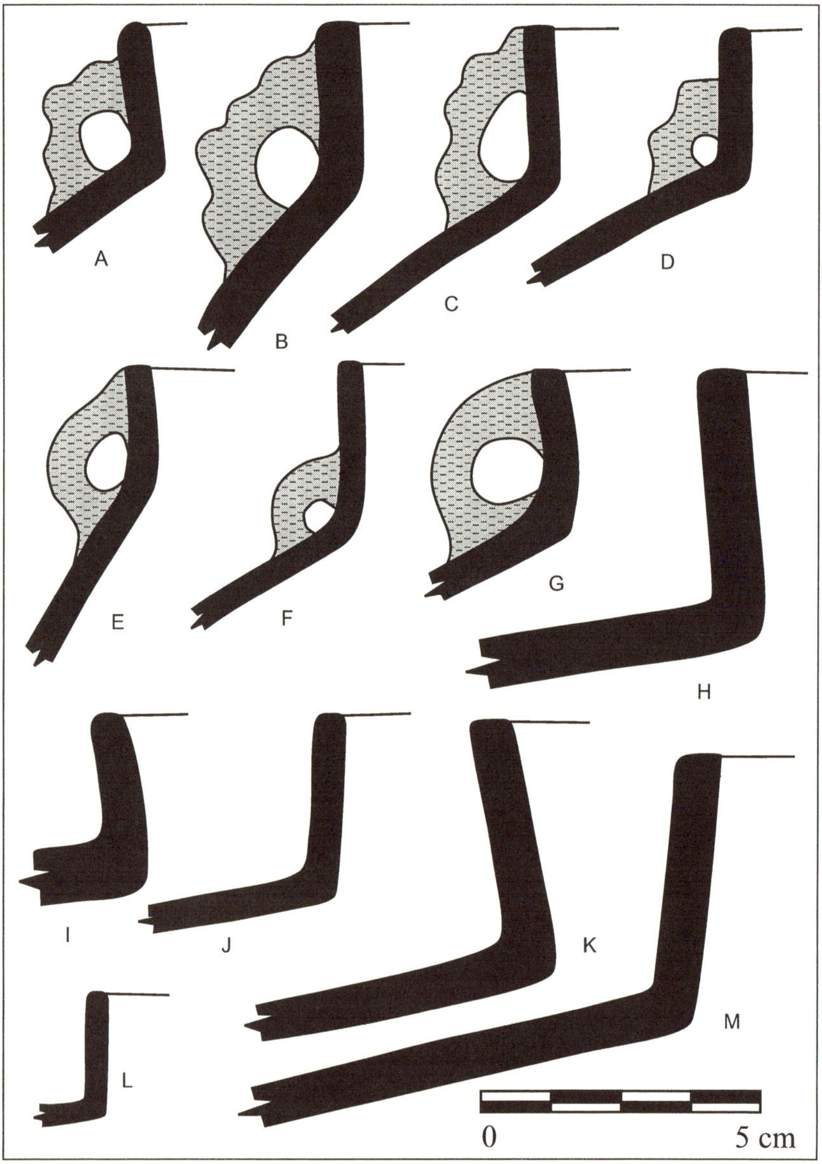


Figure 3.17. Oneota-like jar rim profiles: a–d, direct angled neck with notched intermediate loop/strap handle; e,f, direct angled neck with thick strap handle; g, direct angled neck with loop handle; i–m, direct angled neck.

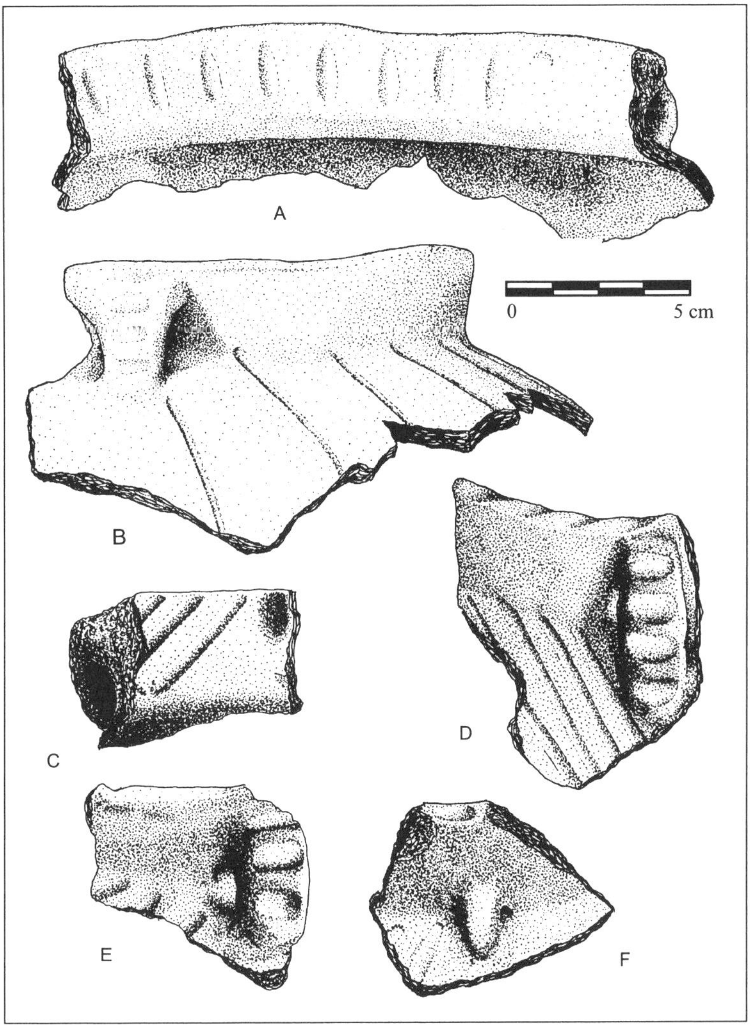


Figure 3.18. Oneota-like ceramics: a, interior dashes (interior of b); b, notched intermediate loop/strap handle and trailed design; c, interior dash and trailed lines (interior of e); d, notched intermediate loop/strap handle, trailed design, and notched lip; e, notched intermediate loop/strap handle and trailed design; f, loop handle, trailed design, and punctated lip.

tion consists primarily of a series of vertical or diagonal dashes or notches (Figures 3.18a,c and 3.19a,c,f,g). Dashes are sometimes associated with trailed chevrons (Figures 3.18a and 3.19a). Diagonal notches are the primary lip decoration found on the top of the lip (Figures 3.18d and 3.20c). Other decorative treatments associated with Oneota-like jar lips include dashes, a groove, and oblong or circular punctations (Figure 3.18f).

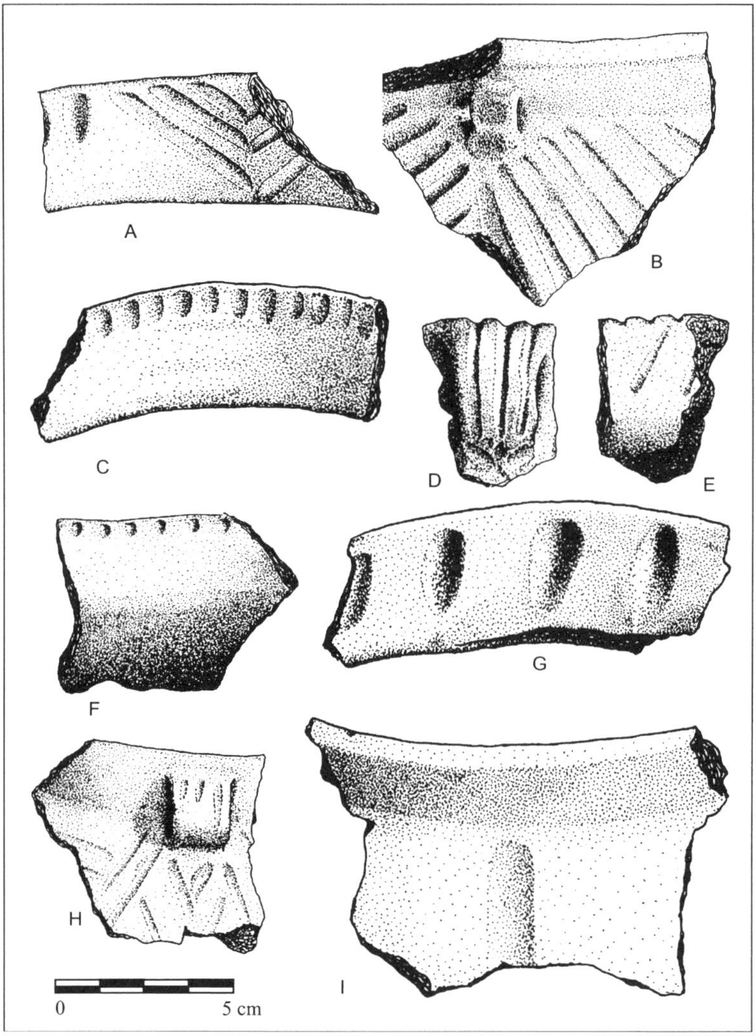


Figure 3.19. Oneota-like ceramics: a, interior trailed chevron and dashes (interior of b); b, notched intermediate loop/strap handle and trailed design; c,f, interior notches (f is interior of h); d, trailed thick strap handle; e,g, interior dashes (e is interior of d); h, trailed thick strap handle and trailed design; i, wide, shallow trailed design.

This type includes jars with plain (37.0 percent) or decorated (63.0 percent) shoulders. Trailing on the exterior surfaces of Oneota-like vessels ranges in width from 2.0 to 10.1 mm, with a mean width of 4.0 mm. In general, trailing on Oneota-like jars is wider and shallower than on Caborn-Welborn Decorated jars (average width of 2.6 mm). Few Oneota-like vessels are deco-

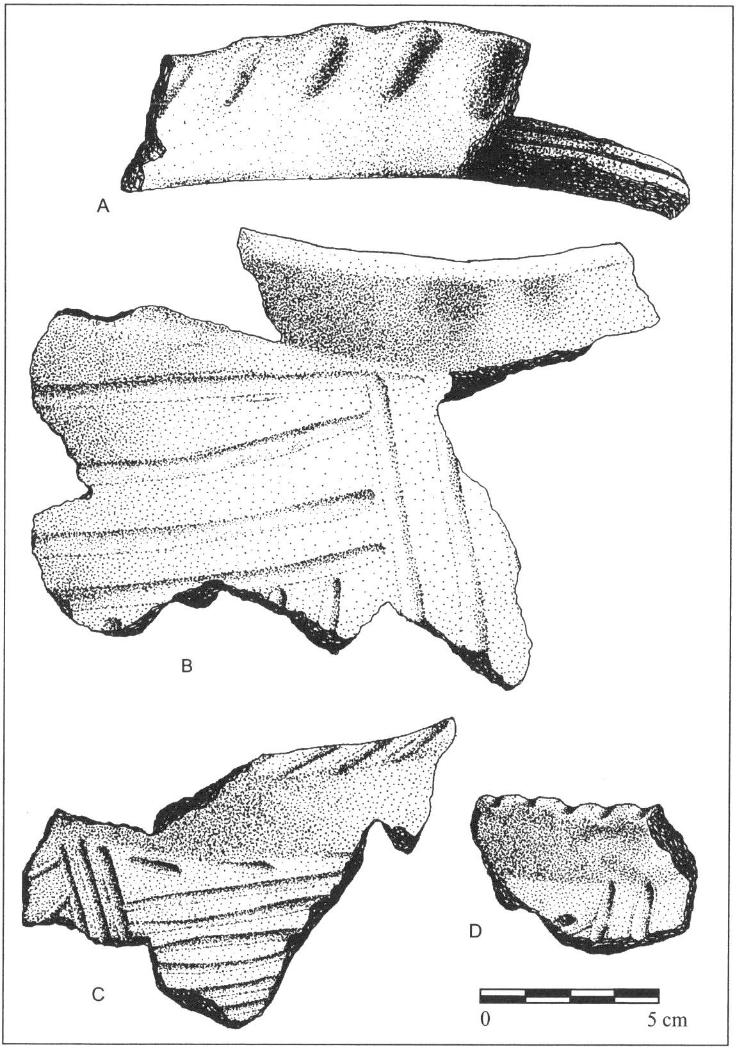


Figure 3.20. Oneota-like ceramics: a, interior diagonal dashes (interior of b); b, trailed design; c,d, trailed design with notched lip.

rated with incised lines or punctations. The only measurable incised line has a width of 2.0 mm. When present, oblong or circular punctations and dashes are primarily used as an exterior border to embellish trailed designs (Figure 3.20b). Trailed lines associated with punctations range in width from 2.9 to 5.5 mm, with a mean width of 4.2 mm.

One trailed design that is fairly common on Oneota-like vessels consists of wide, shallow, parallel vertical or diagonal lines that do not enclose or fill triangular areas (Figures 3.18b and 3.19i). Similar motifs have been observed on Huber Trailed ceramics (Bluhm and Fenner 1961; Bluhm and Liss 1961; Faulkner 1972; Herold et al. 1990:42; Michalik and Brown 1990:203) in northern Illinois and Indiana and Koshkong Bold vessels in Wisconsin (Boszhardt 1994; Hall 1962). This design also is a defining characteristic of Kent Incised (Figure 3.22a) (O'Brien and Fox 1994:37; Phillips 1970), a central Mississippi valley ceramic type. In order to distinguish the Oneota-like ceramics from Kent Incised–like specimens, when this motif was associated with rims having interior lip decoration and a sharply angled rim/neck juncture or extremely wide trailed lines, it was assigned to the Oneota-like group. Rim and body sherds of globular jars with rounded necks and incised or narrow trailed lines were assigned to the type Kent Incised–like (see below). Other designs associated with Oneota-like vessels include lines outlining triangular areas, with these areas filled with diagonal lines (Figures 3.19b and 3.20c) or left plain, and descending chevrons (Figure 3.19h).

### Barton Incised

Decoration on these specimens is located in a zone between the lip and neck of jars (Figure 3.21d). Some designs are similar to those observed on Caborn-Welborn Decorated, but usually only one line was used to lay out rising and descending triangles. One of the Barton Incised rims has an interior-beveled lip that is similar to what House (1993:27) has referred to as the "Memphis Rim Mode." The other Barton rims lack this interior beveling, but all exhibit some degree of exterior lip thickening. Exterior designs on the Barton Incised rims consist primarily of line-filled triangular areas. Designs that incorporate both incising and punctations also are present (see O'Brien and Fox 1994:45). The only appendages associated with this type are nodes and thin straps, some of which are punctated, located between the neck and shoulder.

### Campbell Applique

Campbell Applique (O'Brien and Fox 1994; Phillips 1970) is characterized by a series of applied vertical strips located on the rim between the lip and the neck (Figure 3.21b,c). Most of the applied strips are plain (Figure 3.21b), but some are notched (Figure 3.21c). Campbell Applique jars have direct rims and rounded necks. Vessel orifice diameters range from 4 to 16 cm. Other types of appendages are not associated with any of the Campbell Applique rims, and none of the lips are decorated.

### Campbell Incised

Campbell Incised is similar to Kent Incised. However, on Campbell Incised vessels, the incising extends from the lip or just below the lip to below the shoulder (Chapman and Anderson 1955; O'Brien and Fox 1994) (Figure 3.22b). Most Campbell Incised vessels have recurved rims, but some have direct rims. Campbell Incised jar orifice diameters range from 4 to 10 cm. No

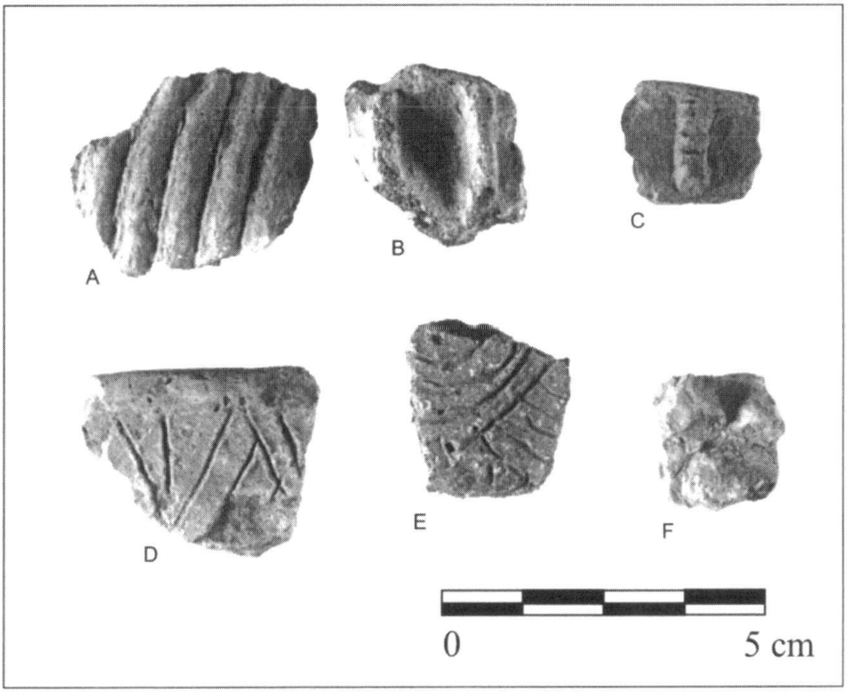


Figure 3.21. Central Mississippi valley–derived types: a, Vernon Paul Applique; b,c, Campbell Applique; d, Barton Incised; e, Ranch Incised-like; f, Fortune Noded.

handles or other appendages were associated with any of the rims, nor was lip decoration observed.

## Campbell Punctate

In contrast to Parkin Punctate, Campbell Punctate is characterized by horizontal rows of punctations (Figure 3.23b). Unlike Manly Punctate, the rows of punctations do not form arches. In the central Mississippi valley, decoration on Campbell Punctate vessels is primarily restricted to an area just below the neck of wide-mouthed bottles and jars (Chapman and Anderson 1955; Lawrence and Mainfort 1995:266; O'Brien and Fox 1994:40, 219). Within Caborn-Welborn collections, this type is primarily restricted to jars.

### *Jars*

At Caborn-Welborn sites, from one to five horizontal rows of oblong, triangular, circular, crescent, or U-shaped punctations are found on Campbell Punctate vessels. Occasionally there is a single incised or trailed line above the punctated area, and sometimes circular or triangular punctations also were placed on the lip.

Jar vessel orifice diameter ranges from 4 to 18 cm. Handles associated with

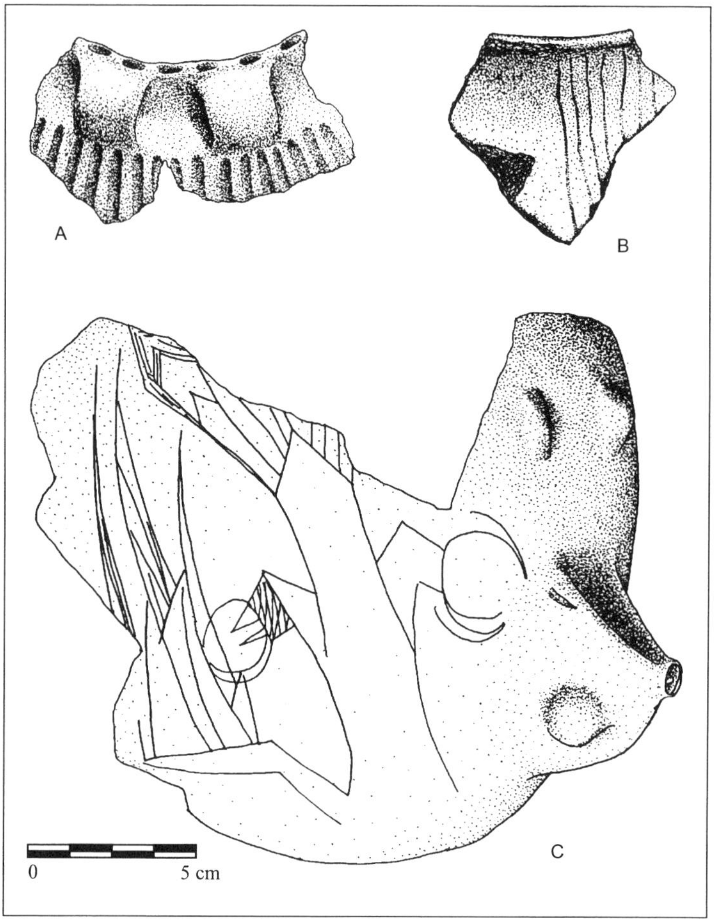


Figure 3.22. Central Mississippi valley–derived types: a, Kent Incised–like with eight thin strap handles and punctated lip; b, Campbell Incised; c, Walls Engraved, fish effigy bowl with engraved hawk(?).

Campbell Punctate vessels have a mean thickness to width ratio of 3.1 to 1 and can be either thin or thick straps. Some vessels have as many as 16 (arcaded) handles (Figure 3.23b). The only other type of appendage associated with Campbell Punctate jars is a bifurcated lug.

*Bottles*

Campbell Punctate bottle rims have a wide mouth and three rows of punctations about 2 cm below the rim. They have an orifice diameter of 8 cm. The only appendage associated with this vessel form is a small node (see O'Brien 1994:230). Campbell Punctate bottle rims also are characterized by the interior-beveled lip that House (1993:27) refers to as the Memphis Rim Mode.

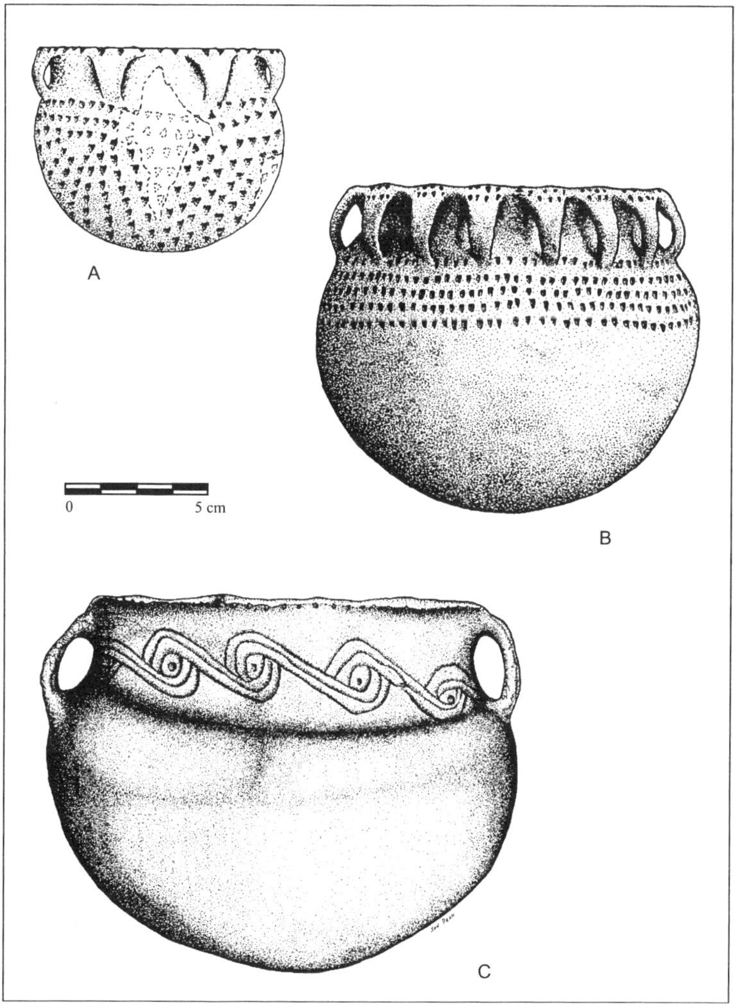


Figure 3.23. Central Mississippi valley jars and miscellaneous jars: a, Parkin Punctate with 8 thick strap handles and punctated lip; b, Campbell Punctate with 16 thick (arcaded) strap handles and punctated lip; c, Miscellaneous Incised/Trailed, with opposing thin strap handles and punctated lip.

## Fortune Noded

Fortune Noded is characterized by nodes placed over a vessel's exterior surface (Phillips 1970) (Figure 3.21f). Little can be said about vessel form, as no Fortune Noded rims have been found at Caborn-Welborn sites. However, one large vessel section appears to be part of a noded bowl that has a Bell Plain paste.

## Kent Incised–Like

As noted, jars having rounded necks and shoulders decorated with a series of vertical or diagonal lines (Figure 3.22a) that do not enclose or fill triangular areas were classified as Kent Incised–like (Phillips 1970). Lines on Kent Incised–like jars can cover the entire shoulder area, or they can occur as clusters of three to four lines with plain areas between them. A slight majority of Kent Incised–like sherds are truly incised, while the remaining sherds have trailed lines. Most Kent Incised–like jars have direct rims and rounded necks, but some have outflaring rims and rounded necks, or recurved rims. Their vessel orifice diameters range from 4 to 18 cm.

The primary handle form associated with Kent Incised–like vessels is the thin strap, but some jars are associated with loop handles. Handles on Kent Incised–like jars have a combined mean width to thickness ratio of 3.5 to 1. Other types of appendages associated with Kent Incised–like vessels are paired or multiple lugs and notched lugs. Lip decoration is restricted to oblong punctations on the lip. One Kent Incised–like jar has eight thin strap handles and oblong punctations on its lip, and another has a series of small lugs extending from the lip and encircling the entire jar orifice.

## Parkin Punctate

Sherds that appear to have been part of jars that were punctated from the neck to the bottom of the vessel were classified as Parkin Punctate (Phillips 1970) (Figure 3.23a). Vessel orifice diameters range from 8 to 10 cm. Punctations with a crescent or U-shape, as well as punctations with an adjacent rise (a small elevated ridge of clay next to the hole), are the most common forms.

The only handles associated with the Parkin Punctate vessels are thick straps that have a width to thickness ratio of 2.2 to 1. As many as eight handles occur on some Parkin vessels (Figure 3.23a). In addition to the punctations observed on jar bodies, on some Parkin rims, triangular punctations also were placed on the lip.

## Ranch Incised–Like

The Ranch Incised–Like type is characterized by groups of parallel incised or trailed lines that intersect each other. The design made by these lines has been characterized as resembling fish scales (Phillips et al. 1951:119–120). Only a few Ranch Incised–like body sherds (Figure 3.21e) have been found at Caborn-Welborn phase sites.

## Vernon Paul Applique

The type Vernon Paul Applique (O'Brien and Fox 1994:42; Phillips 1970:167–168; Phillips et al. 1951:120) is characterized by a series of vertical ribs applied to exterior jar surfaces (Figure 3.21a). Unlike Campbell Applique where widely spaced vertical strips were attached to the wet body of the vessel, these closely spaced strips were smoothed into the vessel wall. Little can be said about vessel form, as no Vernon Paul Applique rims have been found at Caborn-Welborn sites.

## Walls Engraved

Several sherds with Bell Plain paste have engraved exterior or interior surfaces (Figure 3.22c). These specimens are similar to Walls Engraved, which is a common late Mississippian type in the Memphis area of western Tennessee (Phillips et al. 1951; G. Smith 1990). This type is associated with hemispherical bowls with direct or incurving rims. These vessels range in orifice diameter from 12 to 18 cm. While no bottle rims were recovered, several of the body sherds appear to have been derived from bottles.

Vertical lip notches are present on bowl rims. One of the hemispherical bowls has a small bifurcated lug attached to its rim. Directly below the lip engraved on the outside of the vessel were the head and mouth of an animal baring its teeth. Another specimen consists of a large portion of a bowl with incurving sides. The molded head and fins of a fish had been attached to the side of the vessel. An abstract representation of what may have been a hawk had been engraved on the side of the bowl (Figure 3.22c). A portion of a bird with crude talons is depicted, similar to that on an engraved bottle from Owl Cave in the western Ozarks and the Craig C bird-man from Spiro (J. Brown 1989:191, 200; Lawton 1964, cited in J. Brown 1989:200). Engraved lines on other specimens also could be part of abstract representations of animals. However, the small size of the sherds makes it impossible to interpret these designs with any degree of confidence.

# MISCELLANEOUS DECORATED CERAMIC GROUP

## Miscellaneous Incised/Trailed

This group includes sherds with Mississippi or Bell Plain pastes that could not be assigned to previously defined types with any degree of confidence. Some of the Mississippi paste sherds exhibit incised or trailed lines between the neck and rim, and it is possible that these sherds are from Barton Incised vessels. Unfortunately, the small size of most of these specimens precludes their assignment to this ceramic type.

One whole vessel assigned to this type has opposing strap handles, a punctated lip, and a scroll design on its neck. A single circular punctation had been placed in the center of each scroll (Figure 3.23c). This vessel has a direct rim with an orifice diameter of 14 cm and a rounded neck. While this jar could not be assigned to a specific type, the scroll is similar to those found on jars from Alabama (Steponaitis 1983:55; Walthall 1980:162).

Several of the Bell Plain paste sherds exhibit one or more parallel trailed lines. Others exhibit parallel curved lines that form semicircular or circular designs.

## SUMMARY

Most Caborn-Welborn site ceramic collections are dominated by five types: Mississippi Plain, Bell Plain, Caborn-Welborn Decorated, Kimmswick Fabric Impressed, and Kimmswick Plain (Figure 3.24). Of these, the most common are Mississippi Plain and Bell Plain. Not surprisingly, these two ceramic types also dominate earlier and contemporary Mississippian ceramic collections throughout the Ohio and Mississippi valleys. Also present in some collections are minor amounts of Kimmswick Net Impressed, Shell Tempered Cordmarked, and Tolu Fabric Impressed.

As with most Mississippian ceramic collections, Caborn-Welborn assemblages contain a variety of vessel forms (Figure 3.24), including jars, bowls, pans, bottles, plates, and funnels. Jars and bowls, both hemispherical and shallow with outslanting walls, are the most common vessel forms, followed by pans, bottles, plates, and funnels. The jars tend to have direct rims with rounded necks and thin strap handles. A variety of appendages including lugs, nodes, and notched horizontal strips are associated with jars.

Though found on jars, horizontal applied strips and nodes are more common on bowls. Lugs, however, are less common on bowls than on jars. Human and animal effigy bowls also are common. Some animal effigy bowls have a modeled head and sometimes a tail attached to the rim (e.g., ducks, humans, and other unknown animals). Others (e.g., fish and humans in supine positions) were shaped by modeling the vessel wall to depict a head and other major features, such as legs or a tail, and by adding small lugs to indicate minor features, such as ventral fins.

Lip notching is the primary form of decoration associated with shallow bowls. However, the lips of shallow bowls with castellated rims rarely are notched.

Within all Caborn-Welborn collections, Caborn-Welborn Decorated (Figure 3.24k,n–p) is the most common decorated ceramic type. This distinctive ceramic type is characterized by incised, trailed, or punctated designs on jar shoulders. It is present in all Caborn-Welborn collections, but there is intraregional variation in its frequency of occurrence, the thickness of lines, the use of incised or trailed lines to lay out designs, and the use of incised or trailed lines and punctations as fill. Some of this variation reflects temporal trends, and some reflects stylistic cultural differences within the Caborn-Welborn region. This intraregional variation is explored in more detail in subsequent chapters.

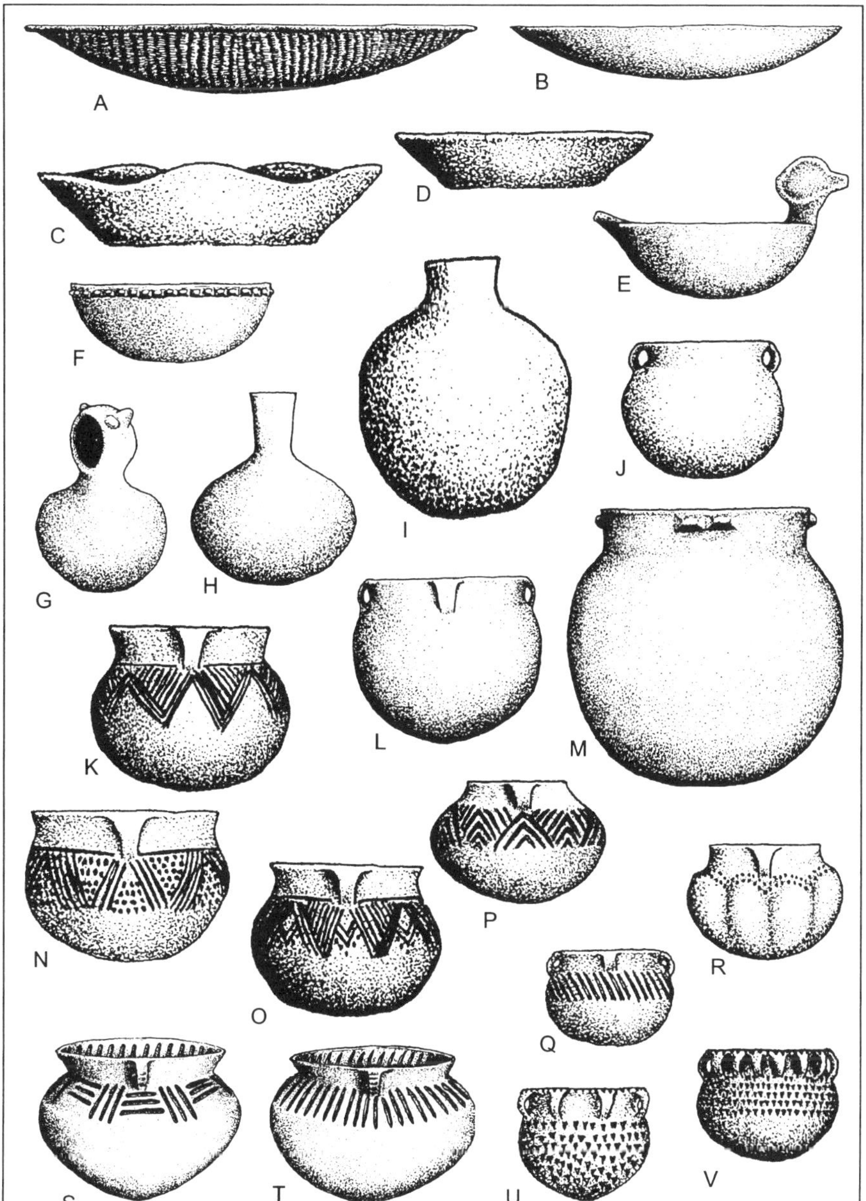


Figure 3.24. Characteristic Caborn-Welborn ceramics: a, Kimmswick Fabric Impressed pan; b, Kimmswick Plain pan; c–f, Bell Plain bowls; g–i, Bell Plain bottles; j,l,m, Mississippi Plain jars; k,n–p, Caborn-Welborn Decorated jars; q, Kent Incised-like jar; r, Manly Punctate jar; s,t, Oneota-like jars; u, Parkin Punctate jar; v, Campbell Punctate jar.

Among the remaining decorated ceramic types, several have a long history of use in the lower Ohio valley, while others point to interaction with groups outside the lower Ohio valley. Ceramic types that reflect continuity with earlier Mississippian groups in the lower Ohio valley include Old Town Red, O'Byam Incised/Engraved, Mound Place Incised, Angel/Kincaid Negative Painted, Manly Punctate, Matthews Incised, and Beckwith Incised. The Oneota-like ceramics reflect interaction with groups to the north of the lower Ohio valley. Types that reflect extraregional interaction with the central Mississippi valley include Barton Incised, Ranch Incised–Like, Parkin Punctate, Campbell Punctate, Kent Incised–Like, Campbell Incised, Walls Engraved, Campbell Applique, Fortune Noded, and Vernon Paul Applique. Taken together, the presence of Oneota-like and central Mississippi valley–derived ceramics within Caborn-Welborn ceramic collections points to some type of economic and social interaction with groups living outside the lower Ohio valley. This interaction will be examined in more detail in chapter 6, and the implications it holds for Caborn-Welborn sociopolitical organization are discussed in chapter 7.

# 4 Site Types and Their Spatial Distribution

Like earlier Mississippian societies of the lower Ohio valley, the Caborn-Welborn settlement system included several different site types. Green and Munson (1978) defined four types: farmsteads, hamlets, small villages, and large villages (see also Green 1977; Muller 1986). A fifth type, blufftop cemeteries not directly associated with a habitation area, was defined during the course of this study (Pollack 1998). The majority of Caborn-Welborn habitation sites are farmsteads, the next most common are hamlets, and small and large villages follow. Unlike earlier Mississippian societies in the lower Ohio valley, however, the Caborn-Welborn settlement system lacked a regional center with a platform mound(s), and no evidence of aboveground corporate architecture has been documented at any Caborn-Welborn sites (Green and Munson 1978).

This chapter defines the five Caborn-Welborn site types used in this study and presents descriptions for a representative sample of sites from which artifact collections were examined or for which information could be obtained from archaeological reports or site forms. The discussion is organized by site type (farmsteads, hamlets, small villages, large villages, and cemeteries). Because Caborn-Welborn sites tend to cluster within one of three subareas (eastern, central, and western), the chapter concludes with an examination of the regional spatial distribution of all types of Caborn-Welborn sites.

## DEFINITIONS, DATA COLLECTION STRATEGIES, AND DATA BIASES

Although a large number of Caborn-Welborn sites have been documented (there are more than 80 known sites), few have been excavated by professional archaeologists. Because of this lack of excavated data, little is known about the internal organization of most Caborn-Welborn settlements, especially farmsteads and hamlets. Likewise, while some Caborn-Welborn villages are known to contain large cemeteries, little is known about Caborn-Welborn mortuary practices.

In the absence of excavated data from well-defined contexts, then, this study relied heavily on surface-collected data to make site type determinations. These data were augmented by information collected from the limited excavations at Hovey Lake and Caborn and the more intensive and extensive investigations at Slack Farm (Munson 1997, 2000; Pollack 1998; Pollack and Munson 1998). There are, however, some problems with relying on surface-collected data to make site type assignments, especially when site size is an important criterion (Anderson 1994:118). The periodic relocation of households within a site or overlapping Caborn-Welborn occupations may make a site appear to be larger than it actually was, which can lead to its being assigned to the wrong site type. On the other hand, deposition of alluvial silts and sands can make a site appear to have been smaller and less intensively occupied than it actually was, which also can lead to its misclassification. Surface artifact assemblages also can be biased by private collectors, who repeatedly collect certain sites. Fortunately, these individuals are generally more interested in chipped and ground stone tools. They rarely collect ceramics, which were the focus of this study.

At all sites, regardless of whether the precise locations of individual artifacts were recorded, all rims, decorated sherds, and appendages were collected. Other potentially diagnostic artifacts, such as triangular points, endscrapers, catlinite disk pipes, copper or brass artifacts, and engraved flat stones, also were collected. The presence or absence of human bone was noted, but none was collected. Materials in museum and private collections also were examined. As noted in chapter 3, the focus of the ceramic analysis was the plain and fabric-impressed rims greater than 4 $cm^2$ and all decorated sherds and appendages regardless of size. Complete and partially reconstructed vessels also were included in the analysis.

In addition to revisiting known sites, selected areas of the Caborn-Welborn region were systematically surveyed in order to record new sites. This surveying involved walking selected areas on transects spaced 10 to 20 m apart. When a site was encountered, determinations were made about whether it dated to the Caborn-Welborn phase, if it contained earlier prehistoric materials, or if it was a later historic site. Only Mississippian sites were systematically collected.

Caborn-Welborn phase sites were distinguished from earlier Angel phase sites on the basis of the presence of three particular classes of artifacts: Caborn-Welborn Decorated ceramics; triangular endscrapers; and Euro-American trade goods, such as brass or copper tubes, coils, and bracelets. These three artifact classes are diagnostic of post–A.D. 1400 components in the lower Ohio valley. Caborn-Welborn Decorated ceramics and triangular endscrapers in particular are found at almost all Caborn-Welborn settlements.

Some projectile point types, such as Nodena Banks or Nodena Elliptical, also are diagnostic of post–A.D. 1400 components. Euro-American trade goods can be used to identify the latest Caborn-Welborn components. These materials in site assemblages, along with the presence of Oneota-like and central Mississippi valley ceramics and the recovery of objects manufactured from nonlocal materials, such as catlinite and marine shell, can provide information on extraregional interaction networks.

In addition to Caborn-Welborn Decorated ceramics, the presence of triangular endscrapers also was used to assign sites to the Caborn-Welborn phase. This distinctive chipped stone tool is diagnostic of post–A.D. 1400 components in the Ohio valley (Green and Munson 1978; Railey 1992). In the Caborn-Welborn region, they are almost always unifacial. These scrapers, which tend to have steep edge-angles, are usually longer than they are wide, with the working edges representing the widest and thickest portions of each tool.

Caborn-Welborn endscrapers occur in three types. Type 1 scrapers (Central Ridge, 37.7 percent) consist of specimens on which 81–100 percent of the original dorsal surface of the blank was removed by intentional retouch (Figure 4.1a–e). Type 2 scrapers (Flat, 49.9 percent) consist of specimens on which 21–80 percent of the dorsal surface displayed retouch (Figure 4.1f–j). Type 3 scrapers (Barely Retouched, 12.4 percent) consist of specimens that had been expediently produced using minimal retouch (up to 20 percent of the dorsal surface).

Triangular point styles typical of post–A.D. 1400 Madison projectile points in the Ohio valley (Railey 1992; Seeman and Munson 1980) also helped to identify Caborn-Welborn components. Most of the triangular points found at Caborn-Welborn phase sites have straight or excurvate sides and a straight base (Types 1 and 2) (Figure 4.1k–m), but specimens with excurvate sides and a concave base (Type 3) (Figure 4.1n) also are common. Some have a thick cross-section and a wide base (Type 4) (Figure 4.1o), and others were classified as crude triangular points. In addition to the Madison points, several of the triangular points were classified as Nodena Banks (Figure 4.1p,q) and a few as Nodena Elliptical (Figure 4.1r) (Justice 1987:232). These point styles are diagnostic of post–A.D. 1400 components in the central Mississippi valley (House 1993; Mainfort 1996; McNutt 1996; Morse and Morse 1983).

Objects manufactured from nonlocal goods have been recovered by professional archaeologists from several sites (Slack Farm, Murphy, Hovey Lake, Blackburn, and Cummings). Not only does the recovery of these materials contribute to our understanding of Caborn-Welborn extraregional interaction, but their presence often confirmed what a collector had reported finding at a particular site (e.g., Slack Farm, Blackburn, and Cummings). Thus, during fieldwork, in addition to ceramic and chipped stone tools, an effort was made to recover objects manufactured from nonlocal materials, such as catlinite, marine shell, copper, brass, or glass, and to document the presence of these materials in museum and private collections. Most of the catlinite objects are disk pipes or pendants, while marine shell occurs as beads, pendants,

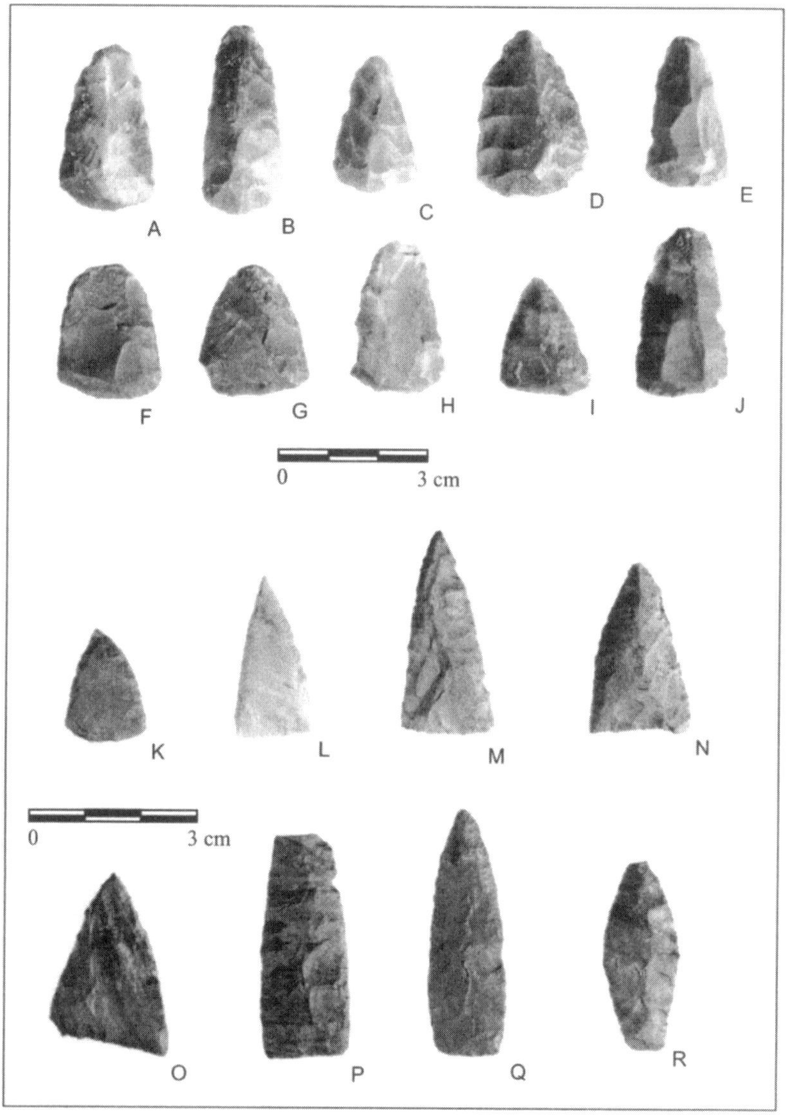


Figure 4.1. Triangular endscrapers and projectile points. Endscrapers: a-e, central ridge (Type 1); f-j, flat (Type 2). Points: k, straight or excurvate sides and straight base (Type 1); l, m, straight sides and longer than it is wide (Type 2); n, excurvate sides and concave base (Type 3); o, thick cross-section and wide base; p, q, Nodena Banks; r, Nodena Elliptical.

and gorgets. Metal artifacts were manufactured from native or European copper or brass (Gersch et al. 1998) and consisted of beads, tubes, coils, and bracelets. Glass beads also have been recovered from Caborn-Welborn sites.

While the presence of objects manufactured from nonlocal materials in poorly provenienced private collections was noted, the lack of site-specific data hampered efforts to use these materials to make intra- or intersite comparisons or to assess intraregional differences in the acquisition of nonlocal goods. Thus, for the most part, the presence of these objects in site collections was used to confirm intersocietal interaction, but these items could contribute little to the intersite or intraregional comparisons.

Although within small site collections, Caborn-Welborn components can be distinguished from earlier Angel phase components, for the most part by the presence of Caborn-Welborn Decorated sherds or triangular endscrapers, the *absence* of these Caborn-Welborn diagnostics within a small site collection does not automatically identify the presence of an earlier Mississippian component. In part, this is owing to the fact that in general there are few early Mississippian diagnostics that, in and of themselves, can be used to date a site. Thus, within the Ohio/Wabash confluence region, small Mississippian site collections often cannot be assigned a temporal or cultural affiliation.

Fortunately, there are diagnostic characteristics of large Mississippian ceramic assemblages that can be used to distinguish earlier Angel phase from later Caborn-Welborn phase ceramic collections (Munson 1994). Earlier collections tend to contain primarily loop or intermediate loop/strap handles and few thin straps. They also contain more flared rim bowls (Hilgeman 1992) and tend to lack bowls with notched or beaded rimstrips (Pollack and Railey 1987) and shallow bowls with outslanting walls (deep rim plates) and castellated rims (Hilgeman 1992). Ramey-like ceramics also may be present in earlier assemblages, and Angel phase collections contain more slipped and negative painted specimens than incised or trailed sherds (Hilgeman 1992).

The primary characteristic used to make site type assignments was site size. Caborn-Welborn settlements range in size from about .3 ha to more than 14 ha. Within this size range, habitations were assigned to the following four types: farmsteads (.25–.50 ha), hamlets (.50–1.25 ha), small villages (1.25–3 ha), and large villages (3–14 ha). Because the size range used in this study was based solely on surface-collected data, it should be viewed as tentative until some of these sites can be intensively and extensively investigated. In addition to size, other criteria used to make site type determinations included the spatial distribution of cultural materials, surface artifact density, the presence or absence of burials (i.e., human bone on the site surface), the number of cemeteries, and the presence of a courtyard or plaza. Thus, using these characteristics, a site that encompassed more than 1.25 ha but had a low surface artifact density and lacked evidence of a cemetery and a courtyard/plaza would have been classified as a farmstead or hamlet. Sites for which there was no information on site size or that had yielded only small surface collections were classified as farmsteads. Of the 80 Caborn-Welborn sites, 53 were classified as farmsteads, 13 as hamlets, 5 as small villages, 4 as large villages, and 5 as cemeteries.

In the remainder of this chapter, each site type is described and representative examples are discussed for each type. For sites that have yet to be assigned a name, only state site number designations that use the Smithsonian trinomial classification system (15 = Kentucky, 12 = Indiana, and 11 = Illinois) are provided. Descriptive information presented for each site varies, depending upon the nature of the investigations that have been carried out there. Descriptions of sites not visited during the course of this study are based on information provided in survey reports and field notes. Artifact distributions for each site and descriptions of all of the Caborn-Welborn sites investigated during this research are presented in Pollack (1998:197–298).

## SITE TYPES

### Farmsteads (.25–.50 Ha in Size)

As with earlier Mississippian settlements in the lower Ohio valley and elsewhere (Blitz 1993a), the smallest Caborn-Welborn habitation site is the farmstead/homestead (Muller 1978; Smith 1978). It was the basic or modular Mississippian site type (Muller 1986:204), representing the building blocks of larger Mississippian settlements (Muller 1978:284). Although no Caborn-Welborn farmstead has been excavated, these types of sites do not appear to have been special-purpose extractive camps but rather family residential areas that were located near agricultural fields. Following Muller (1986:204) and Smith (1978), from one to four families may have lived at Caborn-Welborn farmsteads.

The size range of .25 to .50 ha used here for Caborn-Welborn farmsteads is somewhat larger than Muller's (1986) and Green and Munson's (1978) size range for farmsteads, which was .1 to .3 ha. This somewhat larger size range, however, appears to reflect better the archaeological record of the Caborn-Welborn region.

A total of 53 sites were classified as farmsteads, and they are found throughout the Caborn-Welborn region. Good examples of settlements in this size range are Hart, Site 15He38, Cummings, Site 15He779, Site 15He790, Site 15Un38, Site 15Un96, Site 15Un101, Hooper, Site 15Un178, Site 15Un179, Stull, and Site 11Ga160. It should be noted that some sites identified as farmsteads, such as Rollman and Wessel, exhibit a very light scatter of materials over a relatively large area. They were assigned to this site type because of their low artifact density and the possibility that they represented the relocation of one or more households over an extended period of time. Three representative examples of sites classified as farmsteads are described below.

### *Cummings (15He775)*

The Cummings site is located on a northeast-southwest-trending floodplain levee. It is located 600 m from the Ohio River at an elevation of 106 m and is associated with Huntington silt loam soils (Converse and Cox 1967). Well-developed sloughs are situated on both sides of the levee. This site encompasses an area of 160 × 40 m. Within the boundaries of the Cummings site, four concentrations of materials were observed ranging in size from 20 × 20 m to 20 × 70 m. These concentrations suggest the presence of at least four households or periodic short settlement shifts of one household over an extended period of time.

This site was first recorded as a result of this study, but the locations of individual artifacts were not recorded. Additional materials were collected by the individual who farms the property. Of the 125 analyzed sherds in the Cummings site collection (Table 4.1), four were assigned to Caborn-Welborn Decorated. A total of 30 triangular points and 6 endscrapers were recovered. In addition to ceramics and chipped stone tools, historic trade goods were found. They primarily consisted of beads and tubes manufactured from native copper, European copper, or brass (Gersch et al. 1998). Two turquoise/robin's egg blue drawn glass beads also were found at this site.

### *Hooper (15Un177)*

The Hooper site is situated on a north-south-trending levee bordered on two sides by well-developed swales. It is located 300 m from the Ohio River at an elevation of 106 m and is associated with Huntington silt loam soils (Jacobs 1981). Hooper was first recorded as a result of this study, and these investigations included recording the distribution of surface artifact scatters there.

Materials at the Hooper site are primarily located along the eastern side and top of the levee. This site covers an area measuring 120 × 50 m, but most of the artifacts are found within an area 60 × 40 m in the northern one-half of the site (Figure 4.2). Within this area, concentrations of materials suggest the presence of a least two households (designated C-1 and C-2 on Figure 4.2). Slightly more than 40 percent of the analyzed ceramics from this site were assigned to Caborn-Welborn Decorated (Table 4.1). This small site, which is not well known to collectors, yielded 26 projectile points and 6 endscrapers.

### *Site 11Ga160*

This small Caborn-Welborn site was recorded by Butler et al. (1979:154–156). At that time, only a 10-×-30-m area had good surface visibility, so they were not able to determine its limits. Site 11Ga160 is situated on the north side of an east-west-trending levee that is located 400 m from the Ohio River. The

Table 4.1. Farmstead Large Ceramic Collections.

| Ceramic Types | Hart | | 15Un38 | | Cummings | | Hooper | | Stull | |
|---|---|---|---|---|---|---|---|---|---|---|
| Kimmswick Plain | 1 | 1.0% | | | 9 | 7.2% | | | 4 | 2.5% |
| Kimmswick Fabric Impressed | | | 2 | 3.2% | | | | | 7 | 4.4% |
| Mississippi Plain | 30 | 29.4% | 5 | 8.1% | 97 | 77.6% | 19 | 34.5% | 46 | 28.9% |
| Bell Plain | 3 | 2.9% | 5 | 8.1% | 10 | 8.0% | 13 | 23.6% | 17 | 10.7% |
| Cordmarked | | | | | 1 | 0.8% | | | | |
| Parkin Punctate | | | | | | | | | 1 | 0.6% |
| Caborn-Welborn Decorated | 66 | 64.7% | 46 | 74.2% | 4 | 3.2% | 22 | 40.0% | 84 | 52.8% |
| Manly Punctate | | | 3 | 4.8% | 3 | 2.4% | | | | |
| Old Town Red | 2 | 2.0% | 1 | 1.6% | | | | | | |
| Campbell Applique | | | | | | | 1 | 1.8% | | |
| Vernon Paul Applique | | | | | 1 | 0.8% | | | | |
| Total | 102 | 100% | 62 | 100% | 125 | 100% | 55 | 100% | 159 | 100% |

| Ceramic Types | 11Ga160 | | 15Un96 | | 15Un101 | |
|---|---|---|---|---|---|---|
| Kimmswick Plain | 2 | 2.5% | 17 | 19.5% | | |
| Kimmswick Fabric Impressed | 1 | 1.3% | | | | |
| Mississippi Plain | 23 | 29.1% | 43 | 49.4% | 9 | 20.0% |
| Bell Plain | 19 | 24.1% | 14 | 16.2% | 5 | 11.1% |
| Caborn-Welborn Decorated | 34 | 43.0% | 13 | 14.9% | 31 | 68.9% |
| Total | 79 | 100% | 87 | 100% | 45 | 100% |

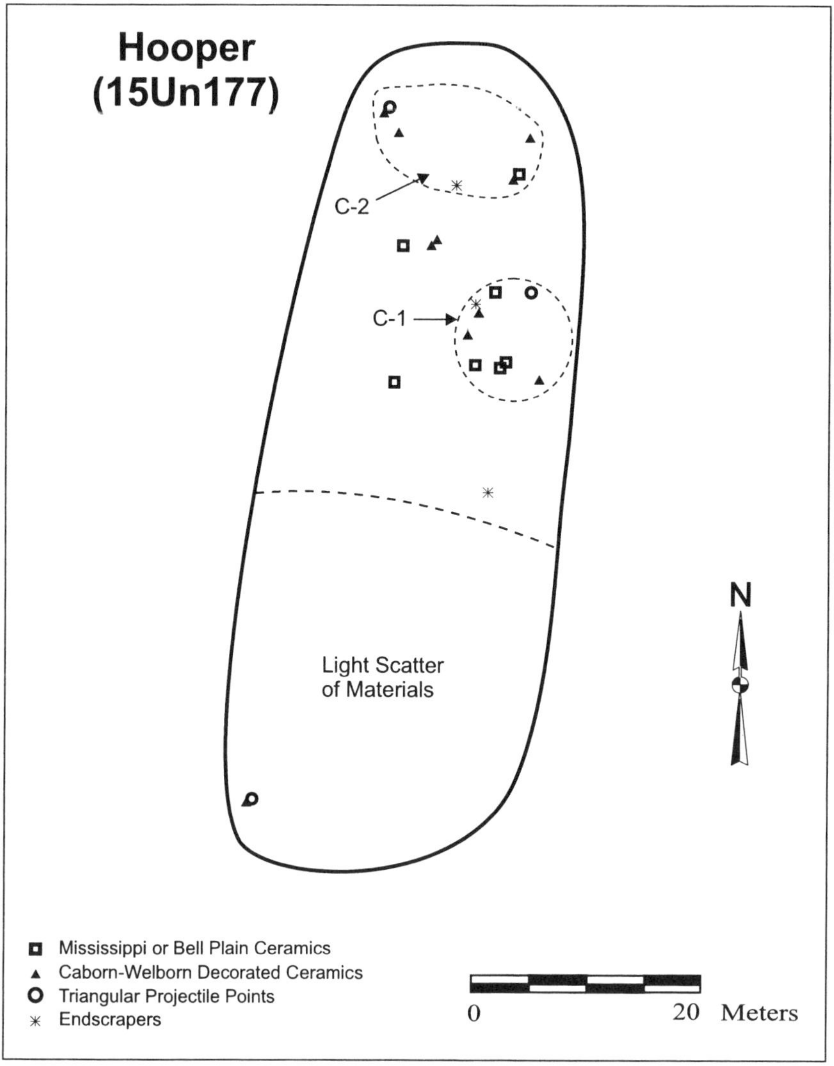


Figure 4.2. Surface distribution of artifacts at the Hooper site.

site is located at an elevation of 105 m and is associated with Allison silty clay loam soils (Wallace and Fehrenbacher 1969). The site measures 110 × 30 m, with most of the materials being found within an area 60 × 30 m (Figure 4.3).

The surface distribution of artifacts at this site was recorded during the course of this study. Of the 79 sherds recovered from the site, 43 percent were assigned to Caborn-Welborn Decorated (Table 4.1). Only one triangular point and four endscrapers were found. Most of these materials were found within one of four concentrations (C1–C4). These concentrations may represent four

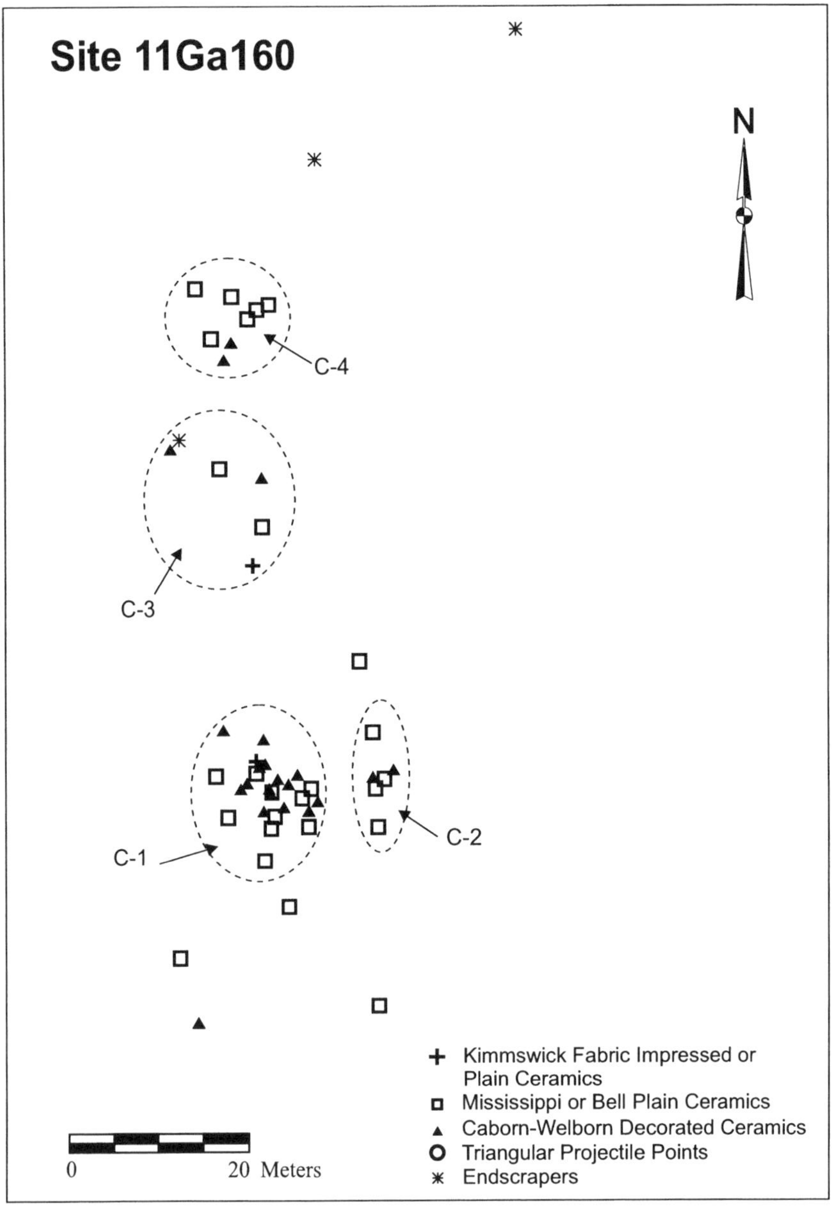


Figure 4.3. Surface distribution of artifacts at Site 11Ga160.

different households or the periodic relocation of one household over an extended period of time. Of the four concentrations, C-1 contained the highest ratio (15 to 11) of Caborn-Welborn Decorated to plain ceramics.

### *Summary*

Farmsteads account for the vast majority of Caborn-Welborn habitation sites. Most exhibit a linear distribution of materials across a narrow floodplain ridge. They range in length from 30 to 125 m and in width from 35 to 50 m. Usually, the site's long axis parallels a narrow floodplain levee bordered by swales or former sloughs. Most Caborn-Welborn farmsteads are located near the embankment of the Ohio River, but a few are situated on toe slopes at the base of the bluffs that overlook the Ohio River floodplain. The location of farmsteads (near the Ohio River as well as near sloughs and swampy areas) suggests that they were situated so as to exploit the fertile floodplain soils as well as the natural resources of the Ohio River and its nearby sloughs and swamps. Whether they were occupied year-round or were seasonally abandoned is not known, but it is possible that, owing to winter and spring floods, many of these farmsteads were only seasonally occupied.

Most Caborn-Welborn farmsteads have low surface artifact densities, and the vast majority of farmsteads yielded less than 30 analyzable sherds. Nevertheless, all farmstead artifact assemblages contain the full range of Caborn-Welborn domestic artifacts. Some farmsteads, such as Hart, Cummings, Stull, Hooper, and Site 11Ga160, did yield relatively large collections (i.e., more than 70 analyzable sherds) (Table 4.1). The higher density of artifacts at these sites may be indicative of longer periods of occupation, or it may be a product of erosion and deep plowing, which brought more materials to the surface. Because no Caborn-Welborn farmsteads have been excavated, it is unclear whether the larger farmsteads represent the clustering of three or four households or the periodic shifting of a single household. In either case, the relatively light surface artifact densities documented for most farmsteads suggest that they represent shorter and less intensive occupations than the more intensively occupied Caborn-Welborn villages.

Farmsteads tend to be located near other farmsteads and are often located in the vicinity of larger Caborn-Welborn settlements. Burials are not common at farmsteads, but when present they tend to cluster within cemeteries with individuals laid out in rows (Pollack 1998). The general lack of burials at farmsteads suggests that the residents of these settlements may have buried their dead at cemeteries associated with hamlets and villages.

## Hamlets (.50–1.25 Ha)

The next largest site in the Caborn-Welborn region is the hamlet. According to Muller (1978, 1986), hamlets were created by the coalescence of 5 to 15 families who chose to live together in a larger settlement. As defined by Parsons (1971), hamlets were communities that lacked obvious ceremonial architecture and were occupied by fewer than 100 persons. For this study, a size range of .50 to 1.25 ha was used for Caborn-Welborn hamlets. This range is similar to Green and Munson's (1978) size range of .25 to 1.0 ha. Only one Caborn-Welborn hamlet, the Caborn site, has been excavated.

Thirteen sites were classified as hamlets: Site 15He37.1, Site 15He43, Site 15He51, Site 15He52, Site 15He110, Site 15He111, Mulligan, Ritz, Mann, Caborn, Big Oeth, Leonard, and Ries-Hasting. In general, hamlets and farmsteads share many characteristics, which can sometimes make it difficult to distinguish one from the other based solely on the surface distribution and density of cultural materials. Repeated use of a locality and short household shifts within a settlement can make a site appear to have been larger or occupied by more households than it actually was, which can lead to the site being misclassified. Unlike farmsteads, however, hamlets are not found throughout the Caborn-Welborn region (see the following section).

Most hamlets that had good surface visibility yielded more than 30 analyzable sherds (e.g., Site 15He110, Mulligan, Ritz, Leonard, and Ries-Hasting) (Table 4.2). Those that produced smaller ceramic collections have been either severely disturbed or destroyed by erosion (e.g., Site 15He43 and Site 15He111) or had poor surface visibility and could not be collected (e.g., Site 15He51 and Site 15He52). Good examples of Caborn-Welborn hamlets are Mulligan, Ritz, and Caborn. These sites are described below.

### *Mulligan (15He625)*

The Mulligan site is located on a north-south-trending floodplain levee about 1 km to the north of the Hooper site (a farmstead). It is situated about 300 m from the Ohio River at an elevation of 106 m and is associated with Huntington silt loam soils (Converse and Cox 1967). The site measures 150 m north-south by 50 m east-west (Figure 4.4). It is in the process of being covered with sand, which accounts for the relatively low surface density of artifacts observed during the course of this study.

Five small concentrations of ceramics and chipped stone tools were identified at this site. These concentrations may correspond to clusters of households. Of the five, Caborn-Welborn Decorated ceramics were most common in Concentration No. 2, which was situated toward the center of the site. Several fragments of human bone were observed in the southern one-third of the site (Figure 4.4) in an area where informants reported finding several burials.

Of the 36 analyzable sherds recovered from the surface, 14 percent were assigned to Caborn-Welborn Decorated. In addition to the surface-collected materials, examination of a private collection of 44 vessels from burial contexts (Table 4.2) documented a similar percentage of whole Caborn-Welborn

Table 4.2. Hamlet Large Ceramic Collections.

| Ceramic Types | Caborn | | 15He37.1 | | 15He110 | | Mulligan | | Ritz | | Ries-Hasting | |
|---|---|---|---|---|---|---|---|---|---|---|---|---|
| Kimmswick Plain | 34 | 7.6% | 3 | 8.8% | 5 | 7.5% | 5 | 6.3% | 2 | 2.4% | 7 | 3.2% |
| Kimmswick Fabric Impressed | 2 | 0.4% | 1 | 2.9% | 8 | 11.9% | | | | | 1 | 0.5% |
| Mississippi Plain | 140 | 31.2% | 22 | 64.7% | 17 | 25.4% | 49 | 61.3% | 22 | 26.2% | 75 | 34.4% |
| Bell Plain | 66 | 14.7% | 6 | 17.6% | 15 | 22.4% | 9 | 11.3% | 22 | 26.2% | 38 | 17.4% |
| Caborn-Welborn Decorated | 202 | 45.0% | 2 | 5.9% | 21 | 31.3% | 11 | 13.8% | 38 | 45.2% | 92 | 42.2% |
| Tolu Fabric Impressed | 1 | 0.2% | | | | | | | | | | |
| Manly Punctate | 2 | 0.4% | | | | | 1 | 1.3% | | | 1 | 0.5% |
| Old Town Red | 1 | 0.2% | | | | | | | | | | |
| Oneota-Like | 1 | 0.2% | | | | | | | | | | |
| Misc. Incised or Trailed | | | | | | | | | | | 2 | 0.9% |
| Campbell Punctate | | | | | 1 | 1.5% | 5 | 6.3% | | | 1 | 0.5% |
| Campbell Applique | | | | | | | | | | | 1 | 0.5% |
| Total | 449 | 100% | 34 | 100% | 67 | 100% | 80 | 100% | 84 | 100% | 218 | 100% |

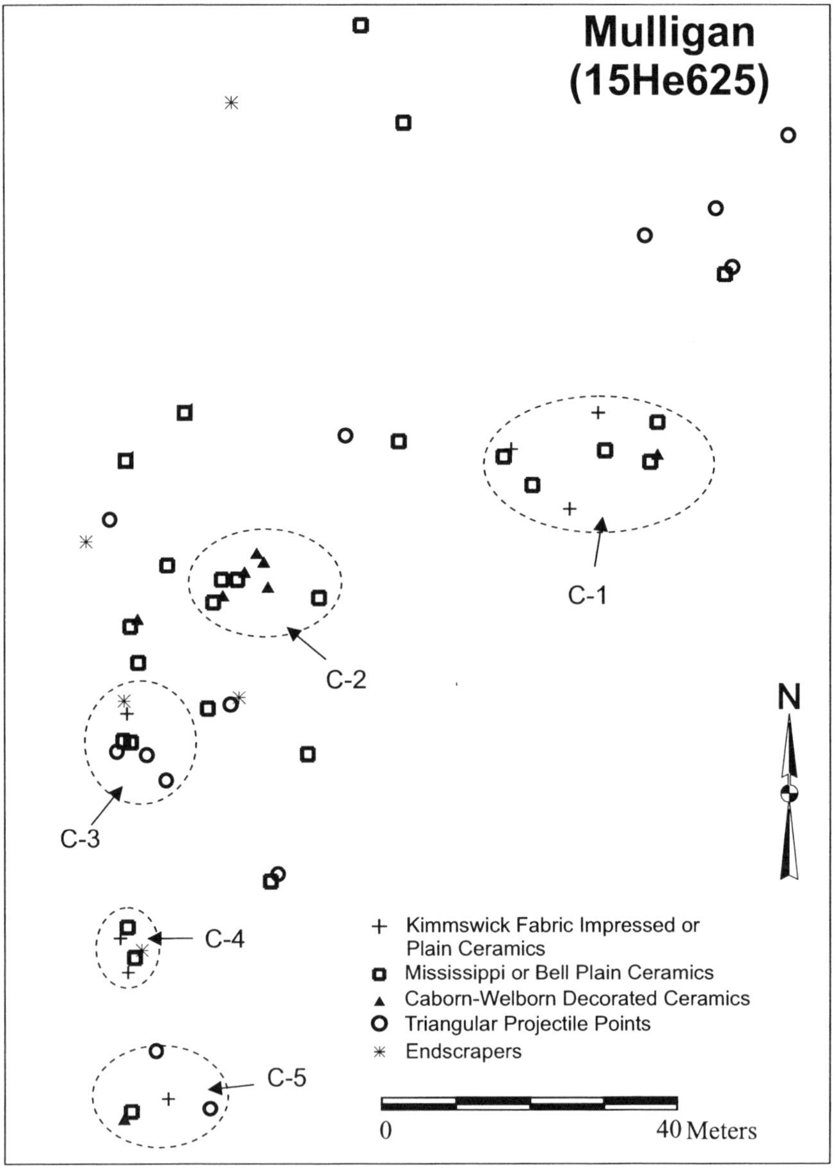


Figure 4.4. Surface distribution of artifacts at the Mulligan site.

Decorated jars (16.6 percent). Other decorated types identified in the private collection included Campbell Punctate (11.4 percent) and Manly Punctate (2.3 percent). A head pot also is reported to have been found at this site. Thus, while Caborn-Welborn Decorated comprises a similar percentage of the surface and mortuary ceramics, more decorated types were identified among the mortuary vessels. Thirteen triangular projectile points and five endscrapers were recovered from this site.

### *Ritz (15He777)*

The Ritz site is located along the edge of the same northeast-southwest-trending levee as Site 15He779 and Site 15He780 (both farmsteads). It is located about 1.2 km east of the Ohio River and 400 m west of Grassy Pond at an elevation of 106 m and is associated with Huntington fine sandy loam soils (Converse and Cox 1967). The edges of this levee undulate, and the lower areas are being filled with sand. Cultural materials were found over an area 220 × 50 m, with the highest concentration of materials found within an 80-×-50-m area near the center of the site (Figure 4.5). Local informants report that a large number of burials have been found at this site; during the course of this study, human remains were observed in the area where the informants reported finding burials. Informants also noted that in the past, artifact densities at this site had been much higher. Of the 84 analyzable sherds found at this site, 42.5 percent were assigned to Caborn-Welborn Decorated (Table 4.2). This site is heavily collected, which probably accounts for the lack of triangular points and endscrapers.

### *Caborn (12Po32)*

The Caborn site was surface collected several times from 1975 to 1987 by Cheryl Ann Munson of Indiana University, who conducted limited excavations there in 1988 (Pollack 1998). It is located on a floodplain levee about 300 m from the Ohio River and is bordered on two sides by former sloughs. The site is situated at an elevation of 109 m and is associated with Nolin silty clay loam soils (McWilliams 1979). Although the site encompasses about 2.2 ha, most of the Caborn-Welborn materials are located within an area 70 × 150 m (1.1 ha) that had been exposed by receding floodwaters.

Munson's initial work at Caborn included a controlled surface collection, which consisted of a total pickup of materials within units ranging from ca 1 to 54 m$^2$. Most of the collection units were placed in the area of greatest artifact density, which is located toward the center of the site.

Limited excavations at Caborn documented the presence of structures, buried midden areas, and large basin-shaped pits. Isolated burials were documented, and there is no evidence to suggest that this site contains a cemetery similar to those identified or reported from several other hamlets, such as Mulligan and Ritz.

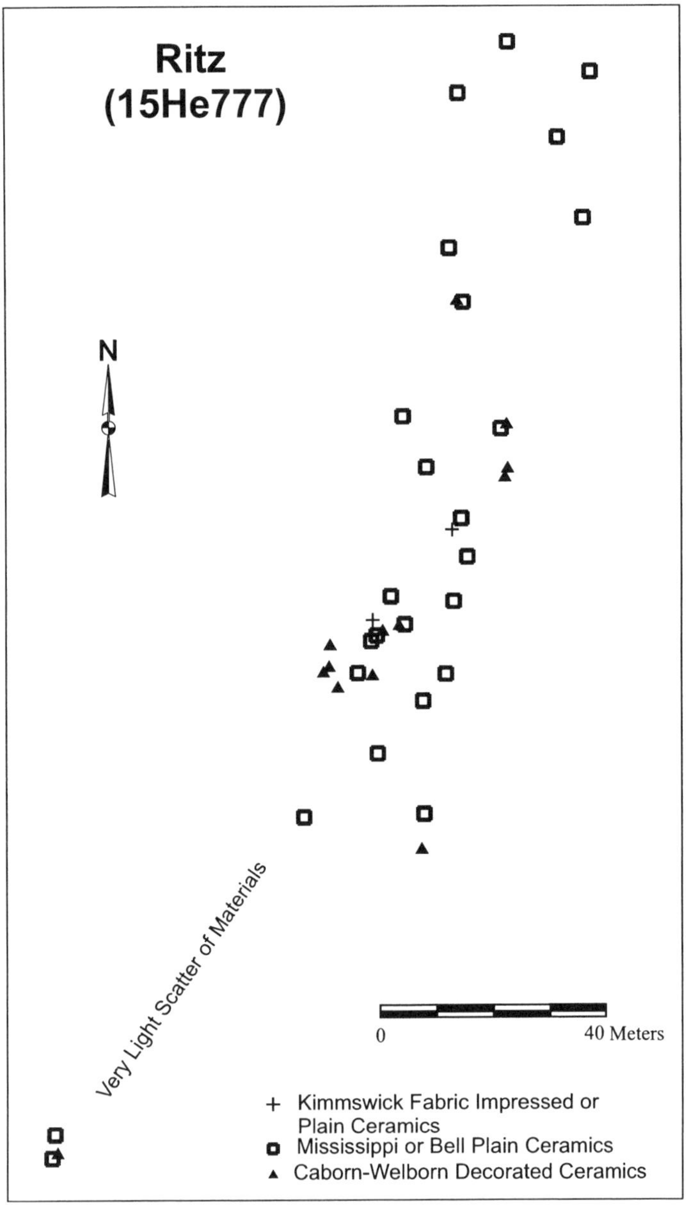


Figure 4.5. Surface distribution of artifacts at Ritz site.

Of the four radiocarbon dates from Caborn, one has midpoints throughout the fourteenth century, one has an early fifteenth century midpoint, and the remaining two dates have late fifteenth century midpoints (Table 2.1). These dates place the Caborn occupation squarely in the fifteenth century. This site had a high percentage of Caborn-Welborn Decorated (45.1 percent) (Table 4.2). A total of 80 triangular points and 42 endscrapers have been found over the years at Caborn.

### *Summary*

Most of the thirteen Caborn Welborn hamlets are located on floodplain levees situated near the Ohio River. Their proximity to the Ohio River, as well as near sloughs and swampy areas, suggests that, as with farmsteads, hamlets were placed to exploit the rich resources of these environmental settings. Many, such as Caborn, Ritz, and Site 15He110, are characterized by a linear distribution of materials. Concentrations of materials within these sites suggest that they consisted of clusters of structures that paralleled a floodplain levee. An exception to this pattern is Site 15He37.1, a hamlet that exhibits a more circular pattern with a central courtyard. Linear sites also may have courtyards, but they are not as easily discernible from surface distributions of materials. As with farmsteads, clusters of artifacts can be documented in hamlet site surface collections. These clusters may correspond to individual households or kin-related family groups.

Cemeteries are associated with several hamlets (e.g., Site 15He43, Site 15He51, Site 15He110, Mulligan, Ritz, and Leonard). Little is known about the composition or organization of these cemeteries, however, but ceramic vessels, pipes, copper/brass objects, and shell beads and gorgets are reported to have been found in association with burials at hamlets, such as Mulligan and Site 15He43. Other hamlets, such as Caborn, contain human burials but lack clearly identifiable cemeteries.

Hamlets and farmsteads share many characteristics. For example, hamlets are situated in similar environmental settings as farmsteads, and in general, similar types of artifacts and features have been identified at both types of sites. Both farmsteads and hamlets exhibit a great deal of variation in the density of materials.

However, hamlets differ from farmsteads in several important ways. Most hamlets are found along levees that are broader than those associated with farmsteads (and narrower than the levees associated with villages), and they tend to have higher surface artifact densities than do farmsteads. While few farmsteads exceed 100 m in length or 50 m in width, most hamlets have a length of more than 150 m and a width of 50 to 75 m. Many hamlets have associated cemeteries, though little is known about them, and some, such as Caborn, have thin midden deposits. These differences suggest that hamlets were occupied by more people and perhaps for longer periods of time than farmsteads.

Hamlets tend to be located near other hamlets and farmsteads, and the clustering of these types of settlements may represent dispersed villages. The relationship of hamlets to small and large villages is not as well defined, but, in general, hamlets tend not to be located near villages. The presence of cemeteries at hamlets and their absence at nearby farmsteads suggests that the residents of these smaller settlements may have buried their dead within the cemeteries at nearby hamlets.

## Small Villages (1.25–3 Ha)

Following Green and Munson (1978:310), the next largest Caborn-Welborn habitation sites were classified as small villages. Their size range for these sites, .25 to 1 ha, is the same as the size range they assigned to hamlets. However, this size seems somewhat restricted for small villages, since they consider that these sites represent the coalescence of hamlets to form larger communities. Therefore, a size range larger than that of Green and Munson's, 1.25 to 3 ha, was used as the size range for small villages in this study. Small villages may have been occupied by from 16 to 50 families.

As with hamlets, small villages lack obvious ceremonial architecture (Parsons 1971). Size and intensity of occupation (as indicated by artifact density and diversity) are the main criteria that were used to distinguish small villages from hamlets. However, as noted by Flannery (1976), in practice, hamlets and small villages represent opposite ends of a continuum, which can make it difficult to distinguish large hamlets from small villages based solely on surface-collected data. Still, because of the differences in size and density of materials documented for hamlets versus small villages in the Caborn-Welborn region, an attempt was made to distinguish between the two. Within the Caborn-Welborn region, small villages also are distinguished from hamlets in that they tend not to have as linear a distribution of materials.

Five sites were assigned to this site type: Gough, Moore, Blackburn, Alzey, and Welborn (Table 4.3). They occur throughout the Caborn-Welborn region, and none has been excavated. Three representative examples of sites classified as small villages are described below.

### *Alzey (15He37.2)*

The Alzey site was recorded by Hoffman (1966), who described it as measuring 1365 × 455 m (i.e., 62 ha). Subsequent work led to its subdivision into two sites, Site 15He37.1 and Alzey (Site 15He37.2), with Alzey being the larger of the two. This site is located on a very broad northeast-southwest-trending floodplain levee. It is located 450 m south of the Ohio River and 560 m southwest of Site 15He37.1, a hamlet, at an elevation of 109 m. It is associated with

Huntington silt loam soils (Converse and Cox 1967). The site covers an area that measures 170 x 120 m. The distribution of materials at Alzey is suggestive of a U-shaped community or two linear concentrations of households (Figure 4.6). In either case, the central area may have functioned as a plaza, as few artifacts were found in this area.

A high percentage of Caborn-Welborn Decorated was recovered from the surface of Alzey (Table 4.3). These materials tend to cluster in three concentrations within this village (Figure 4.6). In addition to sherds from domestic contexts, several mortuary vessels curated at the Glenn Black Laboratory of Archaeology are reported to have been found in the vicinity of this site. Twenty triangular points and four endscrapers were found at Alzey.

### *Moore (15Un42)*

The Moore site is located on a northeast-southwest-trending levee about 600 m from the Ohio River. It is situated at an elevation of 106 m and is associated with Nolin silty clay loam soils (Jacobs 1981). While the plowed portion of the site encompasses an area 200 m × 40 m wide, the site is actually somewhat wider, probably having a width of 80 to 100 m. During the late nineteenth/early twentieth century, part of the site was used as borrow for the construction of substructure mounds for a house and a barn that were built along the western edge of the site. These activities impacted and covered portions of that edge of the site.

Three concentrations of materials were identified at Moore. Soil cores in Concentration 3 revealed 80 to 90 cm of intact deposits. Zones of burning and charcoal observed in core profiles suggest the rebuilding of structures. In addition to Caborn-Welborn Decorated ceramics, each of the concentrations contained other decorated ceramic types: Barton Incised sherds were recovered from Concentration 1; a Parkin Punctate, and two Old Town Red sherds were found in Concentration 2; and Campbell Applique, Ranch Incised–Like, Old Town Red, and Walls Engraved were associated with Concentration 3 (Figure 4.7). Of the 298 analyzable sherds from this site, 14.4 percent were assigned to Caborn-Welborn Decorated (Table 4.3). One of the Barton Incised jar rims and a Campbell Punctate bottle rim from this site have interior-beveled lips that are similar to the Memphis Rim Mode (House 1993:27). Thirty-five triangular points and 15 endscrapers were found at this site, as well as a hematite stone engraved on both sides with an abstract design.

### *Blackburn (15Un57)*

A small Caborn-Welborn village located on a northeast-southwest-trending floodplain levee, Blackburn is situated 600 m from the Ohio River at an elevation of 106 m and is associated with Huntington silt loam soils (Jacobs 1981). The site covers an area that measures 300 x 100 m (Figure 4.8). A possible plaza/courtyard is evident in the northern one-half of the site, consist-

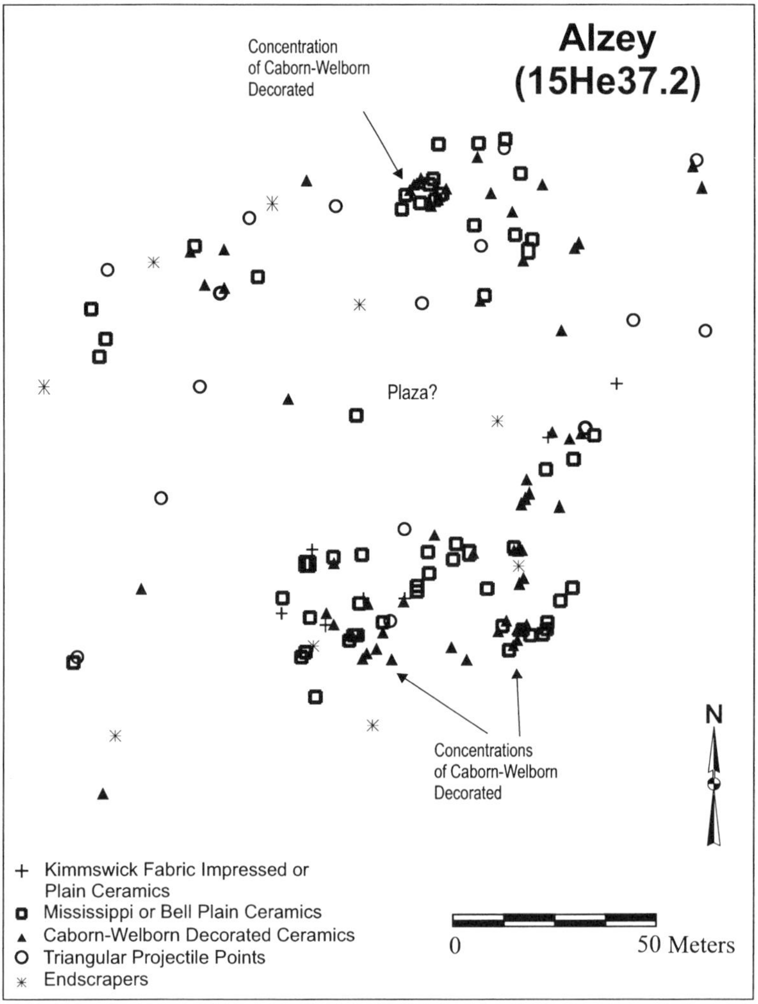


Figure 4.6. Surface distribution of artifacts at the Alzey site.

ing of a 30-m-wide area containing few artifacts. Several concentrations of Caborn-Welborn Decorated, ranging from 4 to 12 sherds, were identified at this site (Figure 4.8). Other decorated ceramic types included Old Town Red, Angel/Kincaid Negative Painted, Mound Place Incised, Parkin Punctate, and Campbell Incised. In general, these types, especially Old Town Red and Angel/Kincaid Negative Painted, appeared to have different distribution patterns than the Caborn-Welborn Decorated specimens, but the decorated sample is too small to interpret these spatial differences with any degree of confidence.

Of the 265 analyzable sherds from Blackburn, 21.5 percent were assigned to Caborn-Welborn Decorated (Table 4.1). Thirty-four triangular points and

Table 4.3. Small Village Large Ceramic Collections.

| Ceramic Types | Alzey | | Welborn | | Gough | | Moore | | Blackburn | |
|---|---|---|---|---|---|---|---|---|---|---|
| Kimmswick Plain | 15 | 4.5% | 10 | 6.7% | 10 | 10.4% | 35 | 11.7% | 33 | 12.2% |
| Kimmswick Fabric Impressed | 2 | 0.6% | 17 | 11.3% | 6 | 6.3% | 6 | 2.0% | 2 | 0.7% |
| Mississippi Plain | 89 | 26.5% | 51 | 34.0% | 38 | 39.6% | 135 | 45.3% | 89 | 33.0% |
| Bell Plain | 46 | 13.7% | 43 | 28.7% | 23 | 24.0% | 59 | 19.8% | 77 | 28.5% |
| Cordmarked | | | | | 1 | 1.0% | | | | |
| Parkin Punctate | | | | | | | 2 | 0.7% | 3 | 1.1% |
| Caborn-Welborn Decorated | 176 | 52.4% | 27 | 18.0% | 17 | 17.7% | 43 | 14.4% | 57 | 21.1% |
| Manly Punctate | 1 | 0.3% | | | | | | | | |
| Matthews Incised | 1 | 0.3% | | | | | | | | |
| Old Town Red | | | 1 | 0.7% | | | 8 | 2.7% | 6 | 2.2% |
| Angel Negative Painted | 2 | 0.6% | | | | | | | 1 | 0.4% |
| Walls Engraved | | | | | | | 1 | 0.3% | | |
| Oneota-Like | 2 | 0.6% | | | 1 | | | | | |
| Beckwith Incised | 1 | 0.3% | | | | 1.0% | | | | |
| Misc. Incised or Trailed | 1 | 0.3% | | | | | 2 | 0.7% | | |
| Barton Incised | | | | | | | 3 | 1.0% | | |
| Mound Place Incised | | | | | | | | | 1 | 0.4% |
| Barton Incised | | | | | | | | | | |
| Campbell Punctate | | | 1 | 0.7% | | | 1 | 0.3% | | |
| Campbell Appique | | | | | | | 1 | 0.3% | | |
| Campbell Incised | | | | | | | 1 | 0.3% | 1 | 0.4% |
| Ranch Incised | | | | | | | 1 | 0.3% | | |
| Total | 336 | 100% | 150 | 100% | 96 | 100% | 298 | 100% | 270 | 100% |

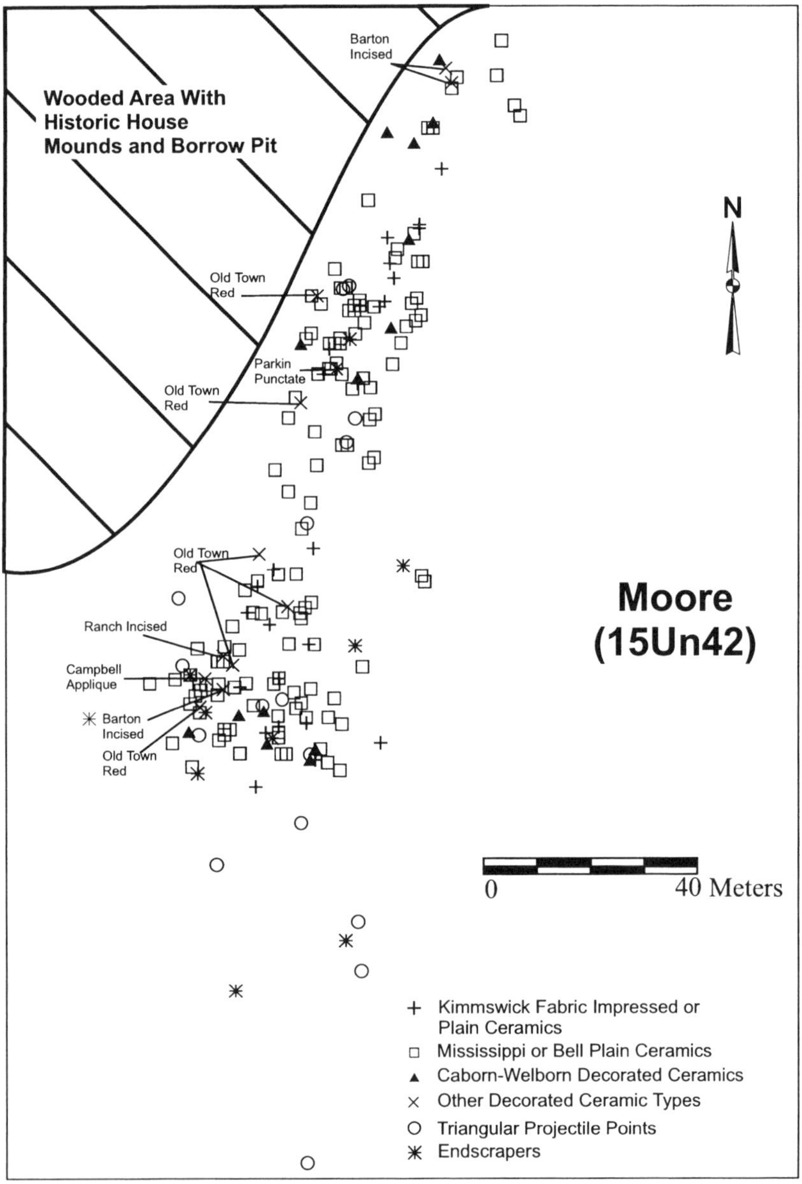


Figure 4.7. Surface distribution of artifacts at the Moore site.

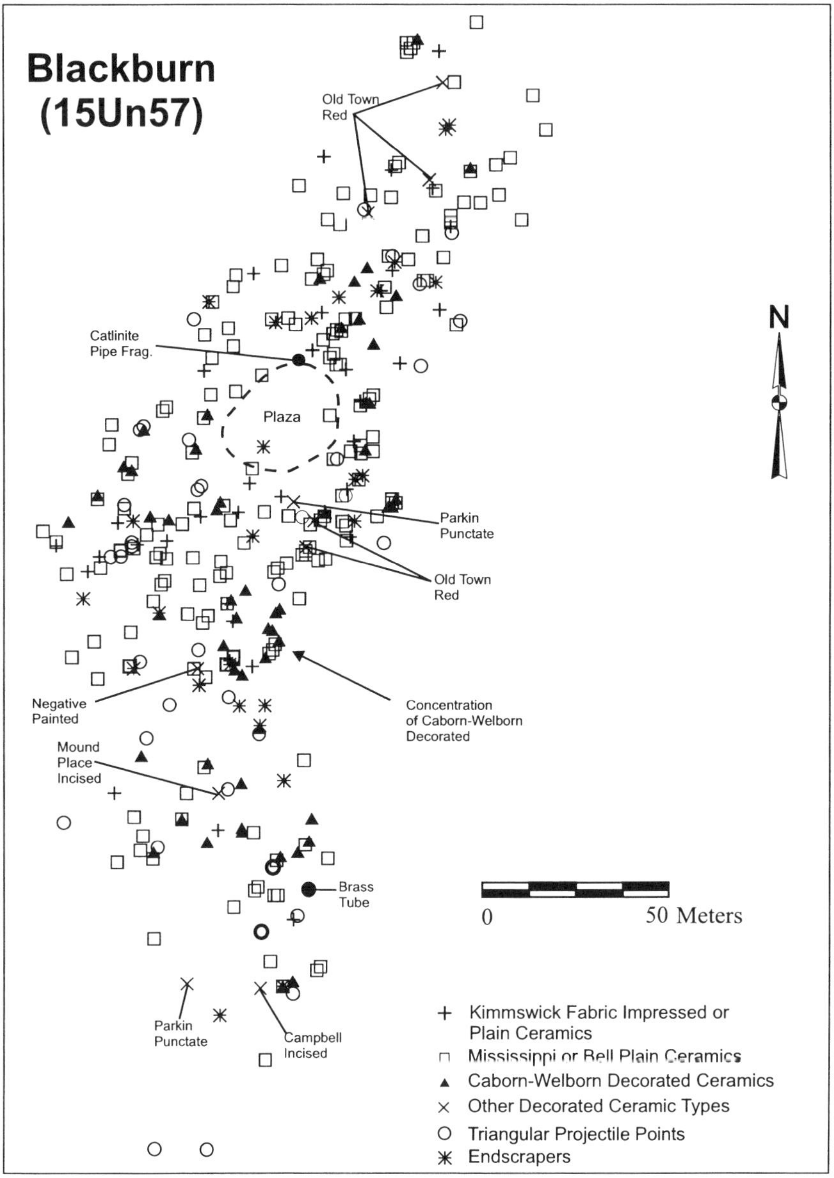


Figure 4.8. Surface distribution of artifacts at the Blackburn site.

25 endscrapers were found on the surface at this site, as were a catlinite disk pipe fragment (Gunderson 1994) and a brass tube (Gersch et al. 1998). An additional catlinite disk pipe and pipe fragment with engraved lines on its sides, along with several other copper and brass artifacts, also are reported to have been found at this site (Mike Moore, personal communication 1994).

### *Summary*

As with the smaller settlements, small Caborn-Welborn villages, which range in size from 1.25 to 3 ha, are primarily found on floodplain levees (the exception being Gough, which is situated on a terrace) near the Ohio River, but they tend to be associated with wider, broader levees than the smaller sites. Small villages, such as Gough, Moore, and Blackburn, exhibit a somewhat linear or arc-shaped distribution of materials, while sites like Alzey exhibit more of a U-shaped distribution. Open areas that may represent a plaza are associated within both arc-shaped and U-shaped villages. Surface artifact concentrations documented for this site type may represent the clustering of structures. Concentrations of Caborn-Welborn Decorated within villages, such as Alzey, point to a different disposal pattern for these jars than for undecorated vessels and suggest that they may have been used for a different set of activities. In addition to concentrations of Caborn-Welborn Decorated ceramics, several other decorated ceramic types that reflect interaction with the central Mississippi valley, including Parkin Punctate, Campbell Applique, Barton Incised, Campbell Incised, and Campbell Punctate, were recovered from two small villages, Moore and Blackburn. Because no small villages have been excavated by professional archaeologists, little else is known about their internal organization.

All of the small villages are characterized by high surface artifact densities, and the full range of Caborn-Welborn artifacts has been recovered from them. Midden deposits, some as thick as 1 m, are present at some villages, such as Moore. The large amount of materials recovered from small villages and the presence of midden at some villages suggest that these types of settlements were occupied for longer periods of time than the smaller settlements. Hamlets tend not to be located near small villages, but farmsteads are common near them.

Within the Caborn-Welborn region, there may be some variability in what constitutes a small village. While this study has used site size and density of materials to distinguish small villages from hamlets and farmsteads, it is possible that clusters of hamlets and farmsteads may represent small dispersed villages, similar to those documented in the Black Bottom region of southern Illinois. In that area, groups of farmsteads, hamlets, and cemeteries have been interpreted as representing small dispersed villages (Butler 1977; Muller 1986). Within the Alzey Bottoms in the eastern section of the Caborn-Welborn region, there is only one small village, but a large number of farmsteads and hamlets, some with cemeteries, do occur. The clustering of these smaller settlements is suggestive of a type of dispersed small village similar to that described for the Black Bottom.

Variation also was noted among these sites with respect to the location of cemeteries. At some villages, such as Alzey and Gough, the dead were interred within the community, while at Moore and Blackburn they appear to have been placed in cemeteries located on the nearby blufftops. The significance of this variation in cemetery location is explored in more detail in subsequent chapters.

In some ways, small villages are similar to large villages. Similar types of ceramics and nonlocal materials were recovered from the surface of both types of sites, and both contain courtyard/plazas. The primary difference is that for large villages, overall site size and the number of associated cemeteries are greater than for small villages.

## Large Villages (3–14 Ha)

This final Caborn-Welborn habitation type as defined here is similar to Green and Munson's (1978) large village, with the primary difference related to settlement size. The size range of 3 to 14 ha used in this study for large villages, like that of small villages, is greater than Green and Munson's (1978) size range of 1 to 4 ha for this site type. Site size and number of cemeteries were the main criteria used to distinguish large from small villages. As with small villages, concentrations of artifacts and surface stains suggest that these communities represent the coalescence of kin-related families to form bigger communities. However, there is no evidence to suggest the presence of monumental architecture in the form of platform mounds or stockades at any large village. It is also possible that the size of some of these sites reflects repeated reuse of a locality and short settlement shifts. Large villages may have been occupied by more than 100 households.

This settlement type includes Slack Farm, the largest and one of the most intensively occupied Caborn-Welborn sites, Murphy, Bone Bank, and Hovey Lake (Table 4.4). Excavations have been conducted at all of these sites, although they vary in the extent of site area examined. Large villages are centrally located within the distribution of Caborn-Welborn phase sites, with two of the large villages, Slack Farm and Murphy, being situated near the mouth of the Wabash River. Two of the four sites classified as large villages are described below.

### *Slack Farm (15Un28)*

The Slack Farm site encompasses slightly more than 14 ha and is located on a terrace that projects from the base of the Ohio River bluffs, as well as on the adjacent broad floodplain levee. It is located 300 m from the Ohio River, at an elevation of 112 m. The portion of the site on the terrace is associated with Wheeling silt loam soils, while the portion on the floodplain is associated with Nolin silty clay soils (Jacobs 1981).

This site was first investigated in 1868 by Sidney S. Lyon (1871), who surveyed and excavated a number of features in the site area as well as earthen mounds (Site 15Un70) on the bluff overlooking the site. Although known to archaeologists for over a century, the Slack Farm site received little professional attention until the Kentucky Heritage Council was informed of looting taking place there in the fall of 1987. In the late winter and spring of 1988, more than 450 looters' holes were investigated by professional archaeologists (Pollack and Munson 1989). Documentation of features and house basins included plan and profile mapping, the collection of artifacts, radiocarbon and flotation samples, and the excavation of the basal portions of a few large pits. However, most materials were recovered from disturbed contexts (looters' holes and backdirt piles).

The most intensively looted portion of site encompassed a ca. 2 ha area on the terrace. Examination of the spatial distribution of partially intact features, houses, and burials within this portion of the site indicated that they tended to occur as discrete clusters surrounding a plaza/courtyard. Within this area, five large (Areas 3–7) and one small (Area 2) residential/mortuary areas were identified (Figures 4.9 and 4.10). To the southwest of these residential/mortuary areas and across a ravine where a small spring-fed stream traverses the site, another large cemetery and associated residential area (Area 1) was documented. Additional residential areas, some with small associated cemeteries, are located in other portions of the site, with many situated on the floodplain. Radiocarbon and fluoride data, along with androcyte comparisons of dental and nonmetric characteristics of human skeletal remains and material culture (Powell et al. 1996; Roach 1995), indicate that all of the large residential/mortuary areas are contemporary (Pollack and Munson 1998). The extent to which this village may have expanded and contracted is not known, but Slack Farm appears to have been occupied for the entire Caborn-Welborn phase.

Features identified in the residential areas at Slack Farm included structures (house basins), posts, small and large pits, and hearths. Although no structure was completely exposed, portions of at least 40 houses were documented. Most appear to have consisted of wall trenches set in shallow basins, and many had prepared clay hearths. The sides of the structures were covered with wattle and daub. Small pits were often located within and in the immediate vicinity of structures. There also is evidence to indicate that when a house was abandoned, old cooking and storage vessels were left behind. This is reflected in the concentrations of Mississippi Plain jars found in the hearths of several structures.

Among the features located near these structures were large pits. Many (n = 30) had diameters or depths of 1.5 to 2.0 m. These "underground silos" were probably used to store dried plant foods. Sprouted corn kernels recovered from some large pits suggest that a portion of the stored corn may have spoiled before it could be consumed. If corn accounted for 65 percent of the diet (and assuming intakes ranging from 2,300 to 3,500 calories a day per person), then the contents of these storage pits could have fed from 7 to 12 individuals for a year. When the contribution of meat, fish, and wild plants to the Caborn-Welborn diet is considered, food stored in these pits may have fed even more individuals.

A comparison of Slack Farm ceramics from house and pit contexts points to differences in the use and discard of ceramic vessels at this large village. In particular, Caborn-Welborn Decorated accounts for only 18.4 percent of the ceramics from house contexts but 53.4 percent of the ceramics from pits (Pollack and Munson 1996). This variation in the contextual association of Caborn-Welborn Decorated ceramics corresponds to differences observed in the distribution of Caborn-Welborn Decorated and other ceramic types at small villages. The presence of a much larger percentage of decorated jars in pit contexts removed from domestic structures at Slack Farm suggests that Caborn-Welborn Decorated vessels may have been used in activities where they were meant to be seen by individuals outside one's immediate family. It is possible that one's cultural or ethnic identity was encoded in the ceramic designs placed on Caborn-Welborn jar shoulders, or perhaps these designs were meant to convey a message to visitors (Allen 1988; DeBoer and Moore 1982; Hodder 1978; Kintigh 1985; Wobst 1977).

Caborn-Welborn Decorated jars may have been used in activities that involved a wider spectrum of the community, such as to prepare food for feasts organized by aspiring elites (Hayden 1995). They also may represent vessels that were used in rituals similar to that of the New Fire and Green Corn ceremonies of Southeastern Historic Indian groups (Swanton 1911, 1946), as has been suggested by Hilgeman (2000:191–203) for Angel/Kincaid Negative Painted ceramics. As noted in chapter 5, the most common motif associated with both Angel/Kincaid Negative Painted plates and Caborn-Welborn Decorated jars is a sun symbol that is depicted by rising and descending triangular areas that are filled with lines and punctations or dots. It is thus possible that these two ceramic types at times served similar functions within their respective societies.

Based on an examination of field and laboratory records, it appears that a minimum of 650 to 750 burials were disturbed by the Slack Farm looters.

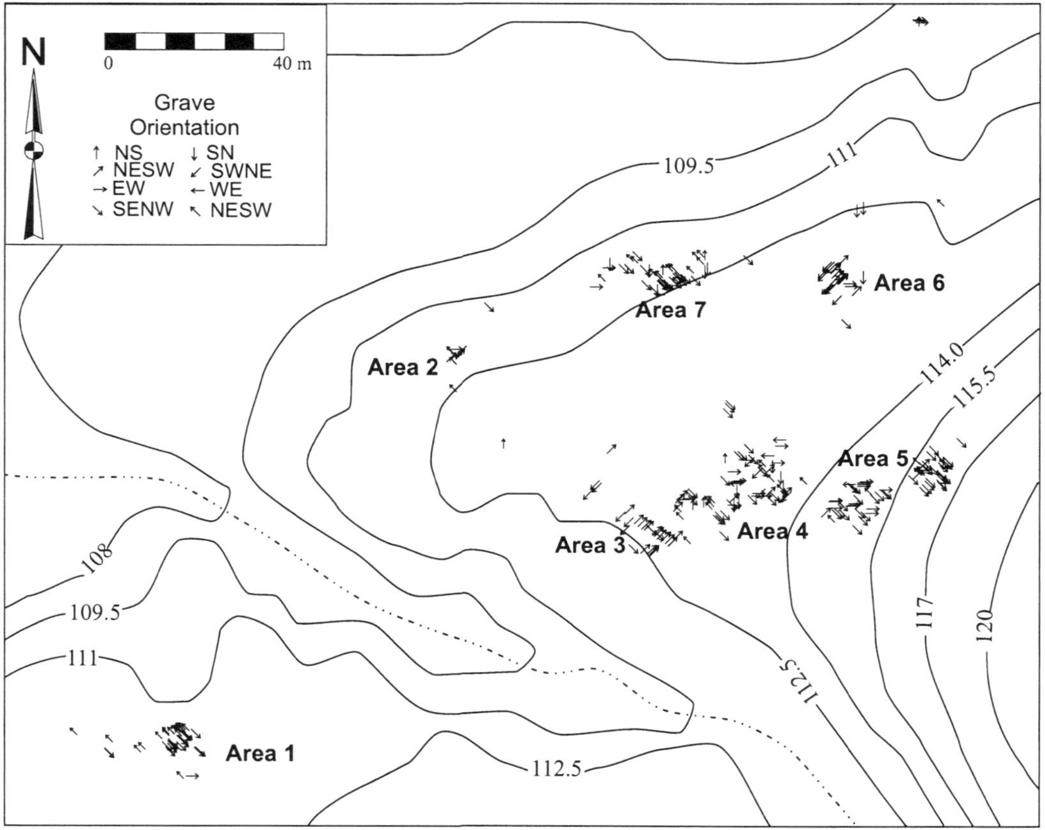


Figure 4.9. Map showing the location of Slack Farm cemeteries and burial orientation.

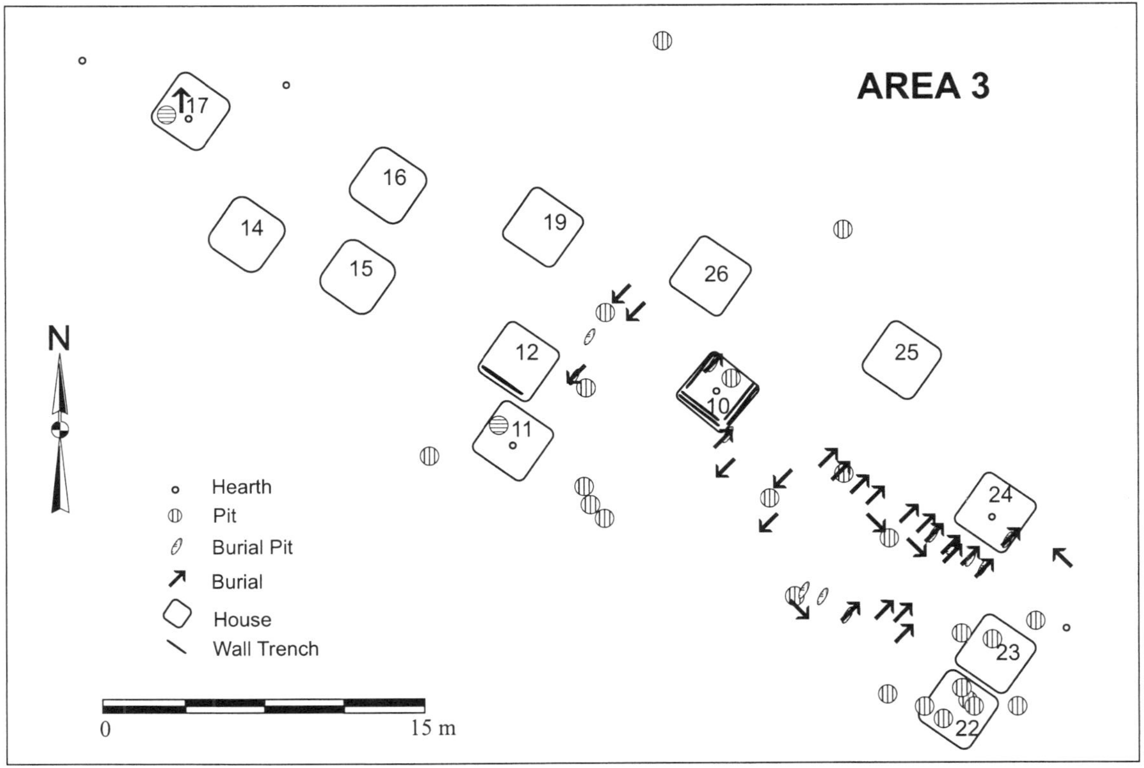


Figure 4.10. Stylized representation of the distribution of houses, storage pits and cemeteries at Slack Farm, Area 3.

Taking into consideration that infants and young children are underrepresented in the site's demographic profile (Powell et al. 1996), it seems reasonable to assume that at least 1,000 individuals were interred in the seven large cemeteries impacted by the looters.

Burials at Slack Farm were typically placed in an extended position. Within each cemetery, they were often laid out in parallel rows (Figures 4.9 and 4.10) and oriented toward the central plaza. Except for Areas 2 and 4, burial orientation was fairly consistent within each cemetery (Figure 4.9), with burials in Areas 3 and 6 being oriented to the northeast or southwest and in Areas 1, 5, and 7 oriented to the southeast or northwest. In Area 4, several individuals were oriented east to west, but most were oriented to the southeast or northwest. In Area 2, there was a slight preference for northeast or southwest orientation. Within each cemetery, individuals occasionally were placed one above another. However, there was little evidence of later burials having disturbed earlier interments. The consistency of burial orientation and general lack of intrusive graves suggest that the mortuary areas were maintained by village residents and that the graves were marked in some fashion.

While most individuals appear to have been interred within one of the large cemeteries, some individuals were buried within houses. Most of these houses were located adjacent to a cemetery, and it is possible that as the cemetery expanded, nearby houses were abandoned and the dead interred within the abandoned house basins. There is little evidence to suggest any similarities with the mortuary program identified at Hovey Lake (Munson and Cook 2000; see below), where some individuals were interred along the inner walls of houses and others were buried in nearby cemeteries. Some of the Slack Farm dead also appear to have been interred in one of the six low mounds (Site 15Un70, see below) on the bluffs overlooking the site.

In general, grave goods were placed near an individual's upper torso, in the area between the hip and the head. Objects recovered from Slack Farm that are known to have been interred with the dead include small Mississippi Plain, Campbell Punctate, Parkin Punctate, Miscellaneous Incised/Trailed jars; long-necked Bell Plain bottles (Figure 4.11) and fish effigy Bell Plain jars; limestone disk pipes; copper or brass beads, tubes, and coils; and shell beads and ear plugs. Other objects reported to have been interred with the dead at Slack Farm include Kent Incised-like and Manly Punctate jars; conch shell bowls; Bell Plain human effigy bowls and Bell Plain bowls with effigy rim riders; Old Town Red bottles; light blue drawn glass beads; and copper/brass bracelets.

Calibrated radiocarbon dates from Slack Farm cluster in the fifteenth century (Table 2.1). These dates yielded an average date of A.D. 1400(1410)1430. Three of the samples have date ranges that extend into the seventeenth century, but the absence of dates with seventeenth century midpoints is somewhat surprising, given the presence of historic trade goods at this site.

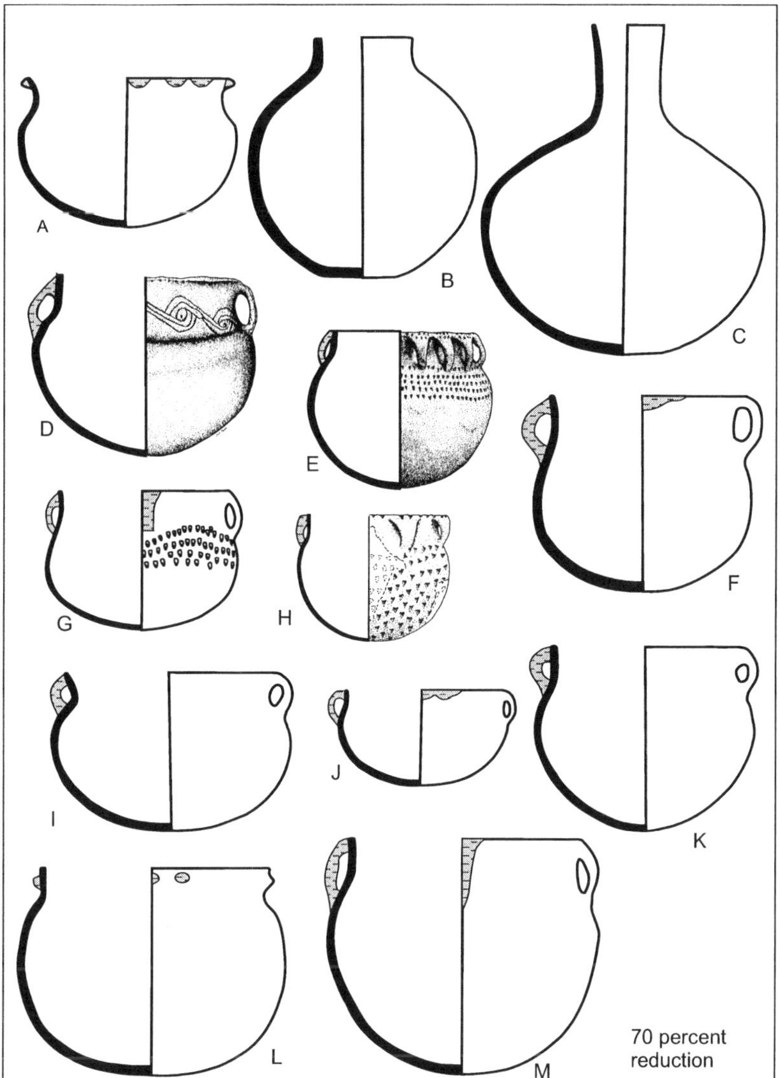


Figure 4.11. Whole or nearly whole vessels from Slack Farm. Mortuary contexts: a,f,i,j,m, Mississippi Plain jars; c, Bell Plain bottle; d, Miscellaneous Trailed/Incised jar; e,h, Campbell Punctate jars; h, Parkin Punctate jar. Unknown contexts: b, Bell Plain bottle; k,l, Mississippi Plain jars.

The 1988 investigations conducted at Slack Farm resulted in the recovery of more than 350,000 sherds, of which slightly more than 15,000 were analyzed as a part of this study (all rims greater than 4 $cm^2$, and all decorated sherds and appendages, regardless of size) (Table 4.4), and 1,075 chipped stone tools (448 triangular projectile points and 627 endscrapers). In addition to these materials, whole vessels in two private collections were examined as part of this study. Caborn-Welborn Decorated accounts for slightly more than 30 percent of the analyzed ceramics from Slack Farm (Table 4.4). Other decorated types that are well represented in this collection include Oneota-like and Manly Punctate, each of which accounts for more than 1.0 percent of the analyzed ceramics.

### *Hovey Lake (12Po10)*

The Hovey Lake site was investigated in 1979 and 1980 by Indiana University field schools under the direction of Cheryl Ann Munson. Additional fieldwork was conducted at this site in 1996 and again in 1997. Although cultural materials at the Hovey Lake site are found over 23.4 ha (Munson 1997), the Caborn-Welborn component is restricted to an 11.8-ha area adjacent to the lake. This component consists of a 2.2-ha habitation area surrounding a central plaza. Several cemeteries are located around the outer margins of the residential area.

Though not as large as Slack Farm, Hovey Lake is, nonetheless, one of the larger Caborn-Welborn villages identified to date. As the name implies, the site is located near Hovey Lake, a large cypress swamp and backwater lake. These wetlands were formed before the site was occupied, the result of Ohio River channel migration. The site is situated on a terrace, about 3.6 km from the Ohio River. It is located at an elevation of 109 m and is associated with Wheeling silt loam soils (McWilliams 1979). Munson (1983) suggests that this community may have contained as many as 100 houses organized around a central plaza.

A controlled surface collection and limited excavations in the late 1970s documented the presence of a large number of surface stains (Figure 4.12). The larger stains may correspond to house basins, while the small stains may be pits or hearths. Some of the stains, which appear to be plow-disturbed burials, were identified in areas between the house basins and to the south and southwest of them. Excavation of one large surface stain revealed the presence of a wall trench house with a central hearth that had been rebuilt at least once. Of particular interest was the presence of burial pits along the northwestern and southeastern walls of the structure (Figure 4.13). The identification of burials in a variety of contexts is suggestive of a mortuary program where status differences were reflected, in part, by how one's body was treated at death (Munson and Cook 2001).

Table 4.4. Large Village Large Ceramic Collections

| Ceramic Types | Murphy | | Hovey Lake | | Slack Farm | |
|---|---|---|---|---|---|---|
| Kimmswick Plain | 37 | 8.2% | 53 | 11.0% | 671 | 4.4% |
| Kimmswick Fabric Impressed | 54 | 12.2% | 51 | 10.5% | 874 | 5.8% |
| Mississippi Plain | 149 | 33.7% | 207 | 42.8% | 4925 | 32.6% |
| Bell Plain | 129 | 29.2% | 121 | 25.0% | 2955 | 19.6% |
| Kimmswick Net Impressed | 1 | 0.2% | 1 | 0.2% | 6 | 0.0% |
| Cordmarked | | | 2 | 0.4% | 22 | 0.1% |
| Tolu Fabric Impressed | 3 | 0.7% | 1 | 0.2% | 39 | 0.3% |
| Parkin Punctate | 1 | 0.2% | 1 | 0.2% | 31 | 0.2% |
| Caborn-Welborn Decorated | 48 | 10.9% | 38 | 7.9% | 4794 | 31.8% |
| Manly Punctate | 3 | 0.7% | 3 | 0.6% | 204 | 1.4% |
| Matthews Incised | | | | | 44 | 0.3% |
| Old Town Red | 5 | 1.1% | 1 | 0.2% | 93 | 0.6% |
| Angel Negative Painted | | | | | 5 | 0.0% |
| Walls Engraved | | | | | 29 | 0.2% |
| O'Byam Incised | 4 | 0.9% | 2 | 0.4% | 9 | 0.1% |
| Oneota-Like | 2 | 0.5% | 1 | 0.2% | 204 | 1.4% |
| Fortune Noded | | | | | 1 | 0.0% |
| Beckwith Incised | | | | | 16 | 0.1% |
| Misc. Incised or Trailed | 2 | 0.5% | | | 50 | 0.3% |
| Kent Incised-Like | 2 | 0.5% | 2 | 0.4% | 53 | 0.4% |
| Mound Place Incised | | | | | 5 | 0.0% |
| Barton Incised | | | | | 1 | 0.0% |
| Campbell Punctate | 2 | 0.5% | | | 45 | 0.3% |
| Campbell Applique | | | | | 13 | 0.1% |
| Campbell Incised | | | | | 9 | 0.1% |
| Total | 442 | 100% | 484 | 100% | 15098 | 100% |

Several partial and complete ceramic vessels were found in association with the burials and on the floor of the structure. Most were small- to medium-sized jars with opposing handles, but one was a large jar with bifurcated lugs, and two were shallow bowls with outslanting walls and flat bottoms (Figure 4.14). The composition of the ceramic assemblage from this house is very similar to the ceramic collections recovered from house contexts at Slack Farm (Pollack and Munson 1996).

Radiocarbon dates from Hovey Lake (Table 2.1) point to long-term use of this locality. However, as will be discussed in chapter 5, the ceramics from this site are indicative of an early Caborn-Welborn occupation. The ceramic data from Hovey Lake points to a shorter period of use than is re-

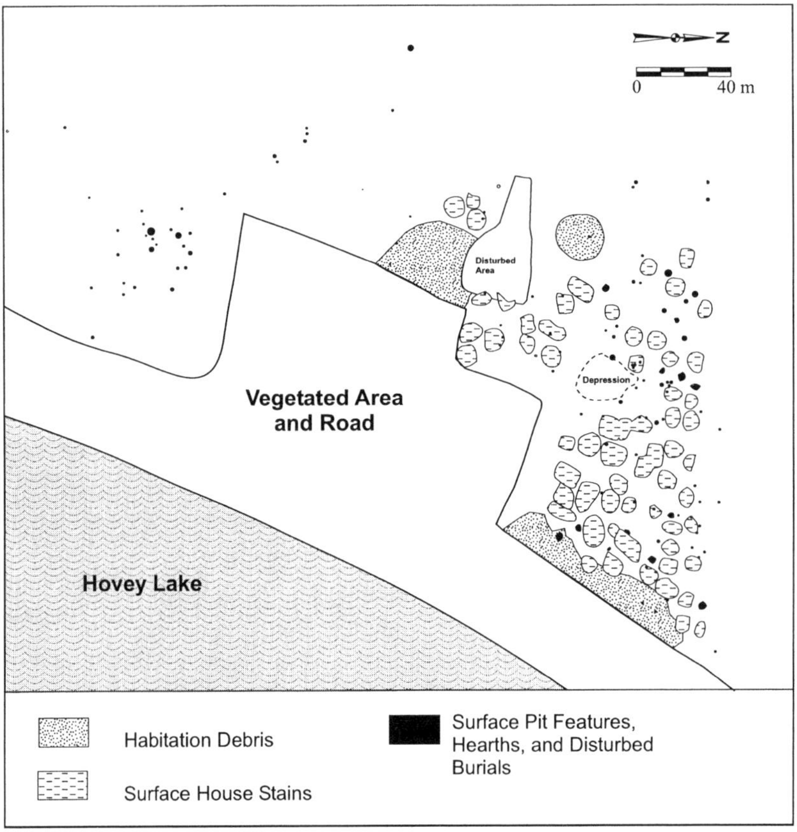


Figure 4.12. Map of Hovey Lake showing the distribution of surface house stains and pit features (based on investigations conducted in 1978–1979).

flected by the five radiocarbon dates from this site which range from A.D. 1280(1305,1367,1373)1410 to A.D. 1490(1657)1950. The four dates that have been corrected for the effects of C12/C13 have midpoints that fall in the late fourteenth/early fifteenth centuries. This suggests that they may be more reliable than the very late date. At present, there is no evidence to suggest that Hovey Lake continued to be occupied into the sixteenth or seventeenth centuries.

The Hovey Lake site artifact assemblage is characterized by a very low percentage (about 7.0 percent) of Caborn-Welborn Decorated ceramics (Table 4.4). Ninety-six triangular points and 51 endscrapers were recovered from this site.

## *Summary*

In general, large villages are found in similar environmental contexts as the smaller communities (i.e., located near sloughs and swales), but they tend to be associated with terraces and thus are not as susceptible to flooding as the

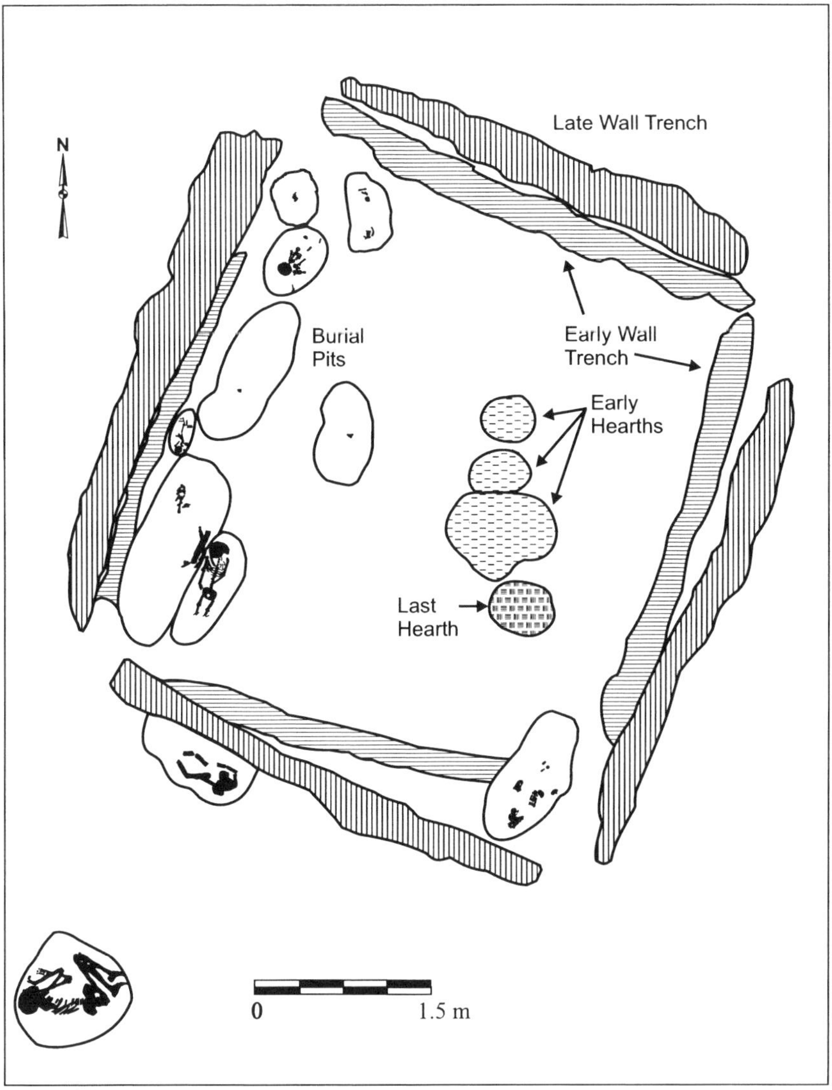


Figure 4.13. Map showing the location of burials within and outside of a house basin at the Hovey Lake site.

other settlement types. Since large villages do not exhibit a linear distribution of materials, they tend to be associated with broader levees and ridges than smaller site types. These areas were selected to accommodate a larger residential population.

Large village sites range in size from 3 to 14 ha, with Slack Farm the largest Caborn-Welborn site documented to date. They are characterized by high artifact densities, thick midden deposits, large storage pits, and plazas. These

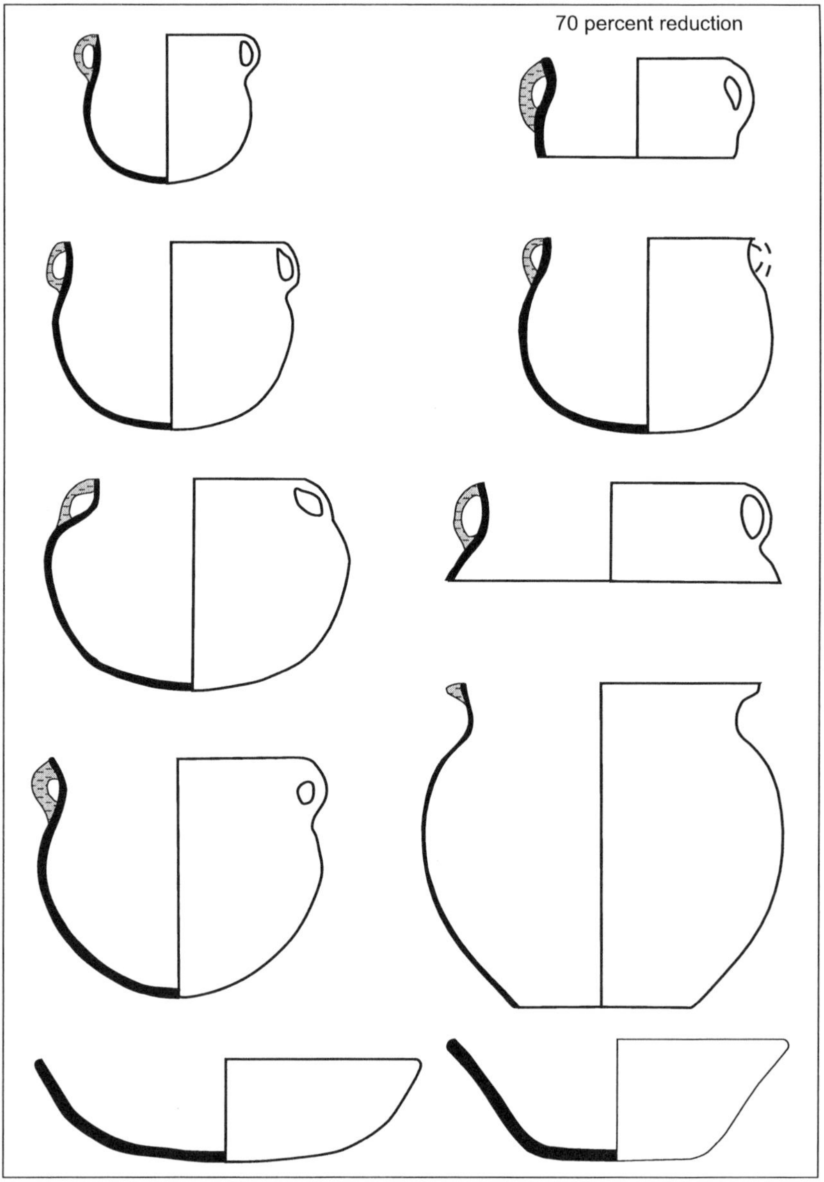


Figure 4.14. Whole or nearly whole ceramic vessels from a house basin at the Hovey Lake site.

villages may have consisted of several distinct groups of houses organized around a central plaza, each with its own associated cemetery. Although the presence of plazas suggests that community or broader region-wide ceremonies and rituals took place at these sites, none of the large villages contain platform mounds or other forms of corporate architecture.

Located near the houses at Slack Farm, and perhaps at other large Caborn-Welborn villages, were large underground storage pits that could feed at least 12 individuals for substantial periods of time. The presence of these large "underground silos" could indicate that they functioned as multifamily storage facilities, that families were able to produce enough food to last more than one year as a hedge against crop failure, or that families were capable of producing a surplus that could be used to help underwrite feasting associated with Caborn-Welborn rituals and ceremonies.

At Slack Farm, differences in the contextual association of Caborn-Welborn Decorated ceramics were identified, with this ceramic type much more common in pit than in house contexts. This pattern, along with the concentrations of Caborn-Welborn Decorated observed at small villages, suggests that these jars may have been used in activities that involved a wide spectrum of the community, such as preparing food for feasts organized by aspiring elites, or in rituals similar to the New Fire and Green Corn ceremonies of Southeastern Historic Indian groups, as has been suggested by Hilgeman (2000:191–203) for Angel/Kincaid Negative Painted plates.

Multiple cemeteries have been documented at most large villages, and within each cemetery, burials were laid out in parallel rows. The clustering of structures within these communities and the presence of more than one cemetery at large villages suggest that several kin-related groups may have occupied these settlements. More detailed investigations aimed at determining the organization of village sites are needed.

Large villages share with small villages high artifact densities and the presence of plazas. But they differ from small villages in terms of size and the presence of multiple cemeteries. All large villages contain large burial populations.

## Cemeteries Not Directly Associated with Habitation Sites

The fifth Caborn-Welborn site type consists of blufftop cemeteries removed from residential sites. Unlike the habitation sites, which tend to be associated with floodplain levees and terraces, these sites are primarily located on the south side of the Ohio River, on top of the bluffs overlooking the river. (Site 15Un40, however, is situated on the upper portion of a spur that extends from the top to the bottom of the bluffs.) Little is known about the mortuary program associated with Caborn-Welborn blufftop cemeteries, since none has been investigated by professional archaeologists.

Among the five sites assigned to this site type, only two, Grundy Hill and Site 15Un40, can be associated with the Caborn-Welborn phase based on material culture documented in private and museum collections. Site 15Un70 was assigned to the Caborn-Welborn phase based on its proximity to Slack Farm. The other two, "The Rocks" Mound and Site 15Un110, were assigned to the Caborn-Welborn phase, based on the recovery of Mississippian ceramics, their proximity to a cemetery (Site 15Un40 and Grundy Hill, respectively) where Caborn-Welborn ceramics are reported to have been found. In addition the general absence of earlier Mississippian habitation sites documented in the region downstream from the mouth of the Wabash and upstream from the mouth of the Saline River provides support for assignment of these sites to the Caborn-Welborn phase. However, it is recognized that some of these sites could actually predate the Caborn-Welborn phase.

Indian Hill, on a blufftop located near the western edge of the Caborn-Welborn region, may represent a Caborn-Welborn cemetery. Unfortunately, little is known about the types of materials found at this site, and a reported Caborn-Welborn habitation site (Site 15Un43) in the floodplain below this site could not be relocated during this study. A Campbell Punctate jar is also reported to have been found on the blufftops slightly downstream from Indian Hill, but the location of this site could not be confirmed. The two most representative blufftop Caborn-Welborn cemetery sites are described below.

### *Grundy Hill (15Un5)*

One of the most well known Caborn-Welborn cemeteries is Grundy Hill, which was investigated by Lyon (1871) in the late nineteenth century (see also DiBlasi and Sudhoff 1978:36, 159). This site consists of several mounds located on the bluffs overlooking the Ohio River at an elevation of 158 m. It is situated 800 m from the Ohio River and is associated with Steinsburg-Frondorf Complex soils (Jacobs 1981).

A small collection of materials from this site was donated to the Smithsonian Institution in the 1960s. These materials were reportedly found by Mr. Thomas Barker Hite in the early 1900s. Lewis (1990:410) notes that among the artifacts from this site that Mrs. Marjorie Jean Hite donated to the Smithsonian were a disk pipe, Barton Incised sherds, and a single astragalus die. Examination of these materials by the author revealed that the Barton Incised sherds are not sherds but a complete Barton Incised jar. Also observed in the collection was a Mississippi Plain jar with opposing pairs of drilled holes about 1 cm below the rim, a Bell Plain bottle lacking a rim, a pestle fragment, and a Caborn-Welborn Decorated jar (Table 4.5). A Fortune Noded vessel also was found at this site (Mike Moore, personal communication 1994). Webb

Table 4.5. Ceramic Collections from Blufftop Cemeteries.

| Ceramic Types | Grundy Hill | | 15Un40 | | 15Un110 | |
|---|---|---|---|---|---|---|
| Mississippi Plain | 1 | 20.0% | 6 | 37.5% | 1 | 33.3% |
| Bell Plain | 1 | 20.0% | 2 | 12.5% | 2 | 66.7% |
| Parkin Punctate | | | 1 | 6.3% | | |
| Caborn-Welborn Decorated | 1 | 20.0% | | | | |
| Matthews Incised | | | | | | |
| Barton Incised | 1 | 20.0% | | | | |
| Fortune Noded | 1 | 20.0% | | | | |
| Campbell Punctate | | | 4 | 25.0% | | |
| Campbell Applique | | | 3 | 18.8% | | |
| Total | 5 | 100% | 16 | 100% | 3 | 100% |

and Funkhouser (1932:382) noted that an "excellent" fluorspar figurine reportedly came from this site. Three fluorspar pendants and two catlinite disk pipes, which are curated at the Kentucky Museum at Western Kentucky University, also are reported to have been found at this site. One fluorspar artifact is described as a bear or owl effigy, another an owl effigy, and the third a human face. On the base of one of the catlinite disk pipes is an engraved bird-man figure with a triangle on its chest, and a broken arrow is engraved on each side of this pipe.

### *Site 15Un40*

Unlike Grundy Hill, the cemetery at Site 15Un40 is located on a ridge-shaped spur that extends from the top to the bottom of the bluffs. This site is located at an elevation of 142 m, is situated 2.5 km from the Ohio River, and is associated with Memphis silty clay loam soils (Jacobs 1981).

Following the publication of an article in the *Courier-Journal* newspaper (1968) about this site, Mike Rodeffer of the University of Kentucky Department of Anthropology visited it and examined 15 ceramic vessels in a private collection. An engraved hematite gorget with an "interesting design" also was examined. Unfortunately, Rodeffer's notes concerning this visit contain little information on the types of ceramic vessels he examined or a description of the design observed on the hematite gorget (fieldnotes on file, Office of State Archaeology, University of Kentucky).

An additional 16 ceramic vessels from this site in a private collection were examined (Mike Moore, personal communication 1994). Campbell Punctate and Campbell Applique account for 43.8 percent of this collection (Table 4.5), which also included a Parkin Punctate vessel.

### Summary

Blufftop cemeteries contain from one to five burial loci. These loci have the appearance of small burial mounds. Unlike the blufftop cemeteries, the bluff spur cemetery consists of a linear distribution of graves. Both types, however, represent cemeteries situated some distance from nearby Caborn-Welborn settlements.

Examination of looters' holes indicates that some of the individuals interred at these sites had been placed in stone boxes. As with earlier Mississippian stone box grave cemeteries, mounds were probably created by the superimposition of graves around the edge of a low rise (Brown 1981; Lane 1998). Through time, the repeated construction of graves on a blufftop increased the height and circumference of the rise and created a moundlike feature on the landscape.

The use of stone boxes and the practice of interring the dead within mounds on blufftops overlooking a habitation site is consistent with mortuary patterns observed at earlier Mississippian sites located downstream from the Caborn-Welborn region, as well as those in the Green River drainage (Lane 1993, 1998). For instance, at Carrsville, a few kilometers downstream from the earlier Mississippian regional center at Tolu, a small Mississippian cemetery is located on the bluffs above a Mississippian habitation site, and in the lower Tennessee-Cumberland region a stone box cemetery was located on the bluffs directly above the Tinsley Hill site (Clay 1997; Lane 1993). Cemeteries removed from habitation areas also have been reported for the Kincaid area (Muller 1986).

## Spatial Distribution of Settlements

As with earlier Mississippian settlements in the lower Ohio valley, such as those of the Angel (Green and Munson 1978) and Kincaid (Muller 1986) chiefdoms, the distribution of Caborn-Welborn settlements reflects, in part, the levee, swale, and slough system of the Ohio River floodplain. Within the 60 km long Caborn-Welborn region, these types of environments are present on both sides of the Ohio River.

Some of the gaps in the distribution of Caborn-Welborn sites correspond to the present locations of Mt. Vernon and Uniontown, coal mines, and other industrial development (Figure 2.2). However, others reflect low-lying areas that are the first to be flooded and are often poorly drained. As such, these areas may not have been as well suited for Caborn-Welborn settlements as other portions of the Ohio River floodplain and may reflect actual breaks in Caborn-Welborn settlement. Based on the observed distribution of the Caborn-Welborn sites, three clusters of sites can be identified in the eastern, central, and western sections (or "subareas") of the Caborn-Welborn region (Figure 4.15).

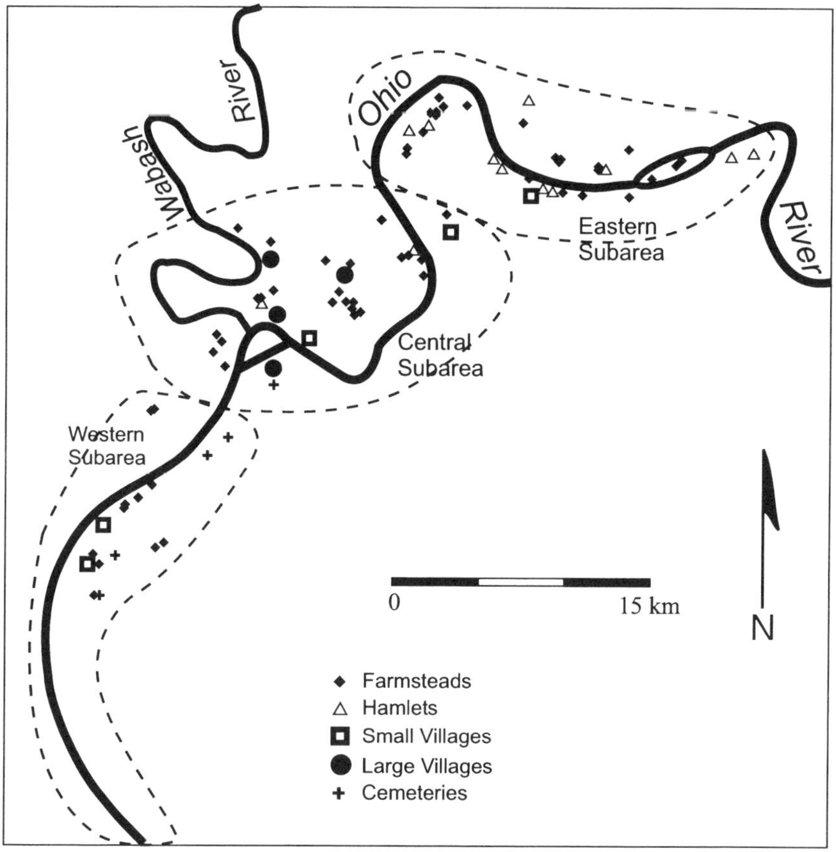


Figure 4.15. Distribution of Caborn-Welborn sites within the three subareas.

The eastern subarea consists of sites located in Cypress Bend and Alzey Bottoms in Kentucky and corresponding areas in Indiana. The central subarea contains sites in Kentucky, Indiana, and Illinois that are located in the vicinity of the mouth of the Wabash. Sites in the western subarea tend to be found on both sides of the river near Shawneetown, Illinois. Assuming that sites located within each subarea shared more in common with each other than with sites in the other two subareas, these subareas can be used as convenient units of analysis for examining the spatial distribution of Caborn-Welborn sites, as well as characteristics of Caborn-Welborn material culture (see chapter 6).

Indeed, when site type is compared and contrasted among the subareas, variation in the number and types of sites found in each subarea can be documented. The eastern subarea (n = 35) is characterized by a concentration of habitation sites that consists of farmsteads (n = 23), hamlets (n = 11), and only one small village, Alzey. Within-community cemeteries are associated with most of the hamlets. Unfortunately, none have been investigated by professional archaeologists, so little is known about their internal structure. Because only one small village is located within this subarea, it is possible that some of the closely spaced farmsteads and hamlets may represent dispersed villages.

The central subarea (n = 28) contains all four of the large Caborn-Welborn villages and two of the five small villages. This subarea also contains 2 hamlets, 19 farmsteads, and a blufftop cemetery. Cemeteries are associated with all the villages, and the large villages contain multiple cemeteries. The large number of villages associated with this subarea may reflect its central location within the distribution of Caborn-Welborn settlements. However, it also may be a reflection of site occupation length owing to the fact that all of the early Caborn-Welborn subdivision villages (Gough, Slack Farm, Welborn, Murphy, and Hovey Lake) are located in this subarea (see discussion in chapter 5). By the beginning of the middle Caborn-Welborn subdivision, two of the large villages (Hovey Lake and Murphy) and both small villages (Gough and Welborn) had been abandoned. One new large village (Bone Bank) had been established. Slack Farm, however, continued to be a large village. This large, centrally located community appears to have been an important Caborn-Welborn settlement throughout the Caborn-Welborn phase. The only blufftop cemetery (Site 15Un70) identified within the central subarea is located in close proximity to Slack Farm.

The western subarea has the fewest sites (n = 17), but among them are 2 small villages, Blackburn and Moore, and 11 farmsteads. Cemeteries are not associated with these small villages. Instead, cemeteries are located on the bluffs southeast of them. In fact, this subarea contains four blufftop cemeteries, the most of any subarea.

Intersubarea variation also is reflected in the location of cemeteries relative to Caborn-Welborn settlements. Cemeteries in the eastern and central subareas are found in clear association with Caborn-Welborn settlements. In the eastern subarea, burials are known from Caborn, Mann, Site 15He1, Site 15He40, Site 15He43, Site 15He51, Mulligan, and Ritz, and in the central subarea they have been recorded at Gough, Slack Farm, Murphy, Bone Bank, Hovey Lake, and Leonard. In the western subarea, however, few individuals appear to have been interred within the village sites of Moore and Blackburn; the dead appear to have been interred primarily on the bluffs overlooking the Ohio River. The only other habitation site in the western subarea that is reported to contain burials is Site 15Un111, a farmstead located near the base of the bluffs.

Cemeteries were often located on the bluffs overlooking a regional center or village (Clay 1997; Lane 1993; Schwartz 1961) in the lower Ohio valley during earlier Mississippian times. Patterns of burial in the western subarea point to a continuation of this practice into the Caborn-Welborn phase.

Within-community cemeteries, however, were common during the earlier Angel phase, and after A.D. 1400 are likewise common in the Caborn-Welborn region upstream from the mouth of the Wabash (i.e., in the central and eastern subareas). This finding points to continuity in burial practices between the earlier local regional Mississippian chiefdom and the local Caborn-Welborn population. Slack Farm is the only site where both within-community and blufftop burial practices are known to have occurred, though most individuals were interred within the village. Why different mortuary programs occurred within the Caborn-Welborn region is not known, but their presence points to cultural differences within the region that are explored in more detail in chapters 6 and 7.

Throughout the Caborn-Welborn region, no Caborn-Welborn farmstead or hamlet is situated more than 20 km from a small or large village, and all the villages are located within 20 km of the centrally located Slack Farm site. This clustering of Caborn-Welborn settlements within the three subareas and the diversity of domestic habitation sites in the Caborn-Welborn region is suggestive of political, as well as social and economic, interaction and interconnectedness between the smaller settlements and nearby villages as well as between villages. The clustering and diversity of settlements also points to the continued presence of a settlement hierarchy within the Caborn-Welborn region during most of the Caborn-Welborn sequence. Slack Farm's central location and size suggest that the residents of this community may have played a prominent role in Caborn-Welborn economic and political life, but, as will be discussed in a later chapter, there is no evidence to suggest that political power was centralized within this or any other Caborn-Welborn community.

The close proximity of these settlements to each other would have provided frequent opportunities for disputes to arise, and leaders would have been needed who could mediate disputes both within *and* between communities. These leaders, who probably resided at the small or large villages situated within each subarea, would have had some measure of control or influence over residents of nearby farmsteads and hamlets. They also would have been needed to schedule religious ceremonies, coordinate agricultural tasks, and negotiate alliances and exchange relationships with external groups.

Following the abandonment of the Angel site, the villages, both small and large, may have taken on many of the roles formerly associated with this regional center. Caborn-Welborn villages thus may have been the focal point of economic, social, and political life within each subarea. If this was the case, then the material culture of village sites, in comparison to that of hamlets and farmsteads, should reflect the wider range of activities that would have been conducted at these types of settlements. This is examined in chapter 6.

## SUMMARY

Caborn-Welborn settlements are found within a 60 km long area on either side of the Ohio River, in an environment that had fertile, easily worked soils and access to animal and plant resources in nearby sloughs and the rivers. In general, farmsteads, hamlets, and small villages are found near the Ohio River in similar environmental contexts: on floodplain levees bordered by sloughs. Large villages tend to be associated with nearby terraces that are less susceptible to flooding. Regardless of size, all Caborn-Welborn habitation sites tend to be associated with very loamy, well-drained soils.

Downstream from the Saline River, the bluffs are situated close to the Ohio River, resulting in a more restricted floodplain than is present in the rest of the Caborn-Welborn region. Although the area immediately downstream from the mouth of the Saline River does not appear to have been occupied during the Caborn-Welborn phase, this area does appear to have supported earlier Mississippian populations, as evidenced by such sites as Tolu and Orr Herrl. Thus, even though floodplain and terrace habitats were more restricted downstream from the mouth of the Saline River, there was still sufficient agricultural soils and other resources in this area to support large Mississippian communities and regional centers. Why the Caborn-Welborn population did not extend into this area is unknown.

Similarly, environmental constraints would not have restricted the expansion of Caborn-Welborn settlements upstream from Cypress Bottoms near Geneva, Kentucky, the eastern edge of the Caborn-Welborn region. In this area, the floodplain and terraces and extensive ridge and swale floodplain deposits remain relatively unconstricted throughout the area inhabited by the earlier Angel population. Sites assigned to the Angel phase are found as far east as the mouth of the Anderson River in southern Indiana, where the floodplain again becomes more constricted. Thus, there is little evidence to suggest that environmental conditions limited or constrained the eastward distribution of Caborn-Welborn settlements, unless environmental degradation contributed to Angel's demise and the environment had not had sufficient time to recover. Again, why the Caborn-Welborn population did not extend into this area of former Angel settlement is unknown, but it may relate to the internal dynamics of Caborn-Welborn society and to the extraregional interaction networks in which the Caborn-Welborn population participated. In essence, households may have found it to their advantage to be within a day's travel of Slack Farm and the mouth of the Wabash, especially if this settlement was the focal point of intra- and extraregional interaction during the Caborn-Welborn phase (see chapter 7).

Within the Caborn-Welborn region, settlements range in size from .3 to more than 14 ha. Based primarily on site size, but also taking into consideration the density and types of materials recovered and how communities were organized, settlements were assigned to one of four types: farmsteads (.25–.50 ha), hamlets (.50–1.25 ha), small villages (1.25–3 ha), and large villages (3–14 ha). As with earlier Mississippian societies in the lower Ohio valley, the majority of Caborn-Welborn sites are farmsteads.

Farmsteads are characterized by low surface artifact densities relative to other Caborn-Welborn settlements, and most exhibit a linear distribution of cultural materials. The smallest farmsteads consist of a single artifact cluster, but some of the larger ones contain two to four clusters. Multiple clusters of artifacts at these sites suggest the presence of one or more households or the periodic shifting of one household. Burials are not common at farmsteads, but when present they tend to be associated with small cemetery areas.

Hamlets are not only bigger than farmsteads, but they tend to have higher artifact densities, and several of the sites assigned to this settlement class have associated cemeteries. As with farmsteads, these sites also tend to exhibit a linear distribution of materials. Artifact clusters within hamlets tend to be larger than at farmsteads, and most hamlets contain two or more clusters of cultural materials. The spatial distribution of artifacts at these sites is suggestive of a larger number of households and a more intensive occupation than has been documented for farmsteads. The spatial clustering of farmsteads and hamlets within portions of the Caborn-Welborn region, especially the Alzey Bottoms in the eastern subarea, suggests that groups of settlements could constitute small dispersed villages.

Small villages have higher artifact densities than farmsteads and hamlets, and public space, in the form of a courtyard/plaza, is present at some small village sites. Small villages tend not to have as linear a distribution of cultural materials as farmsteads and hamlets, being more arc-shaped, circular, or U-shaped. Thick midden deposits are associated with some small villages. Clusters of artifacts within small villages point to extensive residential areas, and concentrations of Caborn-Welborn Decorated ceramics point to differences in the use and discard of these ceramic vessels and other Caborn-Welborn ceramics. Although human remains have not been found at two of the small villages, they are reported for the others. At the two small villages that lack cemeteries, the dead appear to have been interred in cemeteries located on bluffs overlooking these communities.

Large villages have higher artifact densities than farmsteads and hamlets and comparable ones to small villages. In addition, public space, in the form of a plaza, is present at most large village sites. In general, large villages tend to exhibit a more oval distribution of cultural materials than other settlement types. Within large villages, clusters of artifacts and features point to extensive residential areas. Variation in the association of Caborn-Welborn Decorated ceramics within house and pit contexts points to differences in the disposal and use of these vessels within Caborn-Welborn communities, similar to the patterns observed at small villages. These decorated jars may have been used in activities that involved a wide spectrum of the community, such as preparing food for feasts organized by aspiring elites or in rituals similar to the New Fire and Green Corn ceremonies of Southeastern Historic Indian groups. All large villages contain multiple cemeteries, and within these cemeteries, burials were laid out in rows.

A fifth Caborn-Welborn site type was defined as a result of this research: blufftop cemeteries. These cemeteries primarily consist of several small accretional burial mounds located on the bluffs overlooking the Ohio River floodplain. Within these mounds, some of the individuals were interred within stone boxes. The use of stone boxes and the practice of interring the dead within mounds on blufftops overlooking a habitation site is consistent with earlier Mississippian mortuary patterns in areas located downstream from the Caborn-Welborn region.

This study has shown that Caborn-Welborn sites tend to cluster within three subareas, which reflects their own unique characteristics of site type and site frequency (Figure 4.15). The eastern subarea is characterized by a large number of farmsteads and hamlets (dispersed communities that may represent small villages), while the central subarea contains the largest number of villages. The western subarea contains two small villages and several farmsteads but no hamlets or large villages. Within-community cemeteries are the norm in the eastern and central subareas. In contrast, the western subarea is characterized by a preference for interment in blufftop mortuary cemeteries.

Variation in site size, density of surface materials, number of cemeteries, the presence of a plaza, and the composition of site ceramic collections (see chapter 6) attests to the existence of a Caborn-Welborn settlement hierarchy that includes farmsteads, hamlets, and small and large villages. The Caborn-Welborn settlement system, however, lacks a regional center with a platform mound(s) or other signs of corporate architecture. One site, however, based on its central location, size, and density of artifacts, does stand apart from other Caborn-Welborn settlements: Slack Farm, which is located across from the mouth of the Wabash River. It is the largest Caborn-Welborn village documented to date, and it is the only settlement that was occupied for the entire Caborn-Welborn sequence. Its size and large number of cemeteries attests to this community's importance within the Caborn-Welborn settlement system.

# 5 Temporal Trends

Before the Caborn-Welborn population's response to the collapse of the Angel chiefdom can be understood and placed within a broader context, some measure of control of internal Caborn-Welborn developments is needed. Through the identification of Caborn-Welborn temporal trends in material culture, it should be possible to determine whether intersite variation in the distribution of ceramic types and attributes represents Caborn-Welborn cultural developments or if it is related to intraregional cultural differences or site function. Therefore, this chapter focuses on identifying ceramic attributes that reflect Caborn-Welborn diachronic trends, which then can be used to order Caborn-Welborn sites temporally.

Ceramics are compared in this chapter with the intent of highlighting attributes that are shared by both Angel and Caborn-Welborn assemblages, as well as those that can be used to distinguish Caborn-Welborn sites from Angel phase sites. The similarities point to continuities in the manufacture and use of ceramic vessels from Angel 3 to the beginning of the Caborn-Welborn phase, while the differences reflect the unique character of Caborn-Welborn ceramics and the existence of differences relative to the Angel chiefdom with respect to Caborn-Welborn social, political, and economic organization. Of the more than 80 known Caborn-Welborn sites, 22 have yielded 30 or more analyzable specimens (rims, decorated sherds, and appendages). The ceramics from these sites, along with materials from the Angel site, were the focus of the intersite comparisons of ceramic traits and types discussed in this chapter. These comparisons resulted in the identification of temporal trends in Caborn-Welborn ceramic types, decorative styles, and appendages that were used to develop an internal chronology for the Caborn-Welborn phase (Table 5.1).

## COMPARISON OF ANGEL AND CABORN-WELBORN CERAMICS

In order to identify ceramic attributes that reflect internal Caborn-Welborn diachronic trends, some understanding of earlier Mississippian ceramics is needed. Based on an analysis of decorated ceramics and appendages from the Angel site, Hilgeman (1992, 2000) identified the salient characteristics of An-

Table 5.1. Ceramic Types Recovered from the 22 sites with Large Ceramic Collections (Sites are Ordered Temporally)

| Ceramic Types | Early Caborn-Welborn Sites | | | | | | | | E/M/Late | |
|---|---|---|---|---|---|---|---|---|---|---|
| | Murphy | | Welborn | | Hovey Lake | | Gough | | Slack Farm* | |
| Kimmswick Plain | 37 | 8.2% | 10 | 6.7% | 53 | 11.0% | 10 | 10.4% | 671 | 4.4% |
| Kimmswick Fabric Impressed | 54 | 12.2% | 17 | 11.3% | 51 | 10.5% | 6 | 6.3% | 874 | 5.8% |
| Mississippi Plain | 149 | 33.7% | 51 | 34.0% | 207 | 42.8% | 38 | 39.6% | 4925 | 32.6% |
| Bell Plain | 129 | 29.2% | 43 | 28.7% | 121 | 25.0% | 23 | 24.0% | 2955 | 19.6% |
| Kimmswick Net Impressed | 1 | 0.2% | | | 1 | 0.2% | | | 6 | 0.0% |
| Cordmarked | | | | | 2 | 0.4% | 1 | 1.0% | 22 | 0.1% |
| Tolu Fabric Impressed | 3 | 0.7% | | | 1 | 0.2% | | | 39 | 0.3% |
| Parkin Punctate | 1 | 0.2% | | | 1 | 0.2% | | | 31 | 0.2% |
| Caborn-Welborn Decorated | 48 | 10.9% | 27 | 18.0% | 38 | 7.9% | 17 | 17.7% | 4794 | 31.8% |
| Manly Punctate | 3 | 0.7% | | | 3 | 0.6% | | | 204 | 1.4% |
| Matthews Incised | | | | | | | | | 44 | 0.3% |
| Old Town Red | 5 | 1.1% | 1 | 0.7% | 1 | 0.2% | | | 93 | 0.6% |
| Angel Negative Painted | | | | | | | | | 5 | 0.0% |
| Walls Engraved | | | | | | | | | 29 | 0.2% |
| O'Byam Incised | 4 | 0.9% | | | 2 | 0.4% | | | 9 | 0.1% |
| Oneota-Like | 2 | 0.5% | | | 1 | 0.2% | 1 | 1.0% | 204 | 1.4% |
| Fortune Noded | | | | | | | | | 1 | 0.0% |
| Beckwith Incised | | | | | | | | | 16 | 0.1% |

*Continued on the next page*

Table 5.1. *Continued*

| Ceramic Types | Early Caborn-Welborn Sites | | | | | | | | E/M/Late | |
|---|---|---|---|---|---|---|---|---|---|---|
| | Murphy | | Welborn | | Hovey Lake | | Gough | | Slack Farm* | |
| Misc. Incised or Trailed | 2 | 0.5% | | | | | | | 50 | 0.3% |
| Kent Incised-Like | 2 | 0.5% | | | 2 | 0.4% | | | 53 | 0.4% |
| Mound Place Incised | | | | | | | | | 5 | 0.0% |
| Barton Incised | | | | | | | | | 1 | 0.0% |
| Campbell Punctate | 2 | 0.5% | 1 | 0.7% | | | | | 45 | 0.3% |
| Campbell Applique | | | | | | | | | 13 | 0.1% |
| Campbell Incised | | | | | | | | | 9 | 0.1% |
| Total | 442 | 100% | 150 | 100% | 484 | 100% | 96 | 100% | 15098 | 100% |

* Slack Farm was occupied for the entire Caborn-Welborn sequence.

| Ceramic Types | Middle Caborn-Welborn Sites | | | | | | | | | |
|---|---|---|---|---|---|---|---|---|---|---|
| | Caborn | | Hart | | 15He37.1 | | Alzey | | Ritz | |
| Kimmswick Plain | 34 | 7.6% | 1 | 1.0% | 3 | 8.8% | 15 | 4.5% | 2 | 2.4% |
| Kimmswick Fabric Impressed | 2 | 0.4% | | | 1 | 2.9% | 2 | 0.6% | | |
| Mississippi Plain | 140 | 31.2% | 30 | 29.4% | 22 | 64.7% | 89 | 26.5% | 22 | 26.2% |
| Bell Plain | 66 | 14.7% | 3 | 2.9% | 6 | 17.6% | 46 | 13.7% | 22 | 26.2% |
| Caborn-Welborn Decorated | 202 | 45.0% | 66 | 64.7% | 2 | 5.9% | 176 | 52.4% | 38 | 45.2% |
| Tolu Fabric Impressed | 1 | 0.2% | | | | | | | | |
| Manly Punctate | 2 | 0.4% | | | | | 1 | 0.3% | | |

| | | | | | | | | | | |
|---|---|---|---|---|---|---|---|---|---|---|
| Matthews Incised | | | | | | | 1 | 0.3% | | |
| Old Town Red | 1 | 0.2% | 2 | 2.0% | | | | | | |
| Angel Negative Painted | | | | | | | 2 | 0.6% | | |
| Oneota-Like | 1 | 0.2% | | | | | 2 | 0.6% | | |
| Beckwith Incised | | | | | | | 1 | 0.3% | | |
| Misc. Incised or Trailed | | | | | | | 1 | 0.3% | | |
| Total | 449 | 100% | 102 | 100% | 34 | 100% | 336 | 100% | 84 | 100% |

| Ceramic Types | Hooper | | Stull | | 11Ga160 | | Ries-Hasting | | 15Un96 | |
|---|---|---|---|---|---|---|---|---|---|---|
| Kimmswick Plain | | | 4 | 2.5% | 2 | 2.5% | 7 | 3.2% | 17 | 19.5% |
| Kimmswick Fabric Impressed | | | 7 | 4.4% | 1 | 1.3% | 1 | 0.5% | | |
| Mississippi Plain | 19 | 34.5% | 46 | 28.9% | 23 | 29.1% | 75 | 34.4% | 43 | 49.4% |
| Bell Plain | 13 | 23.6% | 17 | 10.7% | 19 | 24.1% | 38 | 17.4% | 14 | 16.2% |
| Parkin Punctate | | | 1 | 0.6% | | | | | | |
| Caborn-Welborn Decorated | 22 | 40.0% | 84 | 52.8% | 34 | 43.0% | 92 | 42.2% | 13 | 14.9% |
| Old Town Red | | | | | | | 1 | 0.5% | | |
| Misc. Incised or Trailed | | | | | | | 2 | 0.9% | | |
| Campbell Punctate | | | | | | | 1 | 0.5% | | |
| Campbell Applique | 1 | 1.8% | | | | | 1 | 0.5% | | |
| Total | 55 | 100% | 159 | 100% | 79 | 100% | 218 | 100% | 87 | 100% |

*Continued on the next page*

Table 5.1. *Continued*

| Ceramic Types | Middle Caborn-Welborn Sites | | | | | | | | | |
|---|---|---|---|---|---|---|---|---|---|---|
| | 15He38 | | 15He110 | | Mulligan | | 15Un101 | | Moore | |
| Kimmswick Plain | | | 5 | 7.5% | 5 | 6.3% | | | 35 | 11.7% |
| Kimmswick Fabric Impressed | 2 | 3.2% | 8 | 11.9% | | | | | 6 | 2.0% |
| Mississippi Plain | 5 | 8.1% | 17 | 25.4% | 49 | 61.3% | 9 | 20.0% | 135 | 45.3% |
| Bell Plain | 5 | 8.1% | 15 | 22.4% | 9 | 11.3% | 5 | 11.1% | 59 | 19.8% |
| Parkin Punctate | | | | | | | | | 2 | 0.7% |
| Caborn-Welborn Decorated | 46 | 74.2% | 21 | 31.3% | 11 | 13.8% | 31 | 68.9% | 43 | 14.4% |
| Manly Punctate | 3 | 4.8% | | | 1 | 1.3% | | | | |
| Matthews Incised | 1 | 1.6% | | | | | | | | |
| Old Town Red | | | | | | | | | 8 | 2.7% |
| Walls Engraved | | | | | | | | | 1 | 0.3% |
| Misc. Incised or Trailed | | | | | | | | | 2 | 0.7% |
| Barton Incised | | | | | | | | | 3 | 1.0% |
| Mound Place Incised | | | | | | | | | | |
| Campbell Punctate | | | 1 | 1.5% | 5 | 6.3% | | | 1 | 0.3% |
| Campbell Applique | | | | | | | | | 1 | 0.3% |
| Campbell Incised | | | | | | | | | 1 | 0.3% |
| Ranch Incised-Like | | | | | | | | | 1 | 0.3% |
| Total | 62 | 100% | 67 | 100% | 80 | 100% | 45 | 100% | 298 | 100% |

Table 5.1. *Continued*

| Ceramic Types | Mid/Late | | Late | |
|---|---|---|---|---|
| | Blackburn | | Cummings | |
| Kimmswick Plain | 33 | 12.2% | 9 | 7.2% |
| Kimmswick Fabric Impressed | 2 | 0.7% | | |
| Mississippi Plain | 89 | 33.0% | 97 | 77.6% |
| Bell Plain | 77 | 28.5% | 10 | 8.0% |
| Cordmarked | | | 1 | 0.8% |
| Parkin Punctate | 3 | 1.1% | | |
| Caborn-Welborn Decorated | 57 | 21.1% | 4 | 3.2% |
| Old Town Red | 6 | 2.2% | 3 | 2.4% |
| Angel Negative Painted | 1 | 0.4% | | |
| Mound Place Incised | 1 | 0.4% | | |
| Campbell Incised | 1 | 0.4% | | |
| Vernon Paul Applique | | | 1 | 0.8% |
| Total | 270 | 100% | 125 | 100% |

gel ceramics and how they changed over time. The ceramic types and attributes that are diagnostic of Angel 3 (A.D. 1325–1450) components are the most relevant to this discussion.

The last and most intensive use of Angel occurred during Angel 3 times, predating, but slightly overlapping, the traditional A.D. 1400 beginning date for the Caborn-Welborn phase (Hilgeman 2000). If the Angel/Caborn-Welborn transition occurred over an extended period of time, one would expect some overlap in the settlement history of the Angel site and the earliest Caborn-Welborn sites. Exactly when this transition began, and whether the period of overlap lasted 10, 20, or 50 years, remains to be determined. For the purposes of this study, Angel 3 is viewed as ending ca. A.D. 1400, which marks the beginning of the Caborn-Welborn phase.

Angel 3 ceramic collections (Hilgeman 1992, 2000:227) are characterized by wide thick and wide thin strap handles; Vanderburgh Stamped short rim plates; notched or beaded horizontal strips on bowls; deep rim plates (shallow bowls with outslanting walls), some with castellated rims; Old Town Red; and Angel Negative Painted. The presence of Old Town Red and Angel Negative Painted in Angel 3 deposits is interpreted by Hilgeman (1992) to represent continuity from the earlier Angel 2 occupation.

Toward the end of Angel 3, ceramic types such as Parkin Punctate, and perhaps Walls Engraved, make their first appearance in the Angel archaeological record. Both Parkin Punctate and Walls Engraved date to some time after ca. A.D. 1350–1400 in the central Mississippi valley, where these types were defined (Mainfort 1996; Morse and Morse 1983:278). The introduction during Angel 3 of these ceramic types, as well as a new bowl form (deep rim plates, that is, shallow bowls with outslanting walls and flat bottoms) and bowl appendages, such as notched or beaded rimstrips, reflects ongoing interaction with Mississippian groups within and to the south of the lower Ohio valley.

Some Angel 3 diagnostic attributes occur with greater frequency on Caborn-Welborn sites than they do on earlier Angel phase sites. This frequency indicates that, following their introduction, the popularity of these decorative styles or vessel forms increased. For instance, only 135 bowls with notched or beaded rims were found at Angel (major excavation) (Hilgeman 2000), which is just slightly more than the 79 recovered from the more limited Caborn investigations (survey and testing) and much less than the 250 specimens recovered from the intensive investigations undertaken at Slack Farm (Pollack and Munson 1998). (Except for intersite comparisons of complete mortuary vessels, counts of vessels presented in this and subsequent chapters are based entirely on rim counts.) Likewise, while 80 bowls with outslanting walls and castellated rims were recovered from Angel, 97 were found during the much more limited investigations at Hovey Lake (survey and testing) and 925 were identified in the Slack Farm collection (Pollack and Munson 1998). The predominance of wide thin strap handles, and bifurcated and round to oval jar lugs in Caborn-Welborn ceramic assemblages also reflects continuity from the earlier Angel phase.

There are a few decorated ceramic types that are present in Angel and Caborn-Welborn ceramic collections that point to continuity from one phase to the other. For instance, Old Town Red is a ceramic type found in both assemblages. This ceramic type has been recovered from good excavated contexts at both Hovey Lake and Caborn. It also is present in the Slack Farm and Murphy collections and in surface collections from six other Caborn-Welborn phase sites: Hart, Moore, Welborn, Ries-Hasting, Blackburn, and Cummings. In addition to Slack Farm, Blackburn and Cummings also have yielded historic trade goods. Thus, based on the present evidence, there is every reason to believe that Old Town Red was a minor component of both Angel and Caborn-Welborn ceramic assemblages, though it was more common at Angel than at any Caborn-Welborn site. The presence of Parkin Punctate and Walls Engraved at Slack Farm and other Caborn-Welborn sites, as well as additional late Mississippian central Mississippi valley types, such as Campbell Punctate, Campbell Applique, Campbell Incised, and Kent Incised-like, indicates that relationships with Mississippian groups in the central Mississippi valley were maintained and continued during the subsequent Caborn-Welborn phase. Again, the presence of similar ceramic types in both Angel and Caborn-Welborn collections is further evidence of continuity.

In addition to ceramic types and attributes, there are several nonvessel ceramic objects that reflect continuity. Among these are pestles, disks, ear plugs, and owl effigy pendants.

Although there are attributes of Angel and Caborn-Welborn ceramic assemblages that point to continuity from one phase to the other, there are differences that serve to distinguish earlier Angel phase assemblages from later assemblages. Perhaps the most striking difference between these ceramic assemblages is a shift from negative painted designs on the interior of plates and the exterior of bottles (Angel) to a preference for trailed, incised, and punctated designs on jar shoulders (Caborn-Welborn). In the Caborn-Welborn region, Angel/Kincaid Negative Painted has been found at fewer sites than Old Town Red. To date, this type has been identified in four Caborn-Welborn collections (Slack Farm, Alzey, Blackburn, and Murphy; Munson 1997:54), where it accounts for less than .6 percent of the analyzed ceramics from each site. Even at the Angel site, Angel/Kincaid Negative Painted may account for only about .3 percent of the ceramics (Munson 1994). However, at the Angel site, Angel Negative Painted ceramics account for 17.9 percent of the decorated and modified sherds reported on by Hilgeman (2000).

At other earlier Mississippian sites in the lower Ohio valley, negative painted ceramics also have a relatively low frequency of occurrence, so one would not expect to find a large number of Angel/Kincaid Negative Painted ceramics at Caborn-Welborn sites. For instance, at the Southwind site, a small Angel phase village located downstream from the Angel site, negative painted sherds account for just .3 percent of the ceramics recovered, and at Chambers, a mid-thirteenth to mid-fourteenth western Kentucky Mississippian village (Pollack and Railey 1987), they account for only .8 percent of the ceramics. (The slightly higher percentages of this type in Caborn-Welborn collections should not be interpreted to mean that this type is more common at some Caborn-Welborn sites than at earlier Mississippian sites. The Caborn-Welborn percentages are based on the analyzed sample of rims and decorated sherds, while the Southwind and Angel percentages include body sherds.)

As with Old Town Red, there is nothing in the archaeological record of the Caborn-Welborn area to suggest that the presence of Angel/Kincaid Negative Painted ceramics in Caborn-Welborn collections reflects the presence of an earlier Mississippian component at these sites. Rather, both types, along with Manly Punctate, Matthews Incised, Beckwith Incised, and Tolu Fabric Impressed, appear to reflect ceramic continuity with earlier Mississippian ceramics of the lower Ohio valley and with the Angel chiefdom in particular. Whether Caborn-Welborn potters continued to make these negative painted ceramics or if these items represent heirlooms remains to be determined.

While Caborn-Welborn assemblages do contain a higher percentage of incised, trailed, and punctated jars (i.e., Caborn-Welborn Decorated ceramics) than their Angel phase counterparts, continuity with the ceramics of the earlier Angel chiefdom is represented. We know this because designs on negative painted ceramics at Angel (Hilgeman 1992, 2000) are similar to those placed on Caborn-Welborn Decorated jar shoulders. The most common design associated with Angel Negative Painted ceramics consists of layout lines that were used to create opposing descending and rising triangles. These triangular areas were usually filled with parallel lines, but dots and chevrons were occasionally used (Hilgeman 2000: Table 5.2). Negative painted plates with this design layout have been interpreted as representing a sun symbol, with the center of the sun in the well of the plate and its rays forming an encircling band of projecting triangular areas around the rim (Curry 1950; Hilgeman 1991). On Caborn-Welborn ceramics, this design is placed on jar shoulders, and, unlike Angel Negative Painted, it is executed through the use of incised/trailed lines and punctations.

Based on the similarity in design layout exhibited by Angel Negative Painted plates and Caborn-Welborn Decorated jars, it is likely that the rising and descending triangular areas found on Caborn-Welborn Decorated vessels also depict a sun symbol, with the center of the sun corresponding to the orifice of the jar. Rather than being painted around the inner rim of a plate, however, Caborn-Welborn potters placed the sun on the outer shoulder of a jar. Thus, while the type of vessel and the technique used to depict the sun may have differed between Angel 3 and the Caborn-Welborn phases (plate vs. jar and painted vs. incised/trailed), similar messages may have been conveyed to Angel and Caborn-Welborn households by the designs placed on these vessels (Pollack and Munson 1996, 1998).

Caborn-Welborn assemblages also can be distinguished from Angel assemblages by the presence of Oneota-like designs and jar forms. Although both Oneota and Caborn-Welborn Decorated jars are characterized by shoulder decoration and the use of trailed lines and punctations to create designs, there are differences, both in the execution of the designs and in the types of appendages that are associated with these designs. The most common design associated with Caborn-Welborn Decorated jars consists of a series of triangular areas demarcated by incised or trailed lines that form opposing series of triangles filled with either parallel diagonal lines or punctations. Decoration on some Oneota jars also consists of alternating panels of lines and punctations (e.g., Boszhardt 1994; Gibbon 1973), but the layout lines on these jars tend to be oriented vertically and rarely intersect each other. Rather than creating triangular areas, the net result is a series of panels or trapezoidal spaces that encircle the vessel. Thus, in general, the orientation of the Caborn-Welborn layout lines and the use of opposing triangular spaces tend to distinguish Caborn-Welborn designs from Oneota designs (Pollack and Munson 1996).

Other attributes of the Oneota-like vessels in Caborn-Welborn ceramic assemblages also contrast with Caborn-Welborn ceramics. Caborn-Welborn handles are much wider and thinner than Oneota handles, and Caborn-Welborn jars are associated with a variety of lugs, nodes, and applied horizontal strips that are rarely found on Oneota jars. Within the Caborn-Welborn region, Oneota-like jars are associated with notched loop or intermediate loop/strap handles and interior lip decoration in the form of notches, dashes, and trailed chevrons. There also are differences in the types and frequency of occurrence of other vessel forms, with bowls, pans, and bottles being much more common in Caborn-Welborn ceramic collections than in Oneota assemblages.

From this review, similarities and differences have been identified in site ceramic collections that can be used to distinguish Angel from Caborn-Welborn phase sites. The similarities demonstrate that important continuities in ceramic tradition exist between Angel 3 and the Caborn-Welborn phase, while the differences illustrate the unique character of Caborn-Welborn ceramics. Both Angel phase and Caborn-Welborn phase ceramic assemblages contain the same Mississippi Plain and Bell Plain vessel forms and appendages and the presence of several decorated types. Shallow bowls with outslanting walls and flat bottoms (deep rim plates), some with castellations; hemispherical bowls with notched or beaded rimstrips; and thin jar strap handles and bifurcated and round to oval jar lugs are good examples of vessels and appendages that are present in both ceramic assemblages. Decorated ceramic types that occur in the ceramic assemblages of both are Old Town Red and, to a lesser extent, Parkin Punctate and perhaps Walls Engraved. The presence of types such as Manly Punctate, Beckwith Incised, Matthews Incised, O'Byam Incised/Engraved, and Tolu Fabric Impressed in Caborn-Welborn assemblages shows continuity not only with the preceding Angel phase but with the lower Ohio valley in general and point to continued connections with this area.

The addition of Caborn-Welborn Decorated jars to Caborn-Welborn phase site ceramic collections clearly distinguishes Caborn-Welborn ceramic assemblages from those of the earlier Angel phase. This ceramic type also distinguishes Caborn-Welborn ceramic assemblages from other earlier regional Mississippian ceramic assemblages in the lower Ohio valley. The presence of Oneota-like jars and several central Mississippi valley ceramic types, such as Kent Incised–like, Campbell Incised, Campbell Punctate, and Campbell Applique, also serve to distinguish Caborn-Welborn ceramic collections from earlier Mississippian ceramic assemblages in the lower Ohio valley, and reflect extraregional interaction with groups living outside the Ohio River valley.

## CABORN-WELBORN CERAMIC TEMPORAL TRENDS

Before it can be determined whether variation in the distribution of Caborn-Welborn ceramic types and attributes represents intraregional cultural differences or is a product of site function, some measure of control of internal Caborn-Welborn temporal trends is needed. Ceramics recovered from the 22 sites that yielded more than 30 analyzable sherds were compared and contrasted to identify temporally sensitive ceramic trends (Table 5.1). A 30-sherd minimum for inclusion in the analysis was used because sampling bias has a greater impact on small samples than on larger ones (Williams 1978). Most of the site ceramic collections that failed to meet this criterion were from small sites that had good surface visibility but low artifact densities, and most were classified as farmsteads. Larger Caborn-Welborn sites with small surface collections had been severely impacted, if not destroyed, by erosion (e.g., Welborn and Site 15He111), had poor surface visibility (e.g., Site 15He51 and Site 15He52), or could not be visited (e.g., Mann).

Of the 22 site collections that contained 30 or more analyzable sherds, 10 are located in the eastern subarea (Caborn, Hart, Site 15He37.1, Alzey, Site

15He38, Site 15He110, Mulligan, Cummings, Ritz, and Hooper), eight are situated in the central subarea (Hovey Lake, Slack Farm, Stull, Gough, Murphy, Welborn, Ries-Hasting, and Site 11Ga160), and four are located in the western subarea (Moore, Blackburn, Site 15Un96, and Site 15Un101). Among these sites are three large villages (Slack Farm, Hovey Lake, and Murphy), five small villages (Alzey, Gough, Moore, Blackburn, and Welborn), six hamlets (Site 15He37.1, Site 15He110, Mulligan, Ritz, Caborn, and Ries-Hasting), and eight farmsteads (Hart, Site 15He38, Cummings, Hooper, Stull, Site 15Un96, Site 15Un101, and Site 11Ga160).

It should be noted that only the surface-collected materials from Caborn and Hovey Lake were included in this study. The excavated materials from both sites were excluded in order to make the size of the Caborn and Hovey Lake collections more comparable to those from other Caborn-Welborn phase sites. No attempt, however, was made to reduce the size of the Slack Farm collection. While the large size of this collection has the potential to overshadow smaller collections, any sampling strategy that might have been employed also had the potential to diminish the significance of Slack Farm as the largest and perhaps most intensively occupied Caborn-Welborn community identified to date. In the end, it was felt that it was best to use the entire Slack Farm collection but to recognize where the size of this collection might potentially bias interpretations of the data.

Since no stratified Caborn-Welborn sites have been excavated, and given the dearth of radiocarbon dates from Caborn-Welborn phase sites, relative dating measures using ceramic data were used to construct this sequence. Some types and attributes were considered to represent early temporal indicators if they were present in earlier Angel 3 assemblages as well as Caborn-Welborn assemblages. Late Caborn-Welborn ceramic traits were identified through an assessment of the salient characteristics of the ceramics recovered from sites that produced historic trade goods manufactured from European copper, brass, or glass (i.e., metal tubes, beads, spirals, and bracelets; and blue glass beads). These sites would have been the latest occupied in the Caborn-Welborn region.

Ceramic characteristics (the presence of certain types and individual attributes) were found to be good temporal indicators: the frequency of occurrence of certain bowl forms and rim shapes; the types of appendages associated with bowls; the relative proportions of Kimmswick Fabric Impressed to Kimmswick Plain; the form of pan rims; the percentage of Caborn-Welborn Decorated jars in the analyzed site assemblage and mean line width of incised and trailed lines on these vessels; the presence of Campbell Applique and the "Memphis Rim Mode"; and jars with 12 to 16 (arcaded) handles. Jar handle shape also was examined to determine if handle width increased and thickness decreased throughout the Caborn-Welborn phase. While thin straps were found to predominate, in general, handle shape proved not to be a good internal temporal indicator.

## Bowls

A bowl form that appears to have increased in popularity from the Angel to Caborn-Welborn phase is the shallow bowl with outslanting sides and a flat bottom (Figures 3.6 and 3.12) (Hilgeman's [2000] deep rim plates). Many of these vessels have castellated rims. As noted, while 80 bowls (.4 percent) with castellated rims were identified among the more than 20,000 rims, decorated sherds, and appendages analyzed by Hilgeman (2000) from the Angel site, almost as many, 55 (11.4 percent of analyzed sample), were recovered from the surface at Hovey Lake, and 764 (5.1 percent of analyzed sample) were identified in the Slack Farm collection (Pollack and Munson 1998). Based on this comparison, it would seem that this bowl rim form is more common at Hovey Lake and Slack Farm than at Angel. It also is well represented in the Welborn, Murphy, Gough, Moore, and Blackburn collections (Pollack 1998:319). Thus the use of this bowl form appears to have increased from the Angel to the Caborn-Welborn phase.

The Caborn-Welborn phase also appears to be marked by an increase, relative to the Angel phase, in the use of applied notched or beaded horizontal strips to decorate bowls. Again, as noted, Hilgeman (2000) identified only 135 notched or beaded rims (.7 percent of analyzed sample) in the earlier Angel collection. In comparison, 250 bowls (1.7 percent of analyzed sample) were identified in the Slack Farm collection (Pollack and Munson 1998). This appendage form also is well represented in other Caborn-Welborn collections. For instance, 31 (6.9 percent of analyzed sample) were identified in the Caborn surface collection, and 19 (6.4 percent of analyzed sample) were recovered from the Moore site (Pollack 1998:319).

## Kimmswick Fabric Impressed and Kimmswick Plain

The Murphy, Welborn, Hovey Lake, and Gough ceramic assemblages are characterized by a high percentage of shallow bowls with outslanting walls and castellated rims and a relatively low percentage of notched and beaded rimstrips on hemispherical bowls. They all also have a high percentage of Kimmswick Fabric Impressed pans (Table 5.1). In contrast to these sites, Kimmswick Fabric Impressed is poorly represented in other Caborn-Welborn site collections, with the exception of Site 15He110 and Slack Farm. In the lower Tennessee-Cumberland region, Clay (1963a) noted that through time, there is a decrease in fabric-impressed pans relative to plain pans. This trend appears to be expressed in the Caborn-Welborn region as well.

Most Kimmswick Fabric Impressed and Kimmswick Plain pan rims have exterior protrusions (Figure 3.14). However, at some sites, such as Cummings and Blackburn, a majority of the Kimmswick rims (66.7 percent and 57.1 percent, respectively) lack this protrusion (Pollack 1998:328). Both of these sites have yielded historic trade goods, such as native and European copper or brass tube beads (Gersch et al. 1998), and Cummings produced blue glass beads. The absence of pans with exterior protrusions at these sites indicates that through time, changes in pan rim forms occurred. Similar temporal trends in pan rim forms have been documented from post–A.D. 1400 Fort Ancient contexts in the middle Ohio valley (i.e., through time, rim protrusions disappear; Turnbow and Henderson 1992).

## Caborn-Welborn Decorated

Intersite variation in the frequency of occurrence of Caborn-Welborn Decorated ceramics within site assemblages may reflect the introduction and growth in popularity of this type within the Caborn-Welborn region: early Caborn-Welborn settlements would be expected to have less Caborn-Welborn Decorated ceramics and later sites would be expected to have higher percentages. As more households were attracted to the Caborn-Welborn area and as more potters began to decorate the shoulders of their jars, use of Caborn-Welborn Decorated jars would have increased.

Sites with relatively low percentages of Caborn-Welborn Decorated (less than about 20 percent) are Hovey Lake, Gough, Welborn, Murphy, Moore, Blackburn, Cummings, and Alzey (Table 5.1). Many of these sites (i.e., Hovey Lake, Gough, Welborn, and Murphy) also are characterized by high percentages of shallow bowls with castellated rims, low percentages of bowls with notched or beaded rim strips, and high percentages of Kimmswick Fabric Impressed pans. Taken together, these attributes can be used to suggest that these four sites date to the early decades of the Caborn-Welborn phase. Slack Farm also appears to contain an early Caborn-Welborn component based on the presence of high percentages of shallow bowls with castellated rims and Kimmswick Fabric Impressed pans. However, unlike the other four sites, the Slack Farm collection contains a relatively high percentage (more than 30 percent) of Caborn-Welborn Decorated ceramics (Table 5.1) and has yielded historic trade goods. These attributes suggest that this site continued to be occupied after sites such as Hovey Lake and Gough were abandoned and that Slack Farm was occupied throughout the entire Caborn-Welborn phase.

Variation in the width of incised and trailed lines and the use of punctation primarily as a border or as fill also could reflect temporal trends. Among Oneota sites in northern Illinois, Brown et al. (1990) suggested that, through time, there was a reduction in the width of trailed and incised lines on vessel shoulders and an increase in the use of punctations as fill rather than as a border to highlight designs.

Table 5.2 Intersite Comparisons of Caborn-Welborn Decorated Mean Line Width.

| Site | Mean Line Width(mm) | Standard Deviation | Frequency |
|---|---|---|---|
| 15He37.1 | 3.05 | 0.64 | 2 |
| Hovey Lake | 2.69 | 1.39 | 32 |
| Gough | 2.64 | 1.24 | 12 |
| Slack Farm | 2.63 | 1.27 | 2331 |
| Hooper | 2.35 | 1.18 | 16 |
| Ritz | 2.30 | 0.74 | 26 |
| Murphy | 2.23 | 1.05 | 21 |
| Alzey | 2.17 | 0.88 | 84 |
| 15He38 | 2.12 | 0.69 | 7 |
| 11Ga160 | 2.07 | 0.76 | 30 |
| Hart | 2.00 | 0.82 | 21 |
| Welborn | 1.96 | 0.85 | 20 |
| Caborn | 1.93 | 0.79 | 159 |
| Stull | 1.78 | 0.79 | 63 |
| Blackburn | 1.74 | 1.04 | 43 |
| Ries-Hasting | 1.70 | 0.80 | 61 |
| Moore | 1.67 | 0.72 | 20 |
| 15Un96 | 1.40 | 0.00 | 1 |
| Mulligan | 1.05 | 0.50 | 2 |
| Cummings | 0.75 | 0.35 | 2 |

A similar trend might be present within Caborn-Welborn assemblages. Sites such as Hovey Lake have a mean line width of 2.7 mm (Table 5.2). Slack Farm, which also has a substantial early Caborn-Welborn component, has a similar mean line width. On the other end of the spectrum are Stull, Ries-Hasting, and Blackburn. These sites have a mean line width of ca. 1.7 mm and much smaller standard deviations: 0.8–1.0 mm compared to 1.4 mm for Hovey Lake. These data suggest that, through time, there may have been a decease in overall line width.

## Other Decorated Ceramic Types

The presence of Campbell Applique, jars with the Memphis Rim Mode (House 1991, 1993), and jars with 12 to 16 (arcaded) handles in Caborn-Welborn site assemblages also may be good temporal indicators. According to Mainfort (1996), Campbell Applique and jars with arcaded handles are diagnostic of post–A.D. 1500 components in the central Mississippi valley, while the Memphis Rim Mode is diagnostic of post–A.D. 1450 components in this region. In the Caborn-Welborn region, sites such as Slack Farm and Moore exhibit one or all of these types and attributes, which indicates that these sites have late Caborn-Welborn components.

## Jar Handles and Appendages

Diachronic trends in the shape of jar handles have been identified throughout the Ohio valley during the Late Prehistoric period (Henderson et al. 1992; Hilgeman 1992; Wesler 1994). The earliest handles tend to be loops, which have a width to thickness ratio of 1.5 to 1.0, and intermediate loop/straps, which have a width to thickness ratio of 1.5–2.0 to 1.0. Through time, handles become wider and thinner, and strap handles are classified as thick (width to thickness ratio of 2.0–3.0 to 1) or thin (width to thickness ratio of >3.0 to 1.0).

As a group, Caborn-Welborn handles have a width to thickness ratio of 3.1 to 1.0. With a starting date of A.D. 1400 for the Caborn-Welborn phase, it is not surprising that the majority of the handles recovered from Caborn-Welborn sites are thin or thick straps. Some examples have width to thickness ratios as high as 7 to 1.0. For the Caborn-Welborn phase, the ratio of handle width to thickness provided little in the way of useful information on the temporal ordering of Caborn-Welborn phase sites, although it did confirm the overall lateness of the phase.

It should be noted, however, that not all handles at Caborn-Welborn sites are straps. A small number of loops and intermediate loop/straps are present in some site assemblages. Their presence does not necessarily indicate an earlier Angel phase Mississippian component, though, because toward the end of the Mississippian period, handles again appear to become smaller and thicker, as evidenced by the vertical applied strips on Campbell Applique vessels and jars with large numbers of small handles (Mainfort 1996; O'Brien and Fox 1994). In addition, some mortuary vessels and other small jars often have small loop or intermediate loop/strap handles, as do the Oneota-like jars in Caborn-Welborn collections. Thus, within any Caborn-Welborn assemblage, one should expect to find a variety of handle types, but thin straps should predominate.

Potential temporal trends were identified in the types of lugs associated with jars and in the placement of notched horizontal strips on jars. There is some evidence to suggest that notched lugs increase in popularity through time at the expense of single plain and bifurcated lugs (Pollack and Munson 1998). At Angel, single lugs predominate and bifurcated lugs are quite common, with some lugs being notched (Hilgeman 2000). Although samples of Caborn-Welborn site jar appendages are rather small, at some sites, such as Caborn and Cummings (historic trade goods have been recovered from Cummings), notched lugs predominate, and at Moore they account for almost as many specimens as single plain lugs (Pollack 1998:316–317). On the other hand, plain and bifurcated lugs dominate the Hovey Lake and Slack Farm jar appendage collections. Notched horizontal strips on jars are not reported from the Angel site, but small amounts have been recovered from several Caborn-Welborn sites, such as Caborn, Cummings, Moore, Ries-Hasting, and Slack Farm, and there appears to be an association between the presence of notched lugs and notched horizontal strips. A larger sample of jar appendages is needed from a variety of sites before the observed trends can be interpreted with any degree of confidence.

### Summary

Intersite comparisons of certain ceramic traits and types from selected Caborn-Welborn sites led to the identification of temporally diagnostic attributes that are interpreted as reflecting ceramic temporal trends, which can be used to develop an internal chronology for the Caborn-Welborn phase. These attributes include an increase through time in the presence of notched or beaded rim strips on bowls; an increase in Kimmswick Plain, coupled with a decrease in Kimmswick Fabric Impressed; an increase in Kimmswick Plain rims that lack exterior protrusions; and a decrease in Caborn-Welborn Decorated line width. The frequency of occurrence of Caborn-Welborn Decorated ceramics increases through time but may have decreased toward the end of the phase. Based on these findings and the presence of historic trade goods of Euro-American manufacture, a Caborn-Welborn internal chronology has been developed and is outlined in the next section.

## INTERNAL CABORN-WELBORN CHRONOLOGICAL SEQUENCE

In developing regional chronological sequences, archaeologists often rely on the identification of horizon markers or stylistic attributes that are temporally sensitive. For the purposes of this study, ceramic decorative styles and attributes and the presence of historic trade goods were used to develop a relative internal chronological sequence for the Caborn-Welborn region (Table 5.3). Unfortunately, radiocarbon dates did not provide much help in developing this chronology. Only a few Caborn-Welborn sites have been dated, and the dates that have been obtained tend to cluster in the fifteenth century (Table 2.1). As with most chronologies, additional research will be needed to clarify and refine the proposed sequence outlined here.

The beginning and ending dates of the proposed chronological sequence are relatively secure, but the end-points of the internal divisions are not and should be viewed as tentative at best. With the available data, it is possible to assign components to one of three temporal units: early (A.D. 1400–1450),

Table 5.3. Caborn-Welborn Temporal Subdivisions Based on Ceramics

| Temporal Subdivision | Ceramic Attributes | Sites |
|---|---|---|
| Early 1400-1450 | High percentage of Kimmswick Fabric Impressed pans with exterior protrusions.<br>Low percentage of Caborn-Welborn Decorated jars.<br>High mean line width on Caborn-Welborn Decorated jars (about 2.6 mm).<br>Preference for a use of lines to fill triangular areas on Caborn-Welborn Decorated jars.<br>High percentage of shallow bowls with outslanting walls and castellations.<br>Small amount of hemispherical bowls with notched or beaded rim strips.<br>Oneota-like ceramics present in site collections. | Hovey Lake, Murphy, Welborn, Gough, Slack Farm |
| Middle 1450-1600 | Increase in Kimmswick Plain and decrease in Kimmswick Fabric Impressed pans.<br>High percentage of Caborn-Welborn Decorated jars.<br>Decrease in mean line width on Caborn-Welborn Decorated jars (about 2.0 mm)<br>Increase in the use of punctation as fill on Caborn-Welborn Decorated jars.<br>Decrease in shallow bowls with outslanting walls and castellations.<br>Increase in hemispherical bowls with notched or beaded rim strips.<br>Oneota-like motifs incorporated into Caborn-Welborn Decorated designs (i.e., hawk motif).<br>Campbell Applique, jars with arcaded handles, and "Memphis Rim Mode." | Caborn, Hart, 15He37.1?, Alzey, 15He38, 15He110, Mulligan, Ritz, Hooper, Moore, Blackburn, Stull, Slack Farm, 11Ga160, Ries-Hasting, 15Un40, Grundy Hill, 15Un101, 15Un96 |
| Late 1600-1700 | Decrease in Kimmswick Plain pans with exterior protrusions.<br>Low percentage of Caborn-Welborn Decorated.<br>Decrease in mean line width (<2.0 mm) on Caborn-Welborn Decorated jars.<br>Handle width may decrease? | Cummings, Blackburn, Slack Farm, Murphy? |

middle (A.D. 1450–1600), and late (A.D. 1600–1700). These subdivisions are meant to be a heuristic device by which Caborn-Welborn components can be temporally ordered so that the dynamics of the development and decline of Caborn-Welborn society can be examined.

Caborn-Welborn begins with the collapse of the Angel chiefdom ca. A.D. 1400. The author acknowledges that the 50-year designation for the early subdivision (A.D. 1400–1450) is rather short, especially given the standard deviations associated with most radiocarbon dates and the paucity of good excavated data from well-defined contexts at a wide range of Caborn-Welborn sites. A 50-year time span, however, reflects the transitional nature of sites assigned to this subdivision. Early Caborn-Welborn ceramic assemblages exhibit characteristics that reflect continuity from the Angel 3 component at the Angel site. In addition, some attributes that are well represented in later Caborn-Welborn collections are poorly represented in these early ceramic collections.

The middle subdivision dates from A.D. 1450 and extends until Native American contact with Europeans could have had an impact on the Caborn-Welborn population (i.e., A.D. 1600). Other researchers in the Ohio valley (e.g., Henderson et al. 1992) have used a date of A.D. 1550 to mark the beginning of the Contact period, since it corresponds to de Soto's expedition through the Southeast and the disruption of Native American culture that followed (G. Smith 1990). For the purposes of this study, a date of A.D. 1600 was used to distinguish middle Caborn-Welborn components from late Caborn-Welborn (i.e., those with Contact period) components. A beginning date of A.D. 1600 for the start of the late Caborn-Welborn subdivision accounts for the period of time it undoubtedly would have taken for historic trade goods to make their way into the lower Ohio valley and for them to occur in sufficiently large numbers that they would be recoverable from archaeological sites in the Caborn-Welborn region. The middle subdivision contains by far the largest number of sites, and it is quite likely that most of the sites that could not be assigned to a temporal unit were occupied during this time period.

A date of A.D. 1700 was selected for the end of the Caborn-Welborn phase, based on the absence of any eighteenth-century historic documents describing Native American settlements in the vicinity of the mouth of the Wabash River. In addition, by the 1700s, European diseases may have greatly impacted the Caborn-Welborn population, contributing to the abandonment of Caborn-Welborn settlements. Undoubtedly, indirect, and perhaps direct, contact with Europeans would have significantly affected the Caborn-Welborn population as well as their trading partners. While some middle subdivision sites may have been occupied into the seventeenth century, only those sites that have yielded historic trade goods were assigned to the late subdivision.

The remainder of this chapter outlines the three-part internal Caborn-Welborn chronological sequence. Although it is primarily based on changes in ceramic attributes, other diagnostic aspects of material culture also are mentioned as appropriate. Site assignments to particular temporal subdivisions are made, site types associated with each temporal unit are identified, and the spatial distribution of sites of each temporal subdivision is described.

## Early Caborn-Welborn Subdivision (A.D. 1400–1450)

The early temporal unit encompasses the Angel to Caborn-Welborn transition. Sites assigned to this phase were settled as Angel phase sites were being abandoned and the Angel elite were losing their power base. By the beginning of the early Caborn-Welborn subdivision or shortly thereafter, the Angel chiefdom had collapsed. This collapse led to the formation of Caborn-Welborn society, as the local population redistributed itself on the natural landscape and reconstructed social, political, and economic relationships.

Early Caborn-Welborn ceramic assemblages contain a low percentage of Caborn-Welborn Decorated jars (Table 5.1). Shoulder designs on many of these vessels are characterized by relatively wide trailed lines and descending triangles that were primarily filled with lines, with only 12.1 percent having been filled with punctations. They also contain a high percentage of shallow bowls with outslanting walls (deep rim plates) and castellated rims and of Kimmswick Fabric Impressed pans that have exterior protrusions. Other characteristics of early Caborn-Welborn include assemblages that have a low number of hemispherical bowls with notched or beaded rimstrips and small amounts of Old Town Red. Some assemblages contain a few Angel/Kincaid Negative Painted sherds, and Oneota-like ceramics are known from some early Caborn-Welborn sites.

Sites with early Caborn-Welborn components are Slack Farm, Murphy, Welborn, Hovey Lake, and Gough (Figure 5.1). All are small or large villages restricted to a 13 km long area within the central subarea. The absence of early Caborn-Welborn farmsteads or hamlets suggests that population aggregation increased immediately following the collapse of the Angel polity. However, caution should be used in interpreting this pattern. Early Caborn-Welborn components are difficult to recognize based solely on small surface collected samples. Thus, the absence of early Caborn-Welborn farmsteads and hamlets may be more a reflection of a sampling problem, with some of the small unassigned Caborn-Welborn sites having early Caborn-Welborn components, than of the archaeological record of this region.

In general, early Caborn-Welborn ceramic collections are distinguished from Angel phase collections by the presence of Caborn-Welborn Decorated jars and an increase in the use of shallow bowls with flat bottoms and castellated rims. They are distinguished from later Caborn-Welborn ceramic assemblages

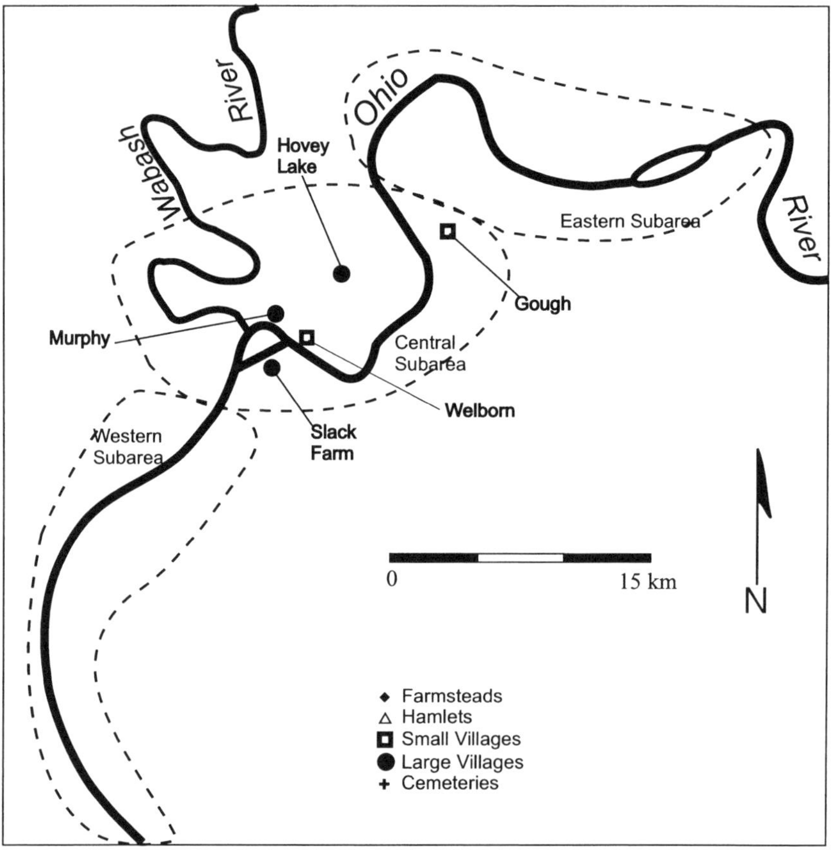


Figure 5.1. Distribution of sites with early Caborn-Welborn subdivision components.

by a low percentage of Caborn-Welborn Decorated jars, a high percentage of Kimmswick Fabric Impressed pans, and a low percentage of hemispherical bowls with notched or beaded rimstrips.

Because Caborn-Welborn Decorated appears to have increased in popularity through time, the low percentage of Caborn-Welborn Decorated at Hovey Lake, Gough, Murphy, and Welborn indicates that they were likely abandoned by ca. A.D. 1450. Slack Farm is an exception, with its higher percentage of Caborn-Welborn Decorated. Had these sites been occupied much longer, as Slack Farm was, they would have yielded much higher percentages of Caborn-Welborn Decorated ceramics.

Attributes of the Slack Farm Oneota-like ceramics, such as wide trailed lines, use of punctations primarily as a border, notched loop handles, and interior lip decoration, date these materials to no later than the early fifteenth century (Boszhardt 1994; Brown and O'Brien 1990). By A.D. 1450, Oneota line width had begun to decrease, and there was a greater use of punctation as fill. The presence of triangular endscrapers, Nodena projectile points, and catlinite disk pipes also distinguishes early Caborn-Welborn collections from Angel phase site assemblages, as does the frequent placement with the dead of a ceramic vessel with a shell spoon inside. Other types of artifacts associated with early Caborn-Welborn sites include central Mississippi valley ceramic types, such as Parkin Punctate, Walls Engraved, and Kent Incised-like; marine shell beads, ear plugs, and gorgets; and objects manufactured from native copper.

## Middle Caborn-Welborn Subdivision (A.D. 1450–1600)

Middle Caborn-Welborn ceramic assemblages (Table 5.3) are characterized by a high percentage of Caborn-Welborn Decorated ceramics, with this type accounting for more than 60.0 percent of the analyzed sherds at some sites (Table 5.1). In general, Caborn-Welborn Decorated jars during this subdivision have thinner trailed lines than those on jars from earlier sites. There also is greater use of punctation as fill. These trends parallel those identified for contemporary Oneota sites to the north of the Ohio valley (Boszhardt 1994; Brown et al. 1990). While Oneota-like jars are rare at middle Caborn-Welborn sites, there is evidence of the incorporation of Oneota decorative motifs, such as the thunderbird or hawk, within the Caborn-Welborn decorative tradition.

Middle Caborn-Welborn collections also are characterized by a paucity of Kimmswick Fabric Impressed pans, although Kimmswick Plain pans continue to be common in site ceramic collections (Table 5.1). Many middle Caborn-Welborn site collections also contain a high percentage of bowls with notched or beaded rimstrips. Some contain ceramics that are diagnostic of post–A.D. 1500 components in the central Mississippi valley, such as small amounts of Campbell Punctate jars with arcaded handles (Table 5.1) (Mainfort 1996), and the jar and bottle rims that exhibit the Memphis Rim Mode (House 1991, 1993). Triangular endscrapers, catlinite disk pipes, and artifacts made from native copper continue to be manufactured during the middle Caborn-Welborn subdivision.

The vast majority of Caborn-Welborn sites with large ceramic collections (i.e., more than 30 analyzable sherds) are assignable to this temporal unit (Figure 5.2). These sites include Hart, Alzey, Site 15He37.1, Site 15He38, Site 15He110, Mulligan, Ritz, Hooper, Slack Farm, Site 11Ga160, Ries-Hasting, Caborn, Site 15Un101, and Site 15Un96. Unlike early Caborn-Welborn sites, which are either small or large villages, most sites assigned to the middle subdivision are farmsteads or hamlets.

Middle Caborn-Welborn sites are found within a 60 km long area that

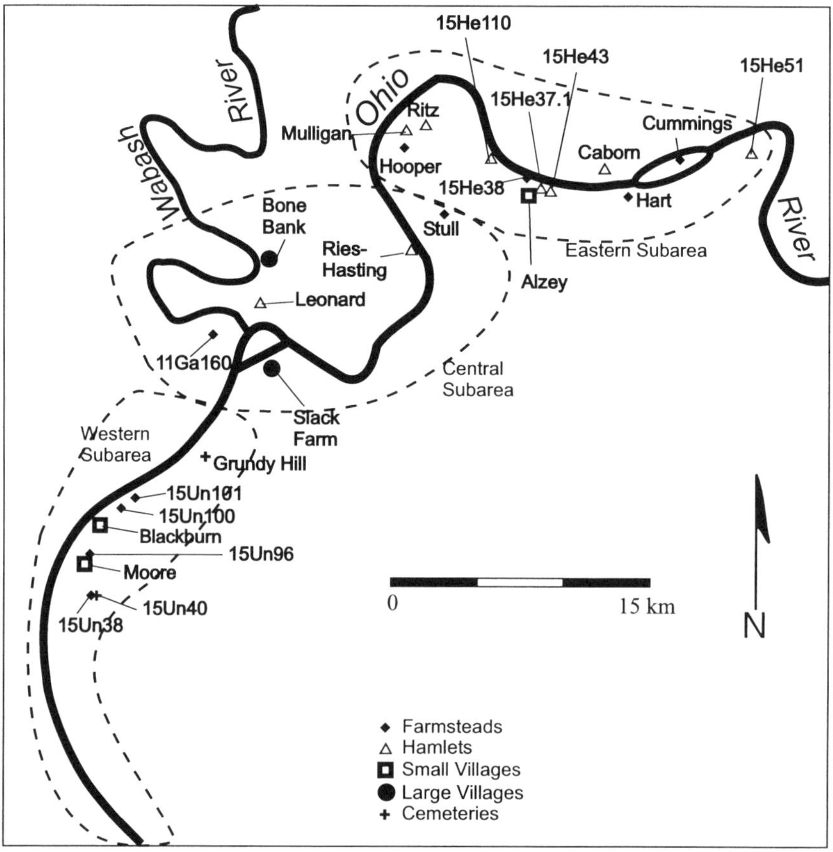


Figure 5.2. Distribution of sites with middle Caborn-Welborn subdivision components.

encompasses the entire Caborn-Welborn region. As such, they are distributed over a larger area than early Caborn-Welborn sites. If the absence of earlier Caborn-Welborn settlements in the eastern and western subareas is not a product of sampling bias, the observed distribution of middle Caborn-Welborn sites points to an expansion of the Caborn-Welborn region and a shift to smaller settlements.

Eastern subarea sites with middle components include Caborn, Hart, Site 15He37.1, Alzey, Site 15He38, Site 15He43, Site 15He51, Site 15He110, Mulligan, Ritz, Hooper, and Cummings. Except for one small village, Alzey, all of the sites in this subarea are farmsteads or hamlets (another may be associated with the Mann site, but at present its existence cannot be confirmed). Several of the hamlets (e.g., Site 15He43, Mulligan, and Ritz) have sizable cemeteries, and a few of the farmsteads (e.g., Bauer) have small cemeteries (Pollack 1998).

In the central subarea, Murphy, Hovey Lake, Welborn, and Gough were apparently abandoned around A.D. 1450. Slack Farm, however, continued to be occupied, and another large village, Bone Bank, may have been established at this time. Unfortunately, very little is known about Bone Bank (Munson 1997). Several hamlets (Leonard and Ries-Hasting) and farmsteads (Stull and Site 11Ga160) in the central subarea appear to have middle Caborn-Welborn components.

Middle Caborn-Welborn sites in the western subarea include farmsteads (Site 15Un38, Site 15Un96, Site 15Un100, and Site 15Un101) and two small villages (Moore and Blackburn). No hamlets have been recorded in this sub area for this temporal unit. In addition to these sites, two of the bluff-top cemeteries (Grundy Hill and Site 15Un40) are assignable to the middle Caborn-Welborn subdivision. The other blufftop cemeteries may be contemporary, but not enough is known about these sites to make a temporal assignment.

Both of the small village sites (Moore and Blackburn) in the western subarea have relatively low percentages of Caborn-Welborn Decorated (15.2 and 21.1 percent, respectively), in contrast with most other sites of this temporal unit. Low percentages of Caborn-Welborn Decorated were used, in part, to argue that sites such as Murphy, Welborn, Hovey Lake, and Gough were abandoned by the beginning of the middle Caborn-Welborn subdivision. The same argument cannot be made for Moore and Blackburn, however. Based on other ceramic traits, such as a paucity of Kimmswick Fabric Impressed pans, the absence of Kimmswick Plain pans with exterior protrusions, and the presence of Caborn-Welborn Decorated jars that are characterized by relatively thin trailed or incised lines, Moore and Blackburn do not appear to have been occupied during the early Caborn-Welborn subdivision. Both appear to have been established some time during the middle subdivision.

Moore and Blackburn also are distinguished from their contemporaries in the eastern subarea by the presence of several central Mississippi valley–derived types, such as Campbell Punctate, Barton Incised, and Walls Engraved. Some of these specimens are rims that have an interior beveled lip, which is the defining characteristic of the Memphis Rim Mode (House 1993: 27). The location of Moore and Blackburn along the western edge of the distribution of Caborn-Welborn settlements also suggests that they may have played a prominent role in extraregional interaction with Mississippi valley groups.

## Late Caborn-Welborn Subdivision (A.D. 1600–1700)

During this last, and protohistoric, Caborn-Welborn subdivision, there is a decrease in Caborn-Welborn Decorated jars, with some late assemblages having very low percentages of Caborn-Welborn Decorated (Table 5.1). A preference for Kimmswick Plain pans continues, with most examples lacking the exterior protrusion that characterized earlier pans. Handles continue to become less functional and more decorative and types, such as Campbell Applique and Campbell Punctate, and rim treatments, such as the Memphis Rim Mode, probably continue into the late Caborn-Welborn subdivision. As with the preceding temporal subdivisions, triangular endscrapers, catlinite disk pipes, and artifacts manufactured from native copper also are associated with late Caborn-Welborn assemblages.

Late Caborn-Welborn artifact assemblages are distinguished from earlier ones by the presence of historic trade goods (copper or brass tubes, beads and bracelets, and glass beads). These materials would have made their way into the Caborn-Welborn region through the same exchange networks as other nonlocal goods, such as catlinite pipes and objects manufactured from native copper.

Only those sites from which historic trade goods have been recovered (Slack Farm, Cummings, Blackburn, and Murphy) were assigned to this subdivision (Figure 5.3). Three are villages; Cummings is a farmstead. Late Caborn-Welborn sites are found throughout the entire Caborn-Welborn region.

Slack Farm continued to be occupied and probably remained a large village during this subdivision. However, it should be noted that the late Caborn-Welborn component at Murphy may represent the presence of a later farmstead or hamlet at the site of a former early Caborn-Welborn village. The few possible historic trade goods associated with burials at Murphy are not consistent with the ceramic collection recovered from the residential areas. Since the spatial relationship of the Murphy site burials with historic trade goods and the residential areas from which the ceramics were recovered is not known, it is possible that two different areas of the site were sampled. Of the remaining two late subdivision sites, Blackburn is a small village in the western subarea that also contains a middle Caborn-Welborn component, and Cummings is a farmstead in the eastern subarea that appears to have been occupied only during the late Caborn-Welborn subdivision.

Of the sites assigned to the late subdivision, Cummings, located in the eastern subarea, is a good example of a late Caborn-Welborn phase farmstead. Based on the presence of historic trade goods (glass beads and artifacts made from European copper and brass), the Cummings site is thought to date to the seventeenth century. The paucity of Caborn-Welborn Decorated (3.2 percent) at this site suggests that toward the end of this subdivision, use of this type was on the decline. Other sites also may have been occupied into the late Caborn-Welborn subdivision, but the presence of historic trade goods has yet to be confirmed at these sites.

Toward the end of the late Caborn-Welborn subdivision, European diseases would have made their way into the lower Ohio valley and protohistoric

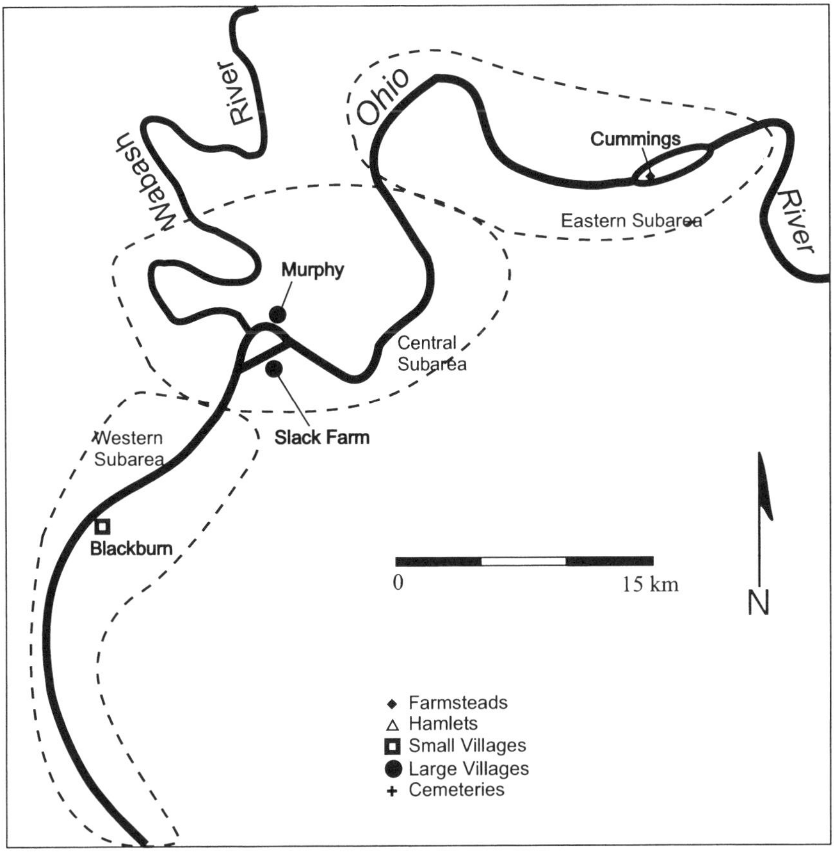


Figure 5.3. Distribution of sites with late Caborn-Welborn subdivision components.

indigenous exchange networks would have begun to break down as interior Native American populations were severely reduced by diseases against which they had little or no immunity. By the early 1700s, most, if not all, of the Caborn-Welborn settlements along the Ohio River had been abandoned, with the population possibly relocating to other regions.

## SUMMARY

Comparison of Angel and Caborn-Welborn ceramics points to a shared ceramic tradition. It is reflected in vessel and appendage forms, several decorated ceramic types, and nonvessel ceramic objects. Shallow bowls with outslanting walls and flat bottoms (deep rim plates), some with castellations, thin jar strap handles and bifurcated and round to oval jar lugs, and hemispherical bowls with notched or beaded rimstrips are good examples of this shared ceramic tradition. Decorated ceramic types found in Caborn-Welborn ceramic assemblages also are associated with Angel phase assemblages as well as with those of other earlier Mississippian groups in the lower Ohio valley. These types include Old Town Red, O'Byam Incised/Engraved, Mound Place Incised, Angel/Kincaid Negative Painted, Matthews Incised, and Beckwith Incised. Among the nonvessel ceramic objects that reflect continuity from the Angel to Caborn-Welborn phase are pestles, disks, ear plugs, and owl effigy pendants.

However, several differences serve to distinguish Caborn-Welborn from Angel phase ceramic assemblages: an increase in the use of shallow bowls with outslanting walls and flat bottoms and of hemispherical bowls with notched or beaded rimstrips. There also is a decrease in the thickness of jar strap handles. The presence of Oneota-like jars within Caborn-Welborn collections is not only an important difference between Angel and Caborn-Welborn ceramic assemblages, but their presence is also temporally diagnostic and indicative of extraregional interaction as well.

Perhaps the biggest difference between Angel and Caborn-Welborn ceramics is in the primary execution of decorative designs and the types of vessels with which these designs are associated. However, this does not necessarily mean that the symbolic message conveyed was different. The most common design associated with both Angel Negative Painted and Caborn-Welborn Decorated vessels consists of a series of triangular areas demarcated by layout lines. These triangular areas were usually filled with either parallel diagonal lines or dots (punctations). On both Angel Negative Painted plates and Caborn-Welborn Decorated jars, these designs may represent a sun symbol. During the Angel phase, negative painted designs were often placed on the interior of plates, but by the beginning of the Caborn-Welborn phase, there was a shift to the use of trailing, incising, and punctation to create similar designs on jar shoulders. Thus, while the type of vessel and the technique used to depict the sun may have differed (plate vs. jar and painted vs. incised/trailed), these similar designs may have conveyed the same messages within Angel and Caborn-Welborn societies.

These analyses also identified some commonalities in the execution of designs placed on Caborn-Welborn and Oneota jars. In particular, Caborn-Welborn potters and Oneota potters shared a preference for the use of trailed/incised lines and punctations to create designs on jar shoulders. These designs are distinguished from each other by the Caborn-Welborn use of diagonal lines to demarcate triangular areas and the Oneota use of lines to create vertical panels. The types of handles and appendages associated with jars also tend to distinguish Caborn-Welborn from Oneota vessels. Caborn-Welborn strap handles are much wider and thinner than the notched loop or intermediate loop/strap handles associated with Oneota vessels recovered from Caborn-

Welborn sites. In addition, Caborn-Welborn jars are associated with a variety of lugs, nodes, and applied horizontal strips that are rarely found on Oneota jars. Within the Caborn-Welborn region, Oneota-like jars are characterized by interior lip decoration in the form of notches, dashes, and trailed chevrons that are not associated with Caborn-Welborn Decorated jars. There also are differences between Oneota and Caborn-Welborn ceramic assemblage characteristics as a whole (i.e., in the types and frequency of occurrence of other vessel forms): bowls, pans, and bottles are much more common in Caborn-Welborn ceramic collections than in Oneota assemblages.

Finally, these analyses identified diachronic ceramic attributes and trends that, combined with information from other diagnostic artifacts (e.g., historic trade goods), permitted the development of a three-part internal Caborn-Welborn chronological sequence. Albeit preliminary, this sequence serves the purpose of temporally ordering Caborn-Welborn site occupations so that issues of Caborn-Welborn developments, interregional cultural differences, and site function can be examined.

The early subdivision (A.D. 1400–1450) represents the initial establishment of Caborn-Welborn communities in the Wabash-Ohio River confluence region, following the collapse of the Angel chiefdom. These settlements consist primarily of small and large villages located in the central subarea near the confluence of the Wabash and Ohio rivers. The absence of smaller settlements may reflect sampling biases, or it could reflect an initial period of population aggregation following the collapse of the Angel chiefdom.

Early Caborn-Welborn ceramic assemblages are characterized by a relatively low percentage of Caborn-Welborn Decorated, relatively broad trailed lines, a high percentage of shallow bowls with outslanting walls and castellated rims, a high percentage of Kimmswick Fabric Impressed pans, and a low percentage of hemispherical bowls with notched or beaded rimstrips. These assemblages also may include Oneota-like vessels, central Mississippi valley–derived ceramic types, triangular endscrapers, Nodena points, catlinite pipes, native copper artifacts, and marine shell objects. The Oneota-like ceramics, triangular endscrapers, and objects manufactured from catlinite and native copper represent the initiation of social and economic interaction with groups to the north of the Ohio valley. Intersocietal interaction with the central Mississippi valley is reflected by the presence of ceramic types, such as Parkin Punctate, Walls Engraved, Campbell Punctate, Barton Incised and Kent Incised-like, Nodena points, and marine shell objects.

During the middle Caborn-Welborn subdivision (A.D. 1450–1600), there is an expansion of settlements into the eastern and western subareas, and all settlement types (farmsteads, hamlets, small villages, large villages, and blufftop cemeteries) are represented. Expansion of the Caborn-Welborn region may have been a result of natural population growth, intraregional competition and factionalism that led to the fissioning of early Caborn-Welborn villages, or segments of neighboring chiefdoms that relocated to the Caborn-Welborn region following their collapse.

Middle Caborn-Welborn ceramic assemblages are marked by an increase in Caborn-Welborn Decorated, with this type accounting for more than 50 percent of the analyzed sherds from several sites. An increase in the decoration of jar shoulders is associated with a decrease in line width and a greater use of punctation as fill. The middle Caborn-Welborn subdivision also is characterized by a decrease in Kimmswick Fabric Impressed pans, an increase in Kimmswick Plain pans, and an increase in hemispherical bowls with notched or beaded rimstrips. Nonceramic objects recovered from middle Caborn-Welborn sites are similar to those found at early Caborn-Welborn sites.

Continued social and economic interaction with Oneota groups north of the Ohio valley is reflected in the incorporation of Oneota decorative motifs within the Caborn-Welborn decorative tradition. It also is reflected by a decrease in incised line width and a greater use of punctation as fill. Interaction with Mississippian groups in the central Mississippi valley is reflected by the presence of the same ceramic types present in early Caborn-Welborn assemblages. Interaction with the central Mississippi valley at this time also is illustrated by Campbell Applique jars, jars with the Memphis Rim Mode, jars with arcaded handles, and the incorporation of vertical notched strips within Caborn-Welborn decorative shoulder designs. The presence of these ceramics within Caborn-Welborn ceramic collections points to some type of social and economic interaction with Mississippian groups living in the central Mississippi valley.

Only a few sites have been assigned to the late Caborn-Welborn (A.D. 1600–1700) subdivision. These sites are located in all three subareas and represent small and large villages and farmsteads. Assignment of sites to this subdivision is based on the presence of historic trade goods. It is expected that as more sites are intensively investigated, additional late Caborn-Welborn components will be identified.

The late Caborn-Welborn subdivision is marked by a decrease in Caborn-Welborn Decorated jars, while handles continue to become less functional and more decorative. A preference for Kimmswick Plain pans continues, with most lacking the exterior protrusion that characterized earlier pans. In general, ceramic trends initiated during the middle Caborn-Welborn subdivision continue into the late Caborn-Welborn subdivision. Nonceramic objects recovered from late Caborn-Welborn sites are similar to those found at middle Caborn-Welborn sites. The most significant characteristic of late Caborn-Welborn artifact assemblages is the presence of historic trade goods (metal ornaments and glass trade beads). These materials, as well as central Mississippi valley types found at late Caborn-Welborn sites, point to continued economic and social interaction with groups outside the Ohio valley. By the end of this subdivision, Caborn-Welborn groups had abandoned most, if not all, of their settlements, bringing to a close the indigenous occupation of the Wabash-Ohio River confluence area.

# 6 Cultural and Functional Ceramic Patterns

With the temporal trends in Caborn-Welborn ceramics identified and a chronological sequence outlined for Caborn-Welborn sites, it is now possible to examine the ceramic data for other patterns, ones that have the potential to provide insights into how the Caborn-Welborn population reconstructed social, political, and economic relationships following the collapse of the Angel chiefdom. Therefore, this chapter examines the distribution by subarea of Caborn-Welborn ceramics as well as ceramic types and attributes that reflect interaction with groups living outside the lower Ohio valley. Comparisons also are made between Caborn-Welborn settlement types.

By examining the spatial distribution of Caborn-Welborn ceramic types and attributes (with regard to both style and form) by subarea, it should be possible to identify intersubarea variation. The identification of such variation could reflect cultural differences that point to the presence of subgroups within the Caborn-Welborn region. These subgroups may represent different factions that emerged as the Caborn-Welborn population reconstructed social and political relationships. Alternatively, they could reflect the presence of households from other regions that relocated to the area in the vicinity of the mouth of the Wabash following the collapse of neighboring chiefdoms.

Assessing the spatial distribution of ceramic types and attributes that are diagnostic of other regions can lead to the identification of settlements that, by virtue of their location or the status of some individuals, had more extensive and intensive intersocietal relationships than others. Though these "nonlocal" ceramic vessels were probably produced locally, their presence within site ceramic assemblages reflects some degree of interaction between Caborn-Welborn settlements and groups living in other regions. When these nonlocally derived ceramic types and attributes are considered along with the presence of objects obtained through long-distance exchange networks, such as marine shell and catlinite, the direction and nature of Caborn-Welborn intersocietal relationships with other groups can be assessed and inferences can be made concerning how the Caborn-Welborn population reconstructed economic relationships.

Finally, an examination of Caborn-Welborn ceramic types and traits and nonlocal ceramic types by settlement type has the potential to provide insights into site function and, therefore, into characteristics of the Caborn-

Welborn settlement hierarchy and how it differed from the earlier Angel settlement system. It can also contribute to an understanding of how Caborn-Welborn political relationships were reconstructed following the demise of the Angel chiefdom.

In making the intersubarea comparisons described in this chapter, it was assumed that similarities among contemporary sites reflect interaction between those communities (Hodder 1978) and that the greater the similarity of ceramic attributes, the greater the social interaction (Rautman 1993). It was assumed further that aspects of ceramic decoration and vessel form convey information (Sherman 1989; Sinopoli 1991; Wobst 1977) concerning the cultural identity of those who manufactured them (Kintigh 1985; Schortman 1989). As noted, except for intersite comparisons of complete mortuary vessels, counts of vessels presented here are based entirely on rim counts.

## INTERSUBAREA CERAMIC COMPARISON: EAST-WEST CULTURAL DIFFERENCES IN THE CABORN-WELBORN REGION

In addition to the ceramics recovered from the 22 Caborn-Welborn sites that have ceramic collections consisting of 30 or more sherds, intersubarea comparisons focused on the spatial distribution of whole vessels from mortuary contexts at 14 sites. The goal of the intersubarea comparisons was to determine if differences could be identified in the distribution of ceramic types and attributes that reflected cultural or ethnic differences within the Caborn-Welborn region. Since intersubarea variation was identified in chapter 4 in the location of Caborn-Welborn cemeteries (within villages vs. blufftop) it was thought that there might be differences in the types of ceramic vessels interred with the dead at these cemeteries. The first part of this section focuses on a comparison of materials recovered from nonmortuary contexts, followed by an examination of the distribution of whole vessels from mortuary contexts and an interpretation of observed patterns.

### Ceramic Types and Attributes from Nonmortuary Contexts

The goal of this analysis was to determine if intraregional variation existed in the distribution of ceramic types and attributes (vessel forms, appendages, and decoration) from nonmortuary contexts. Patterns were evaluated to determine if they reflected the presence of intersubarea cultural differences within the Caborn-Welborn region and the extent to which they reflected involvement in long-distance exchange networks (i.e., if some sites contained more evidence of extraregional interaction in the form of nonlocal ceramic types than others). Since the concern here was strictly with the spatial distribution of ceramic types and attributes, the results of this analysis were evaluated without regard to settlement type or function. Of the 22 sites used in this analysis, 10 are located in the eastern subarea (Caborn, Hart, Site 15He37.1, Alzey, Site 15He38, Site 15He110, Mulligan, Cummings, Ritz, and Hooper), 8 are situated in the central subarea (Hovey Lake, Slack Farm, Stull, Gough, Murphy, Welborn, Ries-Hasting, and Site 11Ga160), and 4 are located in the western subarea (Moore, Blackburn, Site 15Un96, and Site 15Un101) (Figure 6.1).

Pollack presents the results of analysis of the full suite of ceramic types and attributes considered (1998:314–343), but not all of the distributions reflected cultural differences within the Caborn-Welborn region. For example, little in the way of any relevant subarea variation was identified with respect to lip decoration on Mississippi/Bell Plain jars. Likewise, the spatial distributions of some types and attributes could be explained best with reference to time (i.e., jar appendages; bowl appendages; fabric-impressed ceramics and pan rim forms; and the amount of Caborn-Welborn decorated ceramics) or settlement type (i.e., shallow bowls with outslanting walls and flat bottoms; bowl appendage form; and the presence of Oneota-like ceramics). Temporal patterns were discussed in chapter 5, and site function patterns are discussed later in this chapter. Therefore, only those ceramic type and attribute distributions/comparisons considered to reflect intersubarea cultural variation are discussed in this section. Information is presented by ceramic type, and then attributes considered within that type are discussed.

### *Caborn-Welborn Decorated*

Caborn-Welborn Decorated accounts for 3.2 percent to 74.2 percent of site ceramic collections (Table 6.1). In general, sites in the eastern subarea tend to have high percentages of Caborn-Welborn Decorated, those in the western subarea relatively low percentages. In the central subarea, there appears to be wider range of variation in assemblage composition. Most of this variation, especially in the central subarea, can be interpreted as reflecting diachronic trends.

But while the amount of Caborn-Welborn Decorated in site ceramic collections appears to be related to temporal trends, spatial variation in shoulder designs is not. The primary design found on Caborn-Welborn Decorated jars consists of a series of descending and rising triangles demarcated by multiple layout lines, with the descending triangle filled with lines or punctations. Caborn-Welborn Decorated jars from the eastern subarea are distinguished from the other two subareas by a greater use of punctation to decorate jar shoulders and a higher percentage of shoulder designs with descending triangular areas filled with punctations (Tables 6.2–6.3). In contrast, descending triangular areas on jars within the central and western subareas were primarily filled with lines. These patterns are statistically significant (see Table 6.3).

Variation among the subareas also was noted in the distribution of Caborn-

Table 6.1. Caborn-Welborn Decorated in Site Assemblages by Subarea.

| Subarea/Site | Percent |
|---|---|
| *Eastern Subarea* | |
| Caborn | 45.1 |
| Hart | 64.7 |
| 15He37.1 | 5.9 |
| Alzey | 52.4 |
| 15He38 | 74.2 |
| 15He110 | 31.3 |
| Mulligan | 13.8 |
| Cummings | 3.2 |
| Ritz | 45.2 |
| Hooper | 40.0 |
| *Central Subarea* | |
| Murphy | 10.9 |
| Welborn | 18.0 |
| Hovey Lake | 7.9 |
| Slack Farm | 31.8 |
| Gough | 17.7 |
| Stull | 52.8 |
| 15Ga160 | 43.0 |
| Ries-Hasting | 42.2 |
| *Western Subarea* | |
| Moore | 14.4 |
| Blackburn | 21.1 |
| 15Un96 | 14.9 |
| 15Un101 | 68.9 |

Welborn Decorated designs that incorporate Oneota motifs, the most common and easily recognizable the thunderbird or hawk motif (Figures 3.13 and 3.14w-aa) (Benn 1989; Hall 1962). Jars with this design are found at sites in the eastern (Caborn, Alzey, and Ritz) and central (Slack Farm and Site 11Ga160) subareas but not in the western subarea.

## *Other Decorated Types*

Campbell Punctate is the most common central Mississippi valley decorated ceramic type in Caborn-Welborn site collections. Both it and Campbell Ap-

Table 6.2. Intersubarea Comparison of the Use of Lines and Punctations on Caborn-Welborn Decorated Jar Shoulders.

| | East | | Central | | West | |
|---|---|---|---|---|---|---|
| Trailed | 170 | 40.2% | 1644 | 57.8% | 41 | 39.8% |
| Trailed/Punctation | 81 | 19.1% | 346 | 12.2% | 7 | 6.8% |
| Incised | 66 | 15.6% | 481 | 16.9% | 34 | 33.0% |
| Incised/Punctation | 22 | 5.2% | 80 | 2.8% | 5 | 4.9% |
| Punctation | 84 | 19.9% | 295 | 10.4% | 16 | 15.5% |
| Total | 423 | 100.0% | 2846 | 100.0% | 103 | 100.0% |

Table 6.3. Caborn-Welborn Decorated: Lines or Punctations as Fill by Subarea.

| Subarea | Lines Fill | | Punctation Fill | | Total |
|---|---|---|---|---|---|
| Eastern | 54 | 31.2% | 119 | 68.8% | 173 |
| Central | 624 | 61.4% | 392 | 38.6% | 1016 |
| Western | 25 | 58.1% | 18 | 41.9% | 43 |
| Total | 703 | 57.1% | 529 | 42.9% | 1232 |

Pearson Chi-Square, value = 55.06, Degrees of Freedom = 2, Significant at .001

plique are found in all three subareas. However, decorated central Mississippi Valley ceramic types in general (e.g., Parkin Punctate, Kent Incised-like, Campbell Incised, and Walls Engraved) are more common at sites in the central and western subareas than the eastern. The absence in the western subarea of some earlier lower Ohio valley Mississippian decorated types, such as Manly Punctate and Matthews Incised, is somewhat surprising, given the variety of other decorated types found at sites there.

## Ceramic Types and Forms from Mortuary Contexts

The spatial distribution of ceramic types and forms recovered from mortuary contexts also was examined for patterns of intersubarea variation in the Caborn-Welborn region. The goal of this analysis was to ascertain whether the same kinds of ceramic types and forms were interred with the dead throughout the Caborn-Welborn area. It permitted the use of additional Caborn-Welborn ceramic data that, although not recovered with the same precision and control as that recovered from surface-collected and controlled excavation contexts, still contained important information relative to identifying intraregional spatial patterns that could potentially reflect the presence of cultural differences within the Caborn-Welborn region.

A total of 330 ceramic mortuary vessels from blufftop cemeteries (Grundy Hill, Site 15Un40, and Site 15Un110) and from settlements (Site 15He1, Site 15He43, Alzey/Site 15He38, Site 15He51, Mulligan, Site 15Un111, Bone Bank, Leonard, Slack Farm, and Murphy) was targeted in this analysis. Many of these vessels were collected during the early years of American archaeology (Moorehead 1906) or were obtained by private collectors. As such, only minimal site-specific provenience information is available for these vessels. Others can only be assigned to a general area within the Caborn-Welborn region but not to a specific site with any degree of confidence.

## *Ceramic Types*

Caborn-Welborn Decorated mortuary jars are more common in the eastern subarea than they are in the central and western subareas (Table 6.4). Within the eastern subarea, Caborn-Welborn Decorated vessels are reported to have been found with burials at seven sites. Two Caborn-Welborn Decorated jars were found at Site 15He1. At Site 15He43 and Mulligan, Caborn-Welborn Decorated accounts for 15.4 percent and 13.6 percent, respectively, of the mortuary vessels. In addition to these vessels, 78.9 percent of the vessels curated at the Glenn Black Laboratory from the eastern subarea are Caborn-Welborn Decorated jars. Unfortunately, none of these vessels can be assigned to a particular site, but most are thought to have come from either Alzey or Site 15He38, and two may have been found at Site 15He51. The only site outside the eastern subarea to have produced a large number of Caborn-Welborn Decorated vessels is Bone Bank, which is located in the central subarea.

With the exception of Bone Bank, Caborn-Welborn Decorated mortuary vessels are not well represented in mortuary collections from the central subarea (Table 6.4). They are not present in private collections from Slack Farm, nor were any found in association with burials during the professional investigation of this site. Likewise, the Murphy collection contains only two Caborn-Welborn Decorated mortuary jars (Table 6.4). Caborn-Welborn Decorated mortuary vessels also are rare in the western subarea: one is reported to have been found at Grundy Hill, and two were found by Lyon (1871) during his 1868 work in both the central and western subareas.

In contrast, central Mississippi valley–derived types, such as Parkin Punctate, Kent Incised-like, Barton Incised, Campbell Incised, and Fortune Noded, have been found in association with burials at sites in the central and western subareas but are relatively rare in the eastern subarea (Table 6.4). Campbell Punctate is one of the few central Mississippi valley types that is known from all three subareas.

Oneota-like jars, on the other hand, were rarely, if ever, placed with the

Table 6.4. Intersite Comparisons of Mortuary Vessel Ceramic Types (Sites Organized by Subarea).

| Ceramic Types | Eastern Subarea | | | | | | | | | |
|---|---|---|---|---|---|---|---|---|---|---|
| | 15He1 | | Alzey/15He38? | | 15He43 | | 15He51 | | Mulligan | |
| Mississippi Plain | | | 1 | 5.3% | 5 | 38.5% | | | 26 | 59.1% |
| Bell Plain | | | | | 3 | 23.1% | | | 6 | 13.6% |
| Caborn-Welborn Decorated | 2 | 100% | 15 | 78.9% | 2 | 15.4% | 2 | 100% | 6 | 13.6% |
| Manly Punctate | | | 2 | 10.5% | | | | | 1 | 2.3% |
| Campbell Punctate | | | 1 | 5.3% | 3 | 23.1% | | | 5 | 11.4% |
| Total | 2 | 100% | 19 | 100% | 13 | 100% | 2 | 100% | 44 | 100% |
| Ceramic Types | Central Subarea | | | | | | | | | |
| | Murphy[1] | | Bone Bank[2] | | Hovey Lake | | Slack Farm | | Leonard | |
| Mississippi Plain | 27 | 29.3% | | | 4 | 100% | 20 | 30.8% | | |
| Bell Plain | 54 | 58.7% | | | | | 35 | 53.8% | | |
| Parkin Punctate | 1 | 1.1% | | | | | 1 | 1.5% | | |
| Caborn-Welborn Decorated | 2 | 2.2% | 26 | 96.3% | | | | | 1 | 100% |
| Manly Punctate | 2 | 2.2% | | | | | 1 | 1.5% | | |
| Old Town Red | | | | | | | 1 | 1.5% | | |
| O'Byam Incised | 1 | 1.1% | | | | | | | | |
| Misc. Incised or Trailed | 1 | 1.1% | | | | | 1 | 1.5% | | |
| Kent Incised-Like | 2 | 2.2% | | | | | 1 | 1.5% | | |
| Campbell Punctate | 2 | 2.2% | 1 | 3.7% | | | 4 | 6.2% | | |
| Campbell Incised | | | | | | | 1 | 1.5% | | |
| Total | 92 | 100% | 27 | 100% | 4 | 100% | 65 | 100% | 1 | 100% |

Table 6.4. *Continued*

| Ceramic Types | Western Subarea | | | | | | | |
|---|---|---|---|---|---|---|---|---|
| | Grundy Hill | | 15Un40 | | 15Un110 | | 15Un111 | |
| Mississippi Plain | 1 | 20.0% | 6 | 37.5% | 1 | 33.3% | 1 | 50.0% |
| Bell Plain | 1 | 20.0% | 2 | 12.5% | 2 | 66.7% | | |
| Parkin Punctate | | | 1 | 6.3% | | | | |
| Caborn-Welborn Decorated | 1 | 20.0% | | | | | | |
| Matthews Incised | | | | | | | 1 | 50.0% |
| Barton Incised | 1 | 20.0% | | | | | | |
| Fortune Noded | 1 | 20.0% | | | | | | |
| Campbell Punctate | | | 4 | 25.0% | | | | |
| Campbell Applique | | | 3 | 18.8% | | | | |
| Total | 5 | 100% | 16 | 100% | 3 | 100% | 2 | 100% |

[1] Based on copies of photographs and notes made by Cheryl Ann Munson and others.

[2] Bone Bank sample does not include information on plain jars or any other vessels reported to have been found at this site (based on photographs provided to Cheryl Ann Munson by James H. Kellar).

Table 6.5. Intersite Comparisons of Vessel Forms from Mortuary Contexts (Sites Organized by Subarea).

| Vessel Form | Eastern Subarea | | | | | | | | | |
|---|---|---|---|---|---|---|---|---|---|---|
| | 15He1 | | Alzey/15He38? | | 15He43 | | 15He51 | | Mulligan | |
| Bottle | | | | | 1 | 7.7% | | | 1 | 2.3% |
| Jar | 2 | 100% | 20 | 100% | 10 | 76.9% | 2 | 100% | 37 | 84.1% |
| Bowl | | | | | 2 | 15.4% | | | 3 | 6.8% |
| Conch Shell Bowl | | | | | | | | | 1 | 2.3% |
| Pinch Pot Bowl | | | | | | | | | 2 | 4.5% |
| Total | 2 | 100% | 20 | 100% | 13 | 100% | 2 | 100% | 44 | 100% |
| Vessel Form | Central Subarea | | | | | | | | | |
| | Murphy[1] | | Bone Bank[2] | | Hovey Lake | | Slack Farm | | Leonard | |
| Bottle | 23 | 25.0% | | | | | 24 | 36.9% | | |
| Jar | 42 | 45.7% | 27 | 100% | 4 | 100% | 26 | 40.0% | 1 | 100% |
| Bowl | 27 | 29.3% | | | | | 11 | 16.9% | | |
| Conch Shell Bowl | | | | | | | 4 | 6.2% | | |
| Total | 92 | 100% | 27 | 100% | 4 | 100% | 65 | 100% | 1 | 100% |
| Vessel Form | Western Subarea | | | | | | | | | |
| | Grundy Hill | | 15Un40 | | 15Un110 | | 15Un111 | | | |
| Bottle | 1 | 20% | | | 2 | 66.7% | | | | |
| Jar | 4 | 80% | 14 | 87.5% | 1 | 33.3% | 2 | 100% | | |
| Bowl | | | 2 | 12.5% | | | | | | |
| Total | 5 | 100% | 16 | 100% | 3 | 100% | 2 | 100% | | |

[1] Based on copies of photographs and notes made by Cheryl Ann Munson and others.
[2] Bone Bank sample does not include information on plain jars or any other vessels reported to have been found at this site (based on photographs provided to Cheryl Ann Munson by James H. Kellar).

dead anywhere in the Caborn-Welborn region. Oneota-like ceramics are primarily known from nonmortuary contexts at Slack Farm, with only an occasional Oneota-like sherd coming from other sites, such as Murphy, Hovey Lake, Caborn, and Alzey.

### *Ceramic Forms*

Most Caborn-Welborn mortuary vessels are jars, but the Slack Farm and Murphy mortuary vessel collections contain relatively large amounts of, and a diverse assortment of, bottles and effigy vessels. The mortuary collections from these two sites are distinguished by a high percentage of Bell Plain bottles (Table 6.5), with long-necked examples, some with tetrapodal supports, and

Table 6.6. Intersite Comparisons of Bottle Types from Mortuary Contexts (Sites Organized by Subarea).

| | Eastern Subarea | | Central Subarea | | | | Western Subarea | |
|---|---|---|---|---|---|---|---|---|
| Rimform | 15He43 | | Murphy | | Slack Farm | | 15Un110 | |
| Long Neck | | | 7 | 35.0% | 12 | 52.2% | | |
| Hooded | | | 6 | 30.0% | 3 | 13.0% | | |
| Wide Mouth | 1 | 100% | 6 | 30.0% | 6 | 26.1% | 2 | 100% |
| Rounded Neck | | | | | 2 | 8.7% | | |
| Neckless | | | 1 | 5.0% | | | | |
| Total | 1 | 100% | 20 | 100% | 23 | 100% | 2 | 100% |

hooded effigy bottles well-represented in both (Table 6.6). These types of bottles are rare at other Caborn-Welborn sites.

As with bottles, bowls from mortuary contexts also are more common and diverse at Slack Farm and Murphy than at other Caborn-Welborn sites (Table 6.6). Shallow bowls with outslanting walls account for more than 50.0 percent of the mortuary bowls at these two sites (Table 6.7). Fish and human effigy vessels and bowls with effigy rim riders also are more common at these two villages than at other Caborn-Welborn sites, although these types of vessels also are known from Site 15He43 and Mulligan in the eastern subarea.

Other types of effigy vessels from the Caborn-Welborn region include a human head pot that is reported to have been found in the eastern subarea (Mulligan) and conch shell–shaped bowls, which have been found in both the central (Slack Farm) and eastern (Mulligan) subareas. Effigy vessels are not known from the western subarea.

## East-West Cultural Differences

An examination of the spatial distribution of ceramic types and attributes in assemblages recovered from nonmortuary and mortuary contexts in the Caborn-Welborn region identified several patterns that serve to distinguish the subareas from one another: Caborn-Welborn Decorated jar shoulder decoration, the amount of Oneota-like decorative motifs, and the types of decorated jars interred with the dead. Because these patterns cannot be explained with reference to time or function, they could reflect cultural differences that served to distinguish Caborn-Welborn groups living in the eastern subarea from those living in the western subarea, with groups in the central subarea sharing affinities with both. Complementing these ceramic patterns

Table 6.7. Intersite Comparisons of Bowl Types from Mortuary Contexts (Sites Organized by Subarea).

| | Eastern Subarea | | | | Central Subarea | | | |
|---|---|---|---|---|---|---|---|---|
| Rimform | 15He43 | | Mulligan | | Murphy | | Slack Farm | |
| Direct | 1 | 50% | 2 | 66.7% | 8 | 36.4% | 3 | 33.3% |
| Inslanting | | | | | 2 | 9.1% | | |
| Outslanting | 1 | 50% | | | 7 | 31.8% | 5 | 55.6% |
| Outslanting Castellation | | | 1 | 33.3% | 5 | 22.7% | 1 | 11.1% |
| Total | 2 | 100% | 3 | 100% | 22 | 100% | 9 | 100% |

| | Western Subarea | |
|---|---|---|
| Rimform | 15Un40 | |
| Direct | | |
| Inslanting | | |
| Outslanting | 2 | 100% |
| Outslanting Castellation | | |
| Total | 2 | 100% |

are the regional patterns in Caborn-Welborn cemetery location discussed in chapter 4, which also point to cultural differences between the subareas.

### *The Patterns*

Intersubarea variation in Caborn-Welborn Decorated jar design may reflect cultural differences. Descending triangles on Caborn-Welborn Decorated jar shoulders can be filled with either lines or punctations. In the eastern subarea, there is a marked preference for the use of punctation to fill these triangular areas. This pattern stands in sharp contrast to a preference for the use of lines as fill in the central and western subareas. The most variation in the use of lines and punctations as fill was observed in the central subarea, and the greatest consistency was observed in the eastern subarea.

Intersubarea differences identified in the types of decorated jars interred with the dead also can be explained with reference to cultural differences, and perhaps religious differences as well. Caborn-Welborn Decorated vessels accounted for about 15.0 percent of the mortuary vessels at sites in the eastern subarea, yet this ceramic type was rarely placed with the dead in the central and western subareas. In contrast, central Mississippi valley ceramic types were the main kinds of decorated jars interred with the dead in the central and western subareas.

This preference for the use of Caborn-Welborn Decorated mortuary jars in the eastern subarea and the use of central Mississippi valley–derived ceramic types in mortuary contexts in the central and western subareas parallel the ceramic data recovered from nonmortuary contexts in the subareas. These data generally reflect higher frequencies of Caborn-Welborn Decorated sherds in the eastern subarea and higher frequencies of central Mississippi valley ceramic types in the central and western subareas. That the western subarea has more central Mississippi valley types than the eastern subarea is not entirely surprising. Settlements in this subarea would have been the first ones encountered by people traveling up the Ohio River from the central Mississippi valley. However, the absence of some earlier lower Ohio valley Mississippian decorated types from the western subarea, Manly Punctate in particular, which is known from several sites in the eastern and central subareas, is somewhat surprising. The observed spatial differences in the distribution of these types could reflect sampling biases, since outside of Slack Farm these types are not very common.

Intersubarea differences identified in the use of decorated ceramic types in mortuary contexts parallel the regional patterns in grave location discussed in chapter 4. In the eastern subarea, there is a marked preference for within-community burial. In contrast, most individuals in the western subarea were interred in cemeteries located on the bluffs overlooking the floodplain of the Ohio River. Within the central subarea, both types of burial practices have been documented, but there is an overall preference for within-community burial. Considered together, the patterns in these two different sets of data provide strong evidence for the existence of cultural or religious differences within the Caborn-Welborn region.

The patterns in mortuary vessel form distribution may be best explained with reference to site function. Slack Farm and Murphy, which produced higher percentages of Bell Plain and contained a greater variety of bottles and effigy vessels than the other sites for which mortuary ceramic vessel data were available, both represent large villages in the central subarea. Since consideration of this pattern is more relevant to the discussion of Caborn-Welborn settlement hierarchy, it will be discussed in more detail in that section.

And finally, while Oneota-like jars were rarely, if ever, placed with the dead, the presence of Oneota-derived decorative designs in nonmortuary contexts only within the central and eastern subareas also may reflect cultural differences among the subareas (although it also may be a product of sample size, as these motifs are not easily identified in surface collections). The presence of these Oneota-derived motifs (thunderbird/hawk) points to the diffusion and reinterpretation of these motifs in the Caborn-Welborn region. It also suggests that Caborn-Welborn potters incorporated aspects of Oneota decorative designs within their own ceramic tradition through presumed intersocietal interactions with Oneota groups. These data suggest that this Caborn-Welborn/Oneota interaction might have been most intensive, extensive, or sustained in the central and eastern subareas.

### *The Subareas*

In the western subarea, the higher frequency of central Mississippi valley ceramic types and the lower frequency of Oneota-like decorative motifs on Caborn-Welborn Decorated jars suggests that the residents of this subarea interacted socially and economically more often or more intensively with groups living in areas downstream from the mouth of the Wabash River than did those who lived in the eastern subarea. Placement of cemeteries on the bluffs overlooking villages in the western subarea is consistent with earlier Mississippian burial practices in the lower Ohio valley (e.g., Tinsley Hill [Clay 1963b, 1997; Lane 1993]). The presence of blufftop cemeteries in this subarea thus reflects continuation of this earlier practice. Identification of these cemeteries in the Caborn-Welborn region raises the possibility that following the collapse of downstream regional chiefdoms, some households moved upstream, relocating to the Caborn-Welborn region and settling in the western subarea, where they continued the practice of interring the dead in cemeteries removed from residential areas. The greater use of lines as fill in descending triangles on Caborn-Welborn Decorated jar shoulders in this subarea may have served to distinguish residents living downstream from the mouth of the Wabash from those living upstream.

Eastern subarea inhabitants, on the other hand, may have had closer ties to the former Angel chiefdom and possibly to Oneota groups to the north. These relationships are suggested by the greater use of Caborn-Welborn Decorated jars in mortuary contexts and by the higher frequency of Oneota-like decoration on Caborn-Welborn Decorated jars relative to the western subarea. It also is possible that given its proximity to the mouth of the Green River, this subarea had greater interaction with groups living in eastern Tennessee, but this is difficult to document in the archaeological record of the Caborn-Welborn region.

In the eastern subarea, the location of cemeteries within Caborn-Welborn villages and hamlets represents a continuation of the earlier Angel practice of burying the dead near or within residential areas. The primary design found on Caborn-Welborn Decorated jars is similar to the designs on Angel Negative Painted plates, and placement of Caborn-Welborn Decorated jars in graves may have been a reaffirmation of the links between the Angel and Caborn-Welborn populations. Even if the location of cemeteries and the placement of Caborn-Welborn Decorated jars in graves are not, in and of themselves, a reflection of a Caborn-Welborn link to the earlier Angel chiefdom, they still point to cultural differences within the Caborn-Welborn region. That descending triangles filled with punctations occur more frequently on Caborn-Welborn Decorated jars in the eastern subarea also points to cultural differences that may have served to distinguish households living in the eastern subarea from those living in the western subarea.

The central subarea combines elements of both the eastern and western subareas. With the former, the central subarea shares a preference for within-site cemeteries and the incorporation of Oneota motifs within Caborn-Welborn Decorated designs; with the latter, it shares the practice of rarely placing Caborn-Welborn Decorated jars in graves and a preference for filling descending triangles on Caborn-Welborn Decorated jars with lines rather than punctations. These characteristics reflect this subarea's central location within the Caborn-Welborn region. As such, an overlap in the distribution of stylistic elements and mortuary practices would be expected, unless the eastern and western subareas represent separate and distinct entities that had little or no interaction, which does not appear to have been the case. The central subarea also is characterized by initial interaction with Oneota groups to the north of the Ohio valley, as reflected by the large number of Oneota-like jars recovered from this subarea.

### *Discussion*

The patterns discussed here (subarea differences in the distribution of Caborn-Welborn Decorated shoulder decoration, the types of vessels interred with the dead, the amount of Oneota-like decorative motifs, and the location of cemeteries) suggest that Caborn-Welborn society may have been comprised of at least two Mississippian groups that followed slightly different cultural traditions. If this was the case, then it is quite possible that, following the collapse of Angel and the establishment of several Caborn-Welborn villages near the mouth of the Wabash River ca. A.D. 1400–1450, segments of former downstream chiefdoms migrated to the western portion of the Caborn-Welborn region, with the eastern subarea inhabitants thus representing the descendants of the Angel chiefdom.

## SETTLEMENT TYPE, CERAMIC TYPE, VESSEL FORM, AND APPENDAGES COMPARISON: CABORN-WELBORN SETTLEMENT HIERARCHY

The goal of this analysis was to identify patterns in ceramic types and selected ceramic attributes among the four domestic Caborn-Welborn site types (large village, small village, hamlet, and farmstead), defined in chapter 4, in an attempt to determine how they functioned within the Caborn-Welborn settlement hierarchy. Examination of this settlement hierarchy has the potential to provide insights into how the Caborn-Welborn population reconstructed and maintained social and political relationships following the collapse of the Angel chiefdom. The presence of a settlement hierarchy suggests that some aspects of the Caborn-Welborn settlement system were similar to those of the earlier Angel chiefdom, but the absence of a regional mound center and the association of cemeteries with all settlements, not just a regional center, point to changes as well.

The information about ceramic types, vessel forms, and appendages used in this analysis came from the same 22 site assemblages that provided the data used in the intersubarea comparisons. Comparisons were made by settlement type (Table 6.8), irrespective of specific site or subarea association. Because variation in sample size could potentially have affected any observed patterns, comparisons were restricted primarily to those attributes that were well represented in most ceramic collections. Less emphasis was placed on relatively rare ceramic types or attributes that might be present in very large ceramic collections but were not present in smaller ones.

## Assumptions Guiding This Analysis

As discussed in chapter 4, the Caborn-Welborn settlement system was hierarchically organized and consisted of large villages, small villages, hamlets, farmsteads, and blufftop cemeteries (Green 1977; Green and Munson 1978). Its existence points to a measure of cultural continuity between the Angel and Caborn-Welborn phases. But did the Caborn-Welborn settlement hierarchy function in the same way as that of the Angel chiefdom?

If, following the collapse of the Angel chiefdom, large and perhaps small Caborn-Welborn villages assumed many of the roles of this earlier Mississippian regional center, then similar activities should have taken place at both large and small villages, and a wider range or different set(s) of activities would have been conducted at these sites compared to hamlets and farmsteads. These differences should be identifiable in ceramic attributes that reflect site function, such as differences in the proportion of different vessel types in site ceramic collections.

Most archaeologists (Blitz 1993a, 1993b; Hally 1986; Hendrickson and McDonald 1983; Welch and Scarry 1995) assume that, in general, bowls, pans, bottles, and jars were used for different sets of activities. However, it is recognized that the presumed uses of these vessels are not mutually exclusive and that a ceramic vessel could have been used for a variety of purposes before it entered the archaeological record. With this caution in mind, archaeologists have assumed that hemispherical bowls were used to serve food and as individual eating vessels; shallow bowls with outslanting walls and flat bottoms, and pans, were used in activities that involved preparing, serving, and con-

Table 6.8. Ceramic Types Associated with Each Settlement Type.

| Ceramic Types | Farmsteads | | Hamlets | | Sm Village | | L Village | |
|---|---|---|---|---|---|---|---|---|
| Angel Negative Painted | | | | | 3 | 0.3% | 5 | 0.0% |
| Barton Incised | | | | | 3 | 0.3% | 1 | 0.0% |
| Beckwith Incised | | | | | 1 | 0.1% | 16 | 0.1% |
| Bell Plain | 81 | 12.1% | 156 | 16.7% | 248 | 21.6% | 3205 | 20.0% |
| Caborn-Welborn Decorated | 269 | 40.2% | 366 | 39.3% | 320 | 27.8% | 4880 | 30.5% |
| Campbell Applique | 1 | 0.1% | 1 | 0.1% | 1 | 0.1% | 13 | 0.1% |
| Campbell Incised | | | | | 2 | 0.2% | 9 | 0.1% |
| Campbell Punctate | | | 7 | 0.8% | 2 | 0.2% | 47 | 0.3% |
| Cordmarked | 1 | 0.1% | | | 1 | 0.1% | 24 | 0.1% |
| Fortune Noded | | | | | | | 1 | 0.0% |
| Kent Incised-Like | | | | | | | 57 | 0.4% |
| Kimmswick Fabric Impressed | 10 | 1.5% | 12 | 1.3% | 33 | 2.9% | 979 | 6.1% |
| Kimmswick Net Impressed | | | | | | | 8 | 0.0% |
| Kimmswick Plain | 33 | 4.9% | 56 | 6.0% | 103 | 9.0% | 761 | 4.7% |
| Manly Punctate | 3 | 0.4% | 3 | 0.3% | 1 | 0.1% | 210 | 1.3% |
| Matthews Incised | 1 | 0.1% | | | 1 | 0.1% | 44 | 0.3% |
| Misc. Incised or Trailed | | | 2 | 0.2% | 3 | 0.3% | 53 | 0.3% |
| Mississippi Plain | 263 | 39.3% | 325 | 34.9% | 402 | 35.0% | 5281 | 33.0% |

*Continued on the next page*

Table 6.8. *Continued*

| Ceramic Types | Farmsteads | | Hamlets | | Sm Village | | L Village | |
|---|---|---|---|---|---|---|---|---|
| Mound Place Incised | | | | | 1 | 0.1% | 5 | 0.0% |
| O'Byam Incised | | | | | | | 15 | 0.1% |
| Old Town Red | 5 | 0.7% | 2 | 0.2% | 15 | 1.3% | 99 | 0.6% |
| Oneota-Like | | | 1 | 0.1% | 3 | 0.3% | 207 | 1.3% |
| Parkin Punctate | 1 | 0.1% | | | 5 | 0.4% | 33 | 0.2% |
| Ranch Incised | | | | | 1 | 0.1% | | 0.0% |
| Tolu Fabric Impressed | | | 1 | 0.1% | | | 43 | 0.3% |
| Vernon Paul Applique | 1 | 0.1% | | | | | | 0.0% |
| Walls Engraved | | | | | 1 | 0.1% | 29 | 0.2% |
| Total | 669 | 100% | 932 | 100% | 1150 | 100% | 16025 | 100% |

suming food; bottles for both storage and serving liquids; and jars primarily for cooking and storing food. These presumed vessel functions were used to inform the analysis presented here.

## The Data

### *Ceramic Types*

Mississippi Plain, Bell Plain, and Caborn-Welborn Decorated make up the majority of the ceramics at all four settlement types, and Mississippi Plain comprises a similar percentage (between 33.0 percent and 39.3 percent) of the assemblage for all of them (Table 6.8). However, as settlement size increases, the percentage of Bell Plain increases (although the percentage of this type in small villages and large villages is about the same). This pattern is reflected in the ratios of Mississippi Plain to Bell Plain: farmsteads have a ratio of 3 to 1, hamlets a ratio of 2.1 to 1, small villages a ratio of 1.9 to 1; and large villages a ratio of 1.7 to 1 (Table 6.8). As will be discussed in the next section, this pattern is related to patterns in bowls and, in particular, shallow bowls with flat bottoms, which are more common at villages than at farmsteads or hamlets.

A surprising result of this comparison was that Caborn-Welborn Decorated was more common at farmsteads and hamlets than it was at small or large villages. It was expected that there would be a greater need for and use of Caborn-Welborn Decorated jars at larger settlements than at smaller ones. At present, it is not clear if this pattern is related to site function or inter-subarea variation, as most of the farmsteads and hamlets that contained large amounts of Caborn-Welborn Decorated ceramics are located in the eastern subarea.

Farmsteads, hamlets, and small villages produced mainly Kimmswick Plain pans, but at large villages, almost 60 percent of the pans were classified as Kimmswick Fabric Impressed. At first glance, this pattern points to a relationship between settlement size and pan exterior surface treatment that might be related to site function. However, it is most likely a reflection of diachronic stylistic trends: all of the large villages (Hovey Lake, Murphy, and Slack Farm) included in this study have early Caborn-Welborn components. From the beginning to the end of the Caborn-Welborn phase, there was a decline in the use of Kimmswick Fabric Impressed pans, with later sites having only small amounts of Kimmswick Fabric Impressed ceramics. What is relevant to this discussion is that, taken together, Kimmswick Fabric Impressed and Kimmswick Plain account for about 11 percent of the analyzed ceramics at villages and about 7 percent of the ceramics at farmsteads and hamlets (Table 6.8). As will be discussed in the next section, this represents a greater use of pans at villages than at farmsteads and hamlets.

When diversity of ceramic types as a whole is considered (Table 6.8), it is clear that, as a group, small and large villages contain twice as many types as do farmsteads and hamlets. This diversity is even more sharply drawn when the decorated lower Ohio valley and decorated central Mississippi valley ceramic types are considered: two to three Ohio valley types and central Mississippi valley types are associated with farmsteads and hamlets, while six to seven lower Ohio valley types and seven to eight central Mississippi valley types are associated with small and large villages. While it can be argued that, with respect to large villages, this pattern is related to sample size, the same cannot be said for the difference between hamlets and small villages, since a similar number of sherds were analyzed from both settlement types.

Oneota-like ceramics occur at all settlement types except farmsteads. This ceramic type occurs in percentages of less than .5 percent at hamlets and small villages, which is comparable to the frequencies for the decorated lower Ohio valley and decorated central Mississippi valley ceramic types. At large villages, the Oneota-like ceramics occur in percentages slightly greater than 1.0 percent, which is twice the amount of any of the decorated lower Ohio valley and decorated central Mississippi valley ceramic types. This pattern is related to the large number of Oneota-like ceramics recovered from Slack Farm.

### *Vessel Forms*

An examination of Table 6.9 makes it readily apparent that, as settlement size increases, there is an increase in the percentage of bowls and pans and a decrease in the percentage of jars. Bottles remain relatively constant among the four settlement types. There is no evidence to suggest that these trends are related to sample size, as the percentages were relatively consistent among farmsteads and hamlets, and small and large villages. Since general vessel form categories were used for these comparisons, the identified trends do not appear to have been overly influenced by rare examples that may be present in larger collections from villages but usually are not recovered from smaller sites.

The increase in bowls is primarily accounted for by the presence of more shallow bowls with outslanting walls and flat bottoms at large and small villages (Table 6.9). These vessels show a consistent increase from farmsteads to villages, with most of the change accounted for by a single type: shallow bowls with castellated rims (Table 6.9). The largest increase in these bowls is between small and large villages, increasing from 43.7 percent to 73.0 percent. Not surprisingly, an increase in bowls is correlated with an increase in Bell Plain, since most bowls were assigned to this type (Table 6.8). This pattern does not appear to be related to temporal trends within the Caborn-Welborn region but rather to the greater use of shallow bowls at villages than at either farmsteads or hamlets, regardless of when a site was occupied.

The percentage of pans also increases as sites get larger, ranging from

Table 6.9. Settlement Type and Vessel Form Composition.

| | Farmsteads | | Hamlets | | Small Villages | | Large Villages | |
|---|---|---|---|---|---|---|---|---|
| *Vessel Form* | | | | | | | | |
| Pan | 43 | 12.1% | 68 | 13.9% | 136 | 19.0% | 1749 | 19.2% |
| Bottle | 11 | 3.1% | 11 | 2.2% | 21 | 2.9% | 270 | 3.0% |
| Jar | 226 | 63.7% | 269 | 55.0% | 333 | 46.6% | 4239 | 46.6% |
| Bowl | 67 | 18.9% | 135 | 27.6% | 221 | 31.0% | 2764 | 30.4% |
| Plate | 3 | 0.8% | 3 | 0.6% | | | 11 | 0.1% |
| Conch Shell Bowl | | | 1 | 0.2% | | | 12 | 0.1% |
| Pinch Pot Bowl | | | 2 | 0.4% | | | 4 | 0.0% |
| Pinch Pot Jar | | | | | | | 10 | 0.1% |
| Funnel | 5 | 1.4% | | | 3 | 0.4% | 30 | 0.3% |
| Total | 355 | 100% | 489 | 100% | 714 | 100% | 9089 | 100% |
| *Bottles* | | | | | | | | |
| Long Neck | | | | | | | 34 | 12.7% |
| Hooded | | | 1 | 12.5% | | | 30 | 11.2% |
| Wide Mouth | 2 | 20.0% | 5 | 62.5% | 13 | 65.0% | 79 | 29.6% |
| Wide Mouth Rounded Neck | 6 | 60.0% | 1 | 12.5% | | | 90 | 33.7% |
| Wide Mouth Angled Neck | 2 | 20.0% | | | | | 15 | 5.6% |
| Wide Mouth Protrusion at Neck | | | | | | | 6 | 2.2% |
| Neckless | | | 1 | 12.5% | 7 | 35.0% | 13 | 4.9% |
| Total | 10 | 100% | 8 | 100% | 20 | 100% | 267 | 100% |
| *Bowls* | | | | | | | | |
| Direct | 39 | 78.0% | 60 | 58.8% | 106 | 55.8% | 482 | 23.9% |
| Inslanting | 1 | 2.0% | 6 | 5.9% | 1 | 0.5% | 62 | 3.1% |
| Outslanting | 9 | 18.0% | 29 | 28.4% | 54 | 28.4% | 643 | 31.8% |
| Outslanting Castellation | 1 | 2.0% | 7 | 6.9% | 29 | 15.3% | 832 | 41.2% |
| Total | 50 | 100% | 102 | 100% | 190 | 100% | 2019 | 100% |

12.1 percent to 19.2 percent (Table 6.9). Not only were more pans found at villages, but pans from large villages tend to be bigger than those from small villages, hamlets, or farmsteads (Table 6.10). Kimmswick Plain and Kimmswick Fabric Impressed pans from large villages have mean orifice diameters that are about 8 cm larger than those from the other three settlement types. Most of the increase in pan size is attributable to Kimmswick Plain and Fabric Impressed pans from Slack Farm, which have mean orifice diameters of 41.5 and 50.6 cm, respectively. When the Slack Farm pans are removed from this

Table 6.10. Pan Orifice Diameter by Settlement Type.

| Ceramic Type | Farmsteads | | Hamlets | | Small Villages | | Large Villages | |
|---|---|---|---|---|---|---|---|---|
| | Mean | No. | Mean | No. | Mean | No. | Mean | No. |
| Kimmswick Plain | 29.7 | 6 | 32.4 | 20 | 31.5 | 42 | 39.8 | 185 |
| Kimmswick Fabric Impressed | 33.6 | 5 | 41.7 | 7 | 40.4 | 12 | 49.3 | 420 |

comparison, there is no appreciable difference in pan size among the settlement types.

Why there is such an increase in pan size at Slack Farm relative to the other settlements is not easy to explain. It could be owing to sample size, since a much larger sample of pans was recovered from this village than from any other Caborn-Welborn settlement. However, the relative consistency of pan orifice size at all other Caborn-Welborn sites tends to indicate that this is not the case. Rather, the increased pan size at Slack Farm suggests the need for bigger serving vessels at this site, ones that may have been used to serve larger groups than at smaller Caborn-Welborn settlements. This observed difference in pan size is another variable that tends to distinguish Slack Farm from other Caborn-Welborn sites, and, as will be discussed later, it may be related to its function within the Caborn-Welborn settlement hierarchy and its central location within the distribution of Caborn-Welborn settlements (see Chapter 7).

While the number of jars relative to bowls and pans decreases as community size increases, there is no evidence to suggest that jar size is related in any way to settlement size. In fact, mean jar size remains relatively constant among all the settlement types. For example, Mississippi Plain jars with lugs from Cummings, a farmstead in the eastern subarea, have a mean jar orifice diameter of 24.7 cm, which is just slightly larger than similar storage jars from Slack Farm. This distribution of Mississippi Plain jars suggests that, regardless of settlement type, these vessels served similar functions.

And finally, while the overall frequencies of bottles at the four types of settlements are similar, there are differences in the *kinds* of bottles associated with them. Most Caborn-Welborn bottles have wide mouths, but at large villages slightly more than 20 percent are also of the long-necked or hooded variety. The increase in the occurrence of these bottle forms at large villages is owing, in part, to Slack Farm, where these types of bottles are most common. At this site, they were recovered from habitation areas as well as from mortuary contexts (Table 6.6).

Although patterns in mortuary vessel form relative to settlement type were not specifically considered in this analysis, it should be noted that the mortuary assemblages from Slack Farm and Murphy, both large villages, contained a greater variety of bottles and effigy vessels than the other sites for which mortuary ceramic vessel data were available. This variation in the types of vessels interred with the dead is apparently not related to site occupational history. As with the differences in pan orifice size, intersite differences in bottle forms from nonmortuary and mortuary contexts tend to distinguish Slack Farm, and to a lesser extent Murphy, from other Caborn-Welborn communities and may be related to their central location within the Caborn-Welborn region (see chapter 7).

### *Bowl and Jar Appendages*

In general, a greater variety of bowl appendages—lugs (plain, notched, or incised), effigies (as rim riders or molded to vessel walls), and nodes—is present within the ceramic assemblages from large and small villages than those from hamlets and farmsteads (Table 6.11). For example, lugs account for slightly more than 21 percent of all bowl appendages at villages, compared to 13.8 percent at hamlets and 8.3 percent at farmsteads. As with the increase in shallow bowls, pans, and long-necked bottles, this pattern suggests that the kinds of activities requiring the use of effigy vessels and bowls with attached lugs occurred more frequently at villages than at hamlets or farmsteads.

In contrast to lugs, notched or beaded rimstrips on hemispherical bowls account for 64 percent of bowl appendages at farmsteads, hamlets, and small villages but only 37 percent of bowl appendages at large villages (Table 6.11). This pattern probably reflects temporal trends in the use of these types of bowl appendages and is probably not related to settlement function. During the Caborn-Welborn phase, notched or beaded rimstrips appear to have increased in popularity through time (see chapter 5).

Turning to jar appendages, it appears that as site size increases, the number of plain, bifurcated, and multiple lugs (two or more) increases, while the number of notched lugs and horizontal notched applied strips on jars decreases (Table 6.12). Plain, bifurcated, and multiple lugs account for less than 28.0 percent of jar appendages from farmsteads and hamlets but more than 53.0 percent of jar appendages from large and small villages. On the other hand, notched lugs comprise 42.2 percent of jar appendages from farmsteads, and horizontal notched applied strips account for 43.5 percent of jar appendages from hamlets, but only 4.4 percent and 2.3 percent of jar appendages from large and small villages, respectively. It is possible that differences in lug type and notched applied strips may represent temporal, and not functional, trends in the region.

## Discussion

This analysis of ceramic types, vessel forms, and appendages from the four Caborn-Welborn settlement types has identified certain differences among

Table 6.11. Bowl Appendages Associated with Each Settlement Type.

| Appendage Type | Farmsteads | | Hamlets | | Sm Village | | L Village | |
|---|---|---|---|---|---|---|---|---|
| Nodes | | | | | | | | |
| Single | 2 | 5.6% | 3 | 4.5% | 1 | 1.4% | 129 | 17.9% |
| Paired or Multiple | 3 | 8.3% | | | | | 61 | 8.5% |
| Dimpled | | | | | 1 | 1.4% | | |
| Notched or Beaded Strip | | | | | | | | |
| Notched Horizontal | 25 | 69.4% | 53 | 79.1% | 44 | 62.0% | 264 | 36.6% |
| Plain Horizontal | 1 | 2.8% | | | 4 | 5.6% | 32 | 4.4% |
| Notched/Grooved Vertical | | | | | 1 | 1.4% | | |
| Plain Vertical | 1 | 2.8% | | | | | | |
| Lugs | | | | | | | | |
| Plain | 2 | 5.6% | 5 | 7.5% | 14 | 19.7% | 114 | 15.8% |
| Bifurcated | | | | | 2 | 2.8% | 5 | 0.7% |
| Paired or Multiple | | | | | | | 2 | 0.3% |
| Incised | | | | | 1 | 1.4% | 9 | 1.2% |
| Notched/Punctation | | | | | 1 | 1.4% | 3 | 0.4% |
| Notched | 1 | 2.8% | 4 | 6.0% | 1 | 1.4% | 18 | 2.5% |
| Hole in Lug | | | | | | | 7 | 1.0% |
| Effigy | 1 | 2.8% | 2 | 3.0% | 1 | 1.4% | 77 | 10.7% |
| Total | 36 | 100% | 67 | 100% | 71 | 100% | 721 | 100% |

the settlement types. Ceramic type differences (i.e., in the variety of decorated ceramics types) point to a greater use of vessels that reflect extraregional interaction at villages and, with respect to the central Mississippi valley types, more intersocietal interaction between these communities and Mississippian groups living in the central Mississippi valley.

Differences in vessel form have demonstrated that certain vessels (Bell Plain shallow bowls with flat bottoms and outslanting walls, Kimmswick Fabric Impressed and Kimmswick Plain pans, and Bell Plain bowls with effigies) occur in greater quantities at villages than at farmsteads or hamlets. Since shallow bowls with flat bottoms and outslanting walls and pans were probably used to prepare and serve food, the higher percentage of these vessel types at villages of either size suggests that more activities and rituals involving the preparation, serving, and consuming of food (and, perhaps, the entertaining of guests) were conducted at villages than at hamlets or farmsteads (see Pollack and Railey 1987). At the earlier Mississippian Wickliffe site, Wesler (1992, 2001) observed a decrease in jars and pans and a corresponding increase in bowls and plates from early (A.D. 1100–1200) to late Wickliffe (A.D. 1250–

Table 6.12. Jar Appendages Associated with Each Settlement Type.

| Appendage Type | Farmsteads | | Hamlets | | Sm Village | | L Village | |
|---|---|---|---|---|---|---|---|---|
| Nodes | | | | | | | | |
| Node | 2 | 4.9% | 4 | 8.7% | 2 | 4.7% | 104 | 15.6% |
| Paired or Multiple | 3 | 7.3% | | | 2 | 4.7% | 39 | 5.9% |
| Dimpled | | | 2 | 4.3% | | | 11 | 1.7% |
| Notched or Beaded Strip | | | | | | | | |
| Notched Horizontal | 7 | 17.1% | 20 | 43.5% | 5 | 11.6% | 15 | 2.3% |
| Plain Horizontal | | | | | | | 5 | 0.8% |
| Notched/Grooved Vertical | | | 1 | 2.2% | | | 2 | 0.3% |
| Plain Vertical | | | | | | | 5 | 0.8% |
| Lugs | | | | | | | | |
| Plain | 3 | 7.3% | 9 | 19.6% | 19 | 44.2% | 317 | 47.7% |
| Bifurcated | 5 | 12.2% | 1 | 2.2% | 3 | 7.0% | 101 | 15.2% |
| Paired or Multiple | 1 | 2.4% | | | 3 | 7.0% | 28 | 4.2% |
| Incised | 2 | 4.9% | | | | | | |
| Notched/Punctation | | | | | 1 | 2.3% | | |
| Notched | 18 | 43.9% | 7 | 15.2% | 8 | 18.6% | 28 | 4.2% |
| Effigy | | | 2 | 4.3% | | | 10 | 1.5% |
| Total | 41 | 100% | 46 | 100% | 43 | 100% | 665 | 100% |

1350). He suggested that, through time, households may have required a more varied set of vessels or that the increase in bowls and plates could reflect changes in food preparation techniques. It is also possible that the trends observed by Wesler reflect the Wickliffe elite's rise to prominence in the region of the confluence of the Ohio and Mississippi rivers. Perhaps during early and middle Wickliffe times, this settlement was not a regional center, but by late Wickliffe times it may have become one, requiring more entertaining of visitors or the more frequent performance of rituals that required different types of serving vessels.

In comparison to the late Wickliffe assemblage, Caborn-Welborn village ceramic collections contain fewer plates, bottles, and funnels but more bowls and pans. These differences suggest that at Caborn-Welborn villages, shallow bowls with outslanting walls and pans may have been used instead of plates. The higher percentage of bottles at Wickliffe is related to a greater use of hooded bottles, which are not very common on Caborn-Welborn sites.

Greater use of pans and bowls at Caborn-Welborn villages relative to farmsteads and hamlets, however, is not correlated with an increase in the number of bottles. In fact, bottles tend to account for a relatively consistent portion of the assemblage of each settlement type. However, there is greater diversity of bottle types at large villages. If wide-mouthed bottles were primarily used for storage, and long-necked and hooded examples were used to serve liquids, then the higher frequency of occurrence of the latter at large villages (Table 6.9) points to a greater emphasis on serving food at villages in larger quantities to more people during more diverse activities and rituals than at hamlets and farmsteads. This parallels the interpretation discussed for frequency patterns for shallow bowls and pans.

The largest jars on Caborn-Welborn sites, which usually lack handles and have opposing lugs, appear to have been storage vessels. If storage of foodstuffs was important to all households, then large storage jars should be present within the ceramic assemblages from sites of all sizes—exactly what one sees within the Caborn-Welborn region.

If the increased use of certain types of vessels at villages was owing, in part, to activities that involved ritual feasts organized by Caborn-Welborn leaders (which has been documented by Hayden 1995 as an avenue aspiring elites pursued in their quest for power), one might expect overall jar size from villages to be larger or a higher percentage of larger jars to be present at villages than at farmsteads or hamlets (Blitz 1993a, 1993b). However, there is no evidence to support this suggestion, since a similar range of jar sizes appears to be present at all settlement types. In the future, it may be possible to identify patterns within Caborn-Welborn villages that reflect ritual feasts sponsored by Caborn-Welborn leaders, but that will require greater quantities of Mississippi Plain and Caborn-Welborn Decorated jar rims from a variety of well-defined contexts within a small or large Caborn-Welborn village than are currently available.

These analyses documented that hamlets and farmsteads have very similar ceramic assemblages, suggesting that a similar range of activities involving the use of ceramic vessels took place at these sites. These comparisons also indicated that hamlets and farmsteads share more in common with each other than they do with villages and that they played similar roles within the Caborn-Welborn settlement system. As such, hamlets may be viewed as larger versions of farmsteads.

These comparisons also showed that small and large villages share more in common with each other than with the smaller settlements. The characteristics of ceramic assemblages from villages suggest that a similar, but, in comparison to farmsteads and hamlets, a wider range of activities involving ceramics was carried out at these site types. Despite the inability to document ritual feasting conclusively, important Caborn-Welborn ceremonies and rituals would have been carried out at the small and large villages. The close physical proximity of hamlets and farmsteads to these settlements and the presence of plazas at villages (see chapter 4) suggest that residents of hamlets and farmsteads may have visited the villages and participated in these subarea or region-wide activities. Such events would have served to reinforce cultural beliefs and strengthen intercommunity relationships. Community-wide or subarea-wide events sponsored by village leaders would have been a means to reaffirm their status and prestige within Caborn-Welborn society. Coupled with the spatial distribution of settlements described in chapter 4, which points to a clustering of farmsteads and hamlets in the vicinity of villages, these functional differences show the interrelatedness of settlements within each subarea and how these different types of settlements functioned within the Caborn-Welborn settlement hierarchy. Based on these patterns, it appears that Caborn-Welborn villages, both large and small, may have taken on many of the social, political, and economic roles that, prior to the collapse of the Angel chiefdom, had been performed at the Angel site.

## SUMMARY

In this chapter, Caborn-Welborn site ceramic data were examined for the information they contained regarding how the Caborn-Welborn population reconstructed social, political, and economic relationships following the collapse of the Angel chiefdom. Particular attention was paid to identifying whether intraregional variation in ceramic types, ceramic decoration, and the mortuary use of ceramic vessels could be identified that might reflect cultural or ethnic differences within the Caborn-Welborn region and how the functions of the different settlement types varied across the region at large.

The comparisons by subareas of ceramic types and attributes documented east-west spatial variation in the distribution of several ceramic characteristics, particularly the kind of decoration placed on Caborn-Welborn Decorated jar shoulders (punctation as fill preferred in the east and lines as fill in the west) and the kind of decorated ceramic jars interred with the dead (Caborn-Welborn Decorated in the east and central Mississippi valley types in the west). These patterns parallel the geographical differences observed in the location of cemeteries across the Caborn-Welborn region. In the eastern subarea, upstream from Slack Farm, within-community cemeteries are the norm, but in the western subarea, downstream from Slack Farm, the dead were placed in blufftop cemeteries removed from settlements. In the central subarea, both burial practices were identified, with most individuals being interred within villages.

These patterns illustrate that cultural differences existed within the Caborn-Welborn region that could reflect the presence of at least two Mississippian groups that pursued slightly different cultural traditions. If this was the case, then it is possible that, following the collapse of the Angel chiefdom and the establishment of several Caborn-Welborn villages near the mouth of the Wabash River, households of former downstream lower Ohio valley chiefdoms migrated to the western portion of the Caborn-Welborn region.

The intraregional distribution of ceramic types and attributes within the Caborn-Welborn region suggests that individuals or households living in certain subareas interacted socially and economically with particular nonlocal groups more frequently than others. Not surprisingly, much of the observed variation is related to the local geography. Villages that appear to have had the most social and economic interaction with the central Mississippi valley are located in the western or central subarea. The eastern subarea villages may have had more interaction with Mississippian groups in eastern Tennessee, but this is difficult to document based on the Caborn-Welborn archaeological record. Villages in the central and eastern subareas appear to have had more interaction with more northerly Oneota groups than Caborn-Welborn settlements located in the western subarea.

These analyses also identified variation in the composition of ceramic vessel form assemblages associated with the four Caborn-Welborn habitation types. Results showed that large and small villages tend to have similar ceramic assemblages, and hamlets and farmsteads tend to have similar ceramic assemblages. There were important differences between these two groups, particularly the greater frequency of occurrence at villages of pans, shallow bowls with outslanting walls and flat bottoms, and hemispherical bowls with lugs. These ceramic differences suggest that more activities involving the preparation, serving, and consuming of food were undertaken at the larger communities. Whether this involved entertaining village neighbors or families from nearby hamlets or farmsteads is not known.

The proximity of hamlets and farmsteads to a large or small village, as well as the internal structure of villages (i.e., the presence of plazas) points to social, political, and economic linkages among nearby settlements. In general, the observed patterns point to the continued presence of a settlement hierarchy within the Caborn-Welborn region. However, the Caborn-Welborn settlement hierarchy was different from the earlier Angel settlement hierarchy, with the small or large villages taking on many of the social, political, and economic roles that had once been concentrated at a single mound center.

The patterns identified as a result of the analyses discussed provide the data needed to begin to interpret how the Caborn-Welborn population reconstructed social, political, and economic relationships following the collapse of the Angel chiefdom. This topic is considered at length in the next chapter.

# 7 Interpretations and Conclusions

Understanding chiefdom collapse, the consequences of collapse, and the processes by which individual societies reconstruct political, economic, and social relationships following the demise of a complex society have long been of interest to archaeologists (Anderson 1990; Cowgill 1979; Earle 1991; Tainter 1988; Yoffee and Cowgill 1995). However, while the collapse of these kinds of societies has been well documented, researchers often have encountered difficulty determining the response of particular populations. Much of the problem is related to population dispersal and a decline in population density, which often accompany the collapse of a complex society (Anderson 1990; Butler 1991; Muller 1986; Tainter 1988). Dispersed populations are less visible and are often difficult to document in the archaeological record.

This is precisely the situation that has hampered efforts by archaeologists to determine how regional populations responded to the widespread late fourteenth/early fifteenth century collapse of Mississippian chiefdoms in the lower Ohio and upper central Mississippi valleys (Bareis and Porter 1984; Butler 1991; Lewis 1990; McNutt 1996; Milner 1990; Morse and Morse 1983; Muller 1986; Williams 1990). Throughout this area, which has been referred to as the "Vacant Quarter" (Williams 1990) (Figure 1.1), the collapse of Mississippian chiefdoms led to the abandonment of regional mound centers and their associated villages, hamlets, and farmsteads, as local populations either dispersed to widely scattered and smaller settlements or relocated to other regions (Butler 1991; Muller 1986). Throughout the Vacant Quarter, a decline in population density was accompanied by a concomitant reduction in extra-regional interaction.

In the Ohio River/Wabash River confluence area, which is situated near the northern edge of the Vacant Quarter, the Angel collapse represents an exception to this pattern. Although the Angel site and associated small villages, hamlets, and farmsteads were abandoned after the Angel chiefdom's collapse, archaeological manifestations that postdate the demise of this chiefdom are clearly identifiable in the archaeological record of the Ohio River/Wabash River confluence (Green and Munson 1978; Munson 2000; Pollack and Munson 2003). Centered slightly downstream from Angel, at the mouth of the Wabash River, at least 80 Caborn-Welborn sites have been recorded within an area approximately 60 km long. Within this region, Caborn-Welborn settlements are associated with one of three subareas (eastern, central, and western), and within each subarea, farmsteads and hamlets tend to be located near small or large villages (Figure 4.15).

The regional archaeological database does not provide any evidence for population dispersal or a decline in population density after ca. A.D. 1400. Instead, population continuity can be documented as illustrated by similarities in settlement location, subsistence patterns, and ceramic vessel forms and appendages between Caborn-Welborn phase sites (A.D. 1400–1700) and those of the preceding Angel phase (A.D. 1000–1400) (Green 1977; Green and Munson 1978; Pollack 1998). Nevertheless, Caborn-Welborn culture is clearly different from that of Angel, as evidenced by changes in the regional settlement system and in ceramic decoration and by increased involvement in intersocietal exchange and interaction networks as reflected by increased access to nonlocal goods. It is both the continuities and the differences in Caborn-Welborn social, political, and economic organization relative to the preceding Angel chiefdom that provide archaeologists with an opportunity to examine how one regional population responded to the collapse of a Mississippian chiefdom. In order to begin to understand these responses better, this study (1) identified the salient characteristics of Caborn-Welborn ceramics and settlement patterns; (2) developed an internal Caborn-Welborn chronological sequence; and (3) examined the spatial distribution of ceramics (attributes and vessel forms) and site types for the clues they could provide regarding the nature of political, economic, and social linkages between subareas of the Caborn-Welborn region and with groups outside the lower Ohio valley.

In the remainder of this chapter, an overview of the internal Caborn-Welborn chronology is presented, followed by an examination of how Caborn-Welborn potters used and reinterpreted earlier Mississippian and contemporary Oneota design motifs, and of the role that Caborn-Welborn leaders' participation in intersocietal exchange and interaction networks may have played in sustaining these leaders. Caborn-Welborn sociopolitical organization is then examined, and it is suggested that Caborn-Welborn should be considered a small riverine confederacy rather than a simple or group-oriented chiefdom, even though it retained some structural elements of the earlier Angel chiefdom.

## CABORN-WELBORN INTERNAL CHRONOLOGICAL SEQUENCE

In order to identify the Caborn-Welborn response to the collapse of the Angel chiefdom, the development of Caborn-Welborn society needed to be more clearly understood. Therefore, as part of this study, an internal Caborn-Welborn chronological sequence was created. It consists of three subdivisions:

early (A.D. 1400–1450), middle (A.D. 1450–1600), and late (A.D. 1600–1700) (see Table 5.3). In the following section, these temporal units will be discussed with respect to characteristics of site types, material culture, and evidence of participation in extraregional interaction networks.

## Early Caborn-Welborn Subdivision (A.D. 1400–1450)

The late fourteenth/early fifteenth century marks the end of most of the lower Ohio valley Mississippian chiefdoms, as well as those situated in the upper central Mississippi valley (Muller 1986; Williams 1990). The establishment of the first Caborn-Welborn communities in the fifteenth century thus coincides with the widespread collapse of Mississippian chiefdoms throughout the lower Ohio valley.

By the late fourteenth century in the Ohio-Wabash River confluence region, the power and prestige of the Angel elite may have been on the wane (Clay 1997; Green 1977; Green and Munson 1978; Hilgeman 1992; Muller 1986). As competing elites and their followers deserted the Angel chiefdom, some households apparently were attracted to the broad floodplain ridges located near the mouth of the Wabash River in what is now Kentucky, Indiana, and Illinois. Available evidence does not suggest that the collapse of the Angel chiefdom was a sudden and catastrophic event that would have resulted in the simultaneous abandonment of all Angel settlements. Therefore, it is likely that some early Caborn-Welborn villages are contemporary with the latest Angel settlements (although confirmation of such temporal overlap must await the refinement of the local chronological sequence).

All of the sites assigned to the early Caborn-Welborn subdivision are small villages (Gough and Welborn) or large ones (Slack Farm, Murphy, and Hovey Lake) located within a 13 km long area in the central subarea. Of these, Slack Farm, Welborn, and Murphy are located near the mouth of the Wabash River within 3 km of each other. These settlements tend to be situated on terraces located near sloughs or swampy areas and associated with loamy, well-drained floodplain soils (Munson 1995). These characteristics suggest that Caborn-Welborn households preferred localities with fertile, easily worked soils that also provided access to the animal and plant resources of nearby sloughs, swamps, and the Ohio River.

Early Caborn-Welborn villages may have consisted of several residential areas, each having its own cemetery. These residential/cemetery areas often were organized around a central plaza. Residential areas, consisting of structures, large underground storage facilities (about 2 m in diameter and 2 m in depth), and associated domestic activity areas, were located adjacent to a cemetery.

That no early Caborn-Welborn farmsteads or hamlets have been identified points to population aggregation within a few settlements immediately following the collapse of the Angel polity. However, caution should be used in interpreting this pattern. Early Caborn-Welborn sites are difficult to recognize based solely on small surface-collected samples. Thus, the absence of small early Caborn-Welborn settlements may be more of a classification problem than a reflection of the archaeological record. Only after several farmsteads and hamlets have been excavated will it be possible to resolve this issue.

In contrast to the ceramic assemblages from later Caborn-Welborn sites, those from early Caborn-Welborn sites are characterized by a low percentage of Caborn-Welborn Decorated jars. Shoulder decorations on these jars include broad trailed lines. Assemblages also tend to have a high percentage of a particular form of bowl (shallow bowls with outslanting walls, flat bottoms, and castellated rims) and Kimmswick Fabric Impressed pans. Most early Caborn-Welborn pans have an exterior lip protrusion. Ceramic assemblages from sites assigned to the early subdivision also tend to have a low percentage of hemispherical bowls with notched or beaded rimstrips relative to later Caborn-Welborn sites.

Caborn-Welborn interaction with groups outside the lower Ohio valley appears to have been an important component of economic and political relationships throughout the sequence. Interaction with Oneota groups located north of the Ohio valley is represented by the presence of Oneota-like vessels, triangular endscrapers, catlinite pipes, and copper artifacts. The characteristics of the Oneota-like jars, which primarily have been found at Slack Farm—interior lip notching and trailed chevrons, notched loop handles, a sharply angled rim/neck juncture, and wide trailed designs (Figures 3.17–20)—indicate that they are contemporary with pre–A.D. 1450 Oneota ceramics from other regions (Brown et al. 1990). Interaction with central Mississippi valley groups is reflected by the presence of ceramic types, such as Parkin Punctate, Walls Engraved, Campbell Punctate, Campbell Incised, Barton Incised, and Kent Incised–like, and Nodena points.

Continuity in population and certain cultural traditions from the preceding Angel chiefdom, including settlement location, subsistence patterns, and material culture, especially ceramic vessel forms and appendages (Green 1977; Green and Munson 1978), can be documented during the early Caborn-Welborn subdivision. Both Angel and Caborn-Welborn settlements tend to be located on floodplain levees or nearby terraces, and subsistence patterns were geared toward the highly fertile soils of the Ohio River floodplain. Maize accounts for a substantial portion of both the Angel and Caborn-Welborn diet, and native cultigens and nuts also were important sources of food (Edging 1995; Rossen 1995). However, carbon isotope data suggest that maize may have contributed slightly less to the diet of Caborn-Welborn households than to that of Angel households, and beans were an important addition to the Caborn-Welborn diet. Angel and Caborn-Welborn faunal exploitation patterns were the same, geared to the hunting of deer, small mammals, and birds, supplemented by fish and reptiles (Garmiewicz 2000; Terry Martin, personal communication 1997). Caborn-Welborn floral and faunal data indicate that subsistence patterns remained relatively stable throughout the sequence.

Vessel and appendage forms and some decorated ceramic types also point to continuity. For instance, shallow bowls with outslanting walls and flat bottoms (deep rim plates), some with castellations, and hemispherical bowls with notched or beaded rimstrips are found in both Angel and Caborn-Welborn ceramic assemblages, and thin strap handles on jars and bifurcated and single jar lugs also are similar. Several decorated ceramic types reflect continuity with Angel as well as other lower Ohio valley Mississippian groups pre–A.D. 1400. These include Old Town Red, O'Byam Incised/Engraved, Mound Place Incised, Angel/Kincaid Negative Painted, Matthews Incised, and Beckwith Incised.

Along with these similarities, there are important differences in settlement pattern and material culture that distinguish early Caborn-Welborn subdivision sites from earlier Angel sites. Some of these differences are related to changes in sociopolitical organization, while others indicate that new extra-regional relationships were developing. Some simply reflect temporally diagnostic stylistic trends in material culture.

The absence of an administrative mound center similar to that of the Angel site and an increase in Caborn-Welborn village size relative to Angel villages are two important characteristics of the Caborn-Welborn settlement pattern (it should be noted that none of the large Caborn-Welborn villages approach the size of Angel). Together these two attributes suggest that Caborn-Welborn sociopolitical organization was somewhat different from that of the earlier Angel chiefdom. As will be discussed, the absence of a regional administrative center provides one line of evidence to suggest that Caborn-Welborn sociopolitical organization was not characterized by the same degree of political centralization as Angel. An increase in village size relative to earlier Angel villages suggests that Caborn-Welborn leaders may have assumed many of the roles formerly held by the Angel elite. If this was the case, then the increase in Caborn-Welborn village size may reflect a shift from a centralized elite that resided at the Angel site to decentralized lineage heads that resided at one of several villages within the central subarea.

Several characteristics of early Caborn-Welborn material culture serve to distinguish sites assigned to this temporal subdivision from earlier Angel sites. Despite the low frequency of Caborn-Welborn Decorated ceramics, their presence and that of triangular endscrapers are clear horizon markers for the Caborn-Welborn phase. These materials are not found on earlier Angel phase sites. Oneota-like jars, catlinite disk pipes, and Nodena points also are present in early Caborn-Welborn subdivision collections but not in those of Angel phase sites. They reflect changes in extraregional interaction relative to the Angel phase. Temporally stylistic ceramic trends that can be used to distinguish early Caborn-Welborn from Angel sites include increases in the use of shallow bowls with flat bottoms and castellated rims and of hemispherical bowls with notched or beaded rimstrips and a decrease in the thickness of strap handles.

Perhaps the most striking difference between Angel and Caborn-Welborn material culture is how the sun symbol motif is executed and where it is placed on Caborn-Welborn vessels. During the Angel phase, this symbol was a negative painted design often placed on the interior of plates, but by the early Caborn-Welborn subdivision, trailing, incising, and punctating were the techniques used to create this design on jar shoulders. Despite the differences in execution and vessel association, the sun symbol design may still have conveyed similar messages within both societies.

## Middle Caborn-Welborn Subdivision (A.D. 1450–1600)

While early Caborn-Welborn subdivision sites are known only from a 13 km long area within the central subarea, middle Caborn-Welborn subdivision sites are present throughout the 60 km long Caborn-Welborn region. If the absence of early Caborn-Welborn settlements in the eastern and western subareas is not a reflection of sampling bias or a lack of chronological control, then the observed distribution of middle Caborn-Welborn settlements points to an expansion ca. A.D. 1450 of Caborn-Welborn settlements upstream into a portion of the territory encompassed by the earlier Angel chiefdom and downstream from the mouth of the Wabash River into an area that does not appear to have been settled by earlier Mississippian chiefdoms. Although they are found over a larger area than sites assigned to the early Caborn-Welborn subdivision, no middle Caborn-Welborn subdivision settlements have been documented east of Cypress Bottoms near Geneva, Kentucky, or west of the Saline River in southern Illinois.

The expansion of Caborn-Welborn settlements into the eastern and western subareas at the beginning of the middle subdivision could have been the result of intervillage competition and factionalism. It also could have been because of an increase in population as a result of natural growth or possibly the incorporation within Caborn-Welborn society of segments of other lower Ohio valley chiefdoms that moved to the mouth of the Wabash region following the collapse of their respective chiefdoms (see below). The more widespread distribution of middle subdivision Caborn-Welborn settlements also may indicate that after A.D. 1450, the remnants of the earlier Angel chiefdom and surrounding Mississippian polities no longer constituted much of an external threat.

A settlement hierarchy, consisting of villages, hamlets, and farmsteads, is clearly evident by the middle Caborn-Welborn subdivision (Green 1977; Green and Munson 1978). Most middle subdivision sites are hamlets or farmsteads. Unlike earlier villages, which tend to be associated with terraces, middle Caborn-Welborn hamlets and farmsteads tend to be associated with floodplain levees located near sloughs or swampy areas and are associated with loamy, well-drained floodplain soils. The community organization pattern suggested by the distribution of materials at the Caborn site and many other middle Caborn-Welborn hamlets and farmsteads is of a linear arrangement of structures, with storage areas located near each structure.

Middle subdivision villages are located in similar locales as earlier Caborn-Welborn villages. While little is known about their internal organization (few have been excavated by professional archaeologists), they may have been organized in a manner similar to early Caborn-Welborn villages, and most have associated plaza/courtyard areas. Hamlets and villages in the central and eastern subareas tend to have associated cemeteries, but villages in the western subarea lack well-defined, within-site cemeteries. In that subarea, cemeteries are located on the bluffs overlooking Caborn-Welborn settlements.

Middle subdivision site ceramic assemblages are distinguished from those of earlier Caborn-Welborn sites by an increase in Caborn-Welborn Decorated. At some sites, this type accounts for more than 50 percent of the analyzed sherds. This subdivision also is characterized by a decrease in Kimmswick Fabric Impressed pans, an increase in Kimmswick Plain pans, and an increase in hemispherical bowls with notched or beaded rimstrips.

Interaction with Oneota groups north of the Ohio valley continues and is characterized by changes in decoration on Caborn-Welborn Decorated vessels (a decrease in line width and a greater use of punctation as fill) that parallels changes in jar decoration documented at Oneota sites (Michalik and Brown 1990) and by the incorporation within the Caborn-Welborn decorative tradition of Oneota motifs, such as the thunderbird or hawk. Continued interaction with Mississippian groups in the central Mississippi valley is reflected by the presence of central Mississippi valley types, such as Parkin Punctate, Campbell Punctate, and Walls Engraved, that are also found at late Angel sites, and by the introduction of new ceramic types and attributes: Campbell Applique jars (Mainfort 1996); jars with the "Memphis Rim Mode" (House 1991, 1993); arcaded jars (ones with a large number of handles) (Mainfort 1996; O'Brien 1994); and the incorporation of vertical notched strips within Caborn-Welborn shoulder designs.

Intraregional cultural differences appear in the Caborn-Welborn region by at least the beginning of the middle subdivision (A.D. 1450), as evidenced by the spatial distribution of particular attributes of Caborn-Welborn Decorated jar shoulder decorations, the location of cemeteries, and the kinds of jars buried with the dead in these cemeteries. In the eastern subarea, Caborn-Welborn

Decorated jar shoulder decoration is characterized by a greater use of punctations to fill descending triangular areas. Caborn-Welborn Decorated jars were often placed with the dead, who were interred in cemeteries located within communities. In the central and western subareas, however, lines continued to be used as fill more often than punctations. In addition, Caborn-Welborn Decorated jars were rarely interred with the dead. When decorated jars were placed with the dead, they were primarily central Mississippi valley types, such as Parkin Punctate, Campbell Punctate, and Campbell Applique. In the western subarea, burials were primarily placed in cemeteries located on the bluffs overlooking the Ohio River valley, while in the central subarea, as in the eastern, the primary mode of burial was within the community (at the central subarea Slack Farm site, both types of burial treatment were documented).

## Late Caborn-Welborn Subdivision (A.D. 1600–1700)

Only a few sites (n = 4) have components that could be assigned to this subdivision, primarily because late subdivision components are defined by the presence of historic trade goods (ornaments made from reworked European copper and brass kettle parts and glass trade beads). Occupation of some middle Caborn-Welborn sites may have extended into this subdivision, but owing to the lack of recovery of historic trade goods, they were not assigned to this subdivision.

Many middle Caborn-Welborn subdivision characteristics continue into the late Caborn-Welborn subdivision (burial practices, community patterns, and intersubarea differences). As with the middle Caborn-Welborn subdivision, post–A.D. 1600 sites are present throughout the Caborn-Welborn region and are located in similar environmental settings as their predecessors. A settlement hierarchy also is probably present. Of the sites with late subdivision components, one is a large village (Slack Farm), one is a small village (Blackburn), and one is a farmstead (Cummings). The late Caborn-Welborn subdivision component at the Murphy site may be a farmstead or a hamlet.

While ceramic trends initiated in the middle subdivision continue, during the late subdivision there may have been a decline in Caborn-Welborn Decorated jar shoulder decoration, as some very late sites (e.g., Cummings) contain a low percentage of Caborn-Welborn Decorated sherds. A preference for Kimmswick Plain pans continues, with most lacking the exterior protrusion associated with earlier pans. Handles continue to become less functional and more decorative.

Historic trade goods recovered from Caborn-Welborn sites primarily consist of reworked copper and brass objects, such as kettles. Among these are beads, tubes, bracelets, and spirals. Glass beads also have been recovered from these sites.

Along with historic trade goods, indirect contact with Europeans may have brought new diseases to the Caborn-Welborn region (Galloway 1994; Knight 1994; Muller 1986; Pollack and Henderson 1992a; Smith 1987). At present, however, it is difficult to measure the impact that these diseases may have had. Elsewhere, they are known to have severely decimated Native American populations (Dobyns 1983; Ramenofsky 1987). It is possible that the large number of individuals interred within some Caborn-Welborn cemeteries died from European diseases against which the local population had no immunity. However, there is little or no clear evidence for this in the form of mass graves, changes in demographic profiles, or pathologies observed in the human remains from the Slack Farm site (Powell et al. 1996). The orderliness of the Slack Farm cemeteries and the lack of intrusive graves also argue against the large size of these cemeteries being a product of a catastrophic disease event.

Based on available evidence, it also is difficult to measure the impact that indirect contact with Euro-Americans may have had on Caborn-Welborn society. But sometime prior to the Euro-American settlement of the Ohio valley in the late eighteenth century, the Caborn-Welborn population appears to have abandoned its homeland. At present, it is not known if these people relocated to another region where they continued to be a viable group, or if segments of the Caborn-Welborn population moved to different regions where they were assimilated into other groups.

## Summary

Diachronic trends in Caborn-Welborn material culture and settlement patterns reflect how the Caborn-Welborn population organized and maintained itself following the collapse of the Angel chiefdom. These trends illustrate that, as this population reconstructed social, political, and economic relationships, some aspects of earlier Angel society continued with little or no change, while others were reshaped as the Caborn-Welborn population constructed its own identity and subsequent history.

Throughout the Caborn-Welborn sequence, subsistence practices remained fairly constant, and settlements continued to be associated with floodplain environments. The settlement system retained some elements of the earlier Angel hierarchical structure, but no regional mound center was ever established in the Caborn-Welborn region. Economically, Caborn-Welborn groups developed new extraregional exchange relationships with Oneota tribal societies, but they continued to maintain earlier interaction networks with other Mississippian groups. Though the Caborn-Welborn population apparently retained some of the Mississippian rituals of their ancestors, these earlier rituals may have been reinterpreted, as they combined older elements with those incorporated as a result of new extraregional contacts.

Social boundaries that formerly had served to distinguish the elite from others also were different within Caborn-Welborn society. In other words, a restructuring of leadership roles followed the collapse of the Angel chiefdom. As these social boundaries were redefined, aspiring Caborn-Welborn elites would have competed for power in a political environment that was different from that of Angel.

The absence of a Caborn-Welborn regional mound center, coupled with an increase in village size, suggests that leaders of large Caborn-Welborn villages may have assumed many of the roles formerly held by the Angel elite. If this was the case, then as Caborn-Welborn society was developing, ca. A.D. 1400, there may have been a shift from a centralized elite, which had resided at the Angel site, to decentralized lineage heads who resided at one of several small or large villages within the central Caborn-Welborn subarea. These lineage heads may have competed with each other for power and prestige within Caborn-Welborn society.

To be successful, these aspiring Caborn-Welborn elites (lineage heads) would have needed to exert some measure of influence over external as well as internal relationships (Feinman 1995; Spencer 1993, 1994), for it is by controlling both of these domains that elites are able to attain and hold on to power. As Angel collapsed and Caborn-Welborn society formed, aspiring elites may have sought to create a new line(s) of succession and to secure for themselves positions of power and prestige similar to those held by the earlier Angel elite.

## CABORN-WELBORN USE AND REINTERPRETATION OF EARLIER MISSISSIPPIAN AND CONTEMPORARY ONEOTA DESIGN MOTIFS

The widespread collapse of Mississippian chiefdoms throughout the lower Ohio and upper central Mississippi valleys ca. A.D. 1400 may have led to a transformation of many of the chiefly cult institutions that formerly had played important roles in the sanctification of the elite (see Knight 1986:682). This transformation is reflected, in part, by the wide variety of iconography related to the warfare/cosmogony complex of the Southeastern Ceremonial Complex, which often appears as incised or engraved decoration on Walls Engraved ceramics (Knight 1986:682; G. Smith 1990). Caborn-Welborn households may have created their own ritual traditions by reinterpreting early Mississippian rituals and beliefs and incorporating later Mississippian and even Oneota rituals within them. Evidence for this comes from the Caborn-Welborn decorative tradition, which reflects the continued use of earlier Mississippian symbols but which also includes motifs and decorative elements attributable to other late Mississippian groups as well as to Oneota tribal societies.

Within the Caborn-Welborn region, engravings on catlinite disk pipes and on flat pieces of coal, hematite, and slate from Caborn-Welborn sites include Southeastern Ceremonial Cult motifs, such as the weeping eye and thunderbird or bird-man motif (Munson 1997; Pollack and Munson 1998). Other designs are suggestive of a duck with teeth or a snake or are abstract representations of animals. An engraved design on a Walls Engraved bowl from Slack Farm is a portion of a bird with crude talons, similar to those on an engraved bottle from Owl Cave in the western Ozarks and the Craig C bird-man (a Southeastern Ceremonial Cult motif) from Spiro (J. Brown 1989:191, 200; Lawton 1964, cited ibid. 200) (Figure 3.22c).

As discussed, the sun symbol design on Angel Negative Painted plates (Curry 1950; Hilgeman 1992:233–234) also is depicted on Caborn-Welborn Decorated jars. This suggests that these Caborn-Welborn vessels conveyed similar symbolic messages as the Angel plates (Pollack and Munson 1996, 1998; see also Hall 1991; Pauketat and Emerson 1991).

The spatial and contextual distribution of Angel Negative Painted plates at Angel (Hilgeman 1992) and Caborn-Welborn Decorated jars at Caborn-Welborn villages also suggests that these vessels may have served similar purposes. Both types of vessels may, at times, have been used during rituals that involved several households. At Angel, negative painted plates were primarily recovered from pits located near the plaza. This led Hilgeman (1992) to suggest that these vessels were used in conjunction with elite-sponsored rituals that may have been similar to the New Fire and Green Corn ceremonies of Southeastern Historic Indian groups (Swanton 1911, 1946). If this was the case, then it is likely that at those times these vessels were used in public contexts where the designs on them were meant to be seen by others.

The same may have been the case for Caborn-Welborn Decorated jars used at Caborn-Welborn villages. At Slack Farm, these types of jars are more common in pit than house contexts. They also are well represented in a large pit excavated at the Caborn site. Examination of the spatial distribution of surface-collected ceramics from several sites, including Site 11Ga160, Alzey, and Blackburn (see Figures 4.3, 4.6, and 4.8), indicates that Caborn-Welborn Decorated tends to cluster in certain areas of these sites. Whether these surface concentrations of Caborn-Welborn Decorated ceramics correspond to pit or house contexts or other types of activity areas is not presently known, but intrasite variation in the distribution of this ceramic type points to differences in how Caborn-Welborn Decorated ceramic vessels were used and disposed of within these settlements.

The spatial and contextual distribution of Caborn-Welborn Decorated jars suggests that, as with Angel Negative Painted plates, these decorated jars often were used in activities that involved interaction with individuals outside one's immediate household. Perhaps one of these uses was to prepare and serve food at feasts organized by aspiring elites (Hayden 1995). Encoded in the decoration placed on these jars may have been information concerning the social identity of the ritual sponsors and participants (Allen 1988; DeBoer and Moore 1982; Hodder 1978; Kintigh 1985; Wobst 1977).

Caborn-Welborn potters also incorporated selected Oneota motifs and central Mississippi valley ceramic attributes within their ceramic tradition. An important Oneota motif, the hawk or thunderbird, is an easily recognizable design found on Caborn-Welborn ceramics (Figure 3.13). Hall (1991:30) notes that among historic Indian tribes, the thunderbird was associated with the gift of long life. On the other hand, Benn (1989:252) suggests that hawk symbolism was related to warrior themes. In either case, the occurrence of this motif on Caborn-Welborn Decorated jars indicates that Caborn-Welborn potters used and perhaps reinterpretated Oneota-derived designs. Attributes that reflect the incorporation of late Mississippian central Mississippi valley attributes include the placement of vertical applied notched strips and nodes (plain or dimpled) within Caborn-Welborn decorative designs (Figure 3.15). The incorporation of both Oneota and central Mississippi valley decorative attributes and motifs within Caborn-Welborn Decorated designs reflects ongoing interaction between Caborn-Welborn households and groups outside the lower Ohio valley. It also reflects Caborn-Welborn adoption and perhaps reinterpretation of these symbols.

## CABORN-WELBORN EXCHANGE AND INTERACTION NETWORKS

Unlike collapse situations in many regions, where populations became more inward looking, in the aftermath of the collapse of the Angel chiefdom the Caborn-Welborn population appears to have become more outward looking. They established new relationships with Oneota groups living to the north of the Ohio valley and maintained and reaffirmed relationships with Mississippian groups situated to the south of the lower Ohio valley. The widespread distribution of nonlocal materials throughout the Caborn-Welborn region suggests that aspiring Caborn-Welborn elites were not able to control or regulate access to these goods to the same extent as had the earlier Angel elite.

### Reorientation and Expansion of Exchange Networks

The fifteenth century is marked by an increase in the long-distance exchange of goods and interaction among a diverse set of late prehistoric societies (Hall 1991). Research in several regions of the Midwest and the East (Drooker 1997; Hall 1991; Henderson et al. 1992; Pollack and Henderson 1992a, 1992b, 2000) has shown that after A.D. 1400, there was increased participation on the part of tribal societies in intersocietal exchange networks that previously had been the domain of Mississippian elites. The widespread collapse of pre–A.D. 1400

Mississippian chiefdoms in the lower Ohio and central Mississippi valleys appears to have led to, permitted, or encouraged an expansion of Mississippian interaction networks to include these groups (Pollack and Henderson 1992a, 1992b; Pollack et al. 2002).

The inclusion of these tribal societies may have been initiated by Mississippian elites in eastern Tennessee, the central Mississippi valley, or other regions where chiefdoms had not collapsed, as well as by aspiring Caborn-Welborn elites seeking to establish new exchange relationships in order to maintain access to the nonlocal goods and information they needed to validate their positions within their respective societies. Leaders of Fort Ancient and Oneota groups situated on the periphery of these Mississippian chiefdoms may have viewed participation in these expanded exchange networks as a way to enhance prestige within their own societies (see Schortman and Urban 1992).

In examining Caborn-Welborn extraregional relationships, therefore, it is important to keep in mind that the Caborn-Welborn population was part of an extensive and dynamic network of interactors whose transactions not only linked their respective societies but also may have affected their sociopolitical developments (Schortman and Urban 1992:238). Individuals who participated in these networks included Mississippian elites, aspiring Caborn-Welborn elites (lineage heads), and leaders of more egalitarian groups, each of whom would have had different goals and reasons for participating in these transactions. The extent to which these extraregional contacts were important to the sociopolitical complexity of these societies may have depended, in part, on the nature of the interaction, the volume and types of goods exchanged, and the ability of group leaders to use intersocietal contacts to gain privileged access to the loyalty and labor of their adherents (Schortman and Urban 1992:245).

The geographic location of the Caborn-Welborn homeland may have contributed to the successful participation of Caborn-Welborn leaders in these long-distance exchange networks. It is possible that the region's location along the periphery of both the Mississippian and Oneota interaction spheres (Hall 1991) allowed some members of Caborn-Welborn society to function as "middlemen" in the long-distance movement of goods between Mississippian polities to the south and Oneota tribal groups to the north. These individuals may have been able to control or regulate the movement of valued goods through their territory and to use this to their political advantage (Schortman and Urban 1992:242).

Although there is good evidence to support Caborn-Welborn interaction with groups living to the north and south of the lower Ohio valley, there is little evidence to suggest interaction between Caborn-Welborn people and Fort Ancient groups living to the east and upstream in the middle Ohio valley. Both Caborn-Welborn and Fort Ancient groups appear to have had access to similar nonlocal materials, such as catlinite disk pipes and marine shell gorgets, and in both areas triangular endscrapers, a more northerly artifact type, are diagnostic of post–A.D. 1400 components. After A.D. 1600, similar types of historic trade goods, such as copper and brass spirals and tubes, have been recovered from both regions. Though the historic trade goods recovered from Caborn-Welborn sites could have made their way into the lower Ohio valley through exchange relationships with Fort Ancient groups, it is also quite possible that Caborn-Welborn and Fort Ancient people obtained these materials directly from northern tribal groups with whom they had exchange relationships. Though Drooker (1997:332) views the recovery of similar types of nonlocal goods from Caborn-Welborn and Fort Ancient sites as representing interaction between these two areas, there is little evidence in the archaeological record of the lower or middle Ohio valleys that supports this suggestion. For instance, Caborn-Welborn Decorated jars have not been found in the Fort Ancient area, nor have Fort Ancient diagnostics been recovered from Caborn-Welborn sites. At present, the best explanation is that both Caborn-Welborn and Fort Ancient groups interacted with groups living to the north and south of the Ohio valley but had limited interaction with each other.

Following the collapse of the Angel chiefdom, aspiring Caborn-Welborn elites or "aggrandizers" (Clark and Blake 1994; Hayden 1995) appear to have been able to keep former Angel households from dispersing, for Caborn-Welborn villages appear in the central subarea as the Angel chiefdom was collapsing or slightly afterward. One of the ways these aspiring elites may have accomplished this was by retaining the loyalty of a large number of kinsmen and other families through their continued and perhaps increased participation in existing intersocietal exchange networks and interaction spheres and by seeking out and establishing new exchange relationships.

After the collapse of Angel, aspiring Caborn-Welborn elites maintained exchange relationships with other Mississippian societies living in the central Mississippi valley that had been initiated toward the end of the Angel phase. Evidence of continued interaction with Mississippian groups situated in the central Mississippi valley is reflected by the presence of Nodena projectile points and ceramic types such as Parkin Punctate, Campbell Punctate, Campbell Incised, Campbell Applique, Kent Incised–Like, Walls Engraved, and Ranch Incised–Like within site assemblages. Interaction with this region also is reflected by jars that have a large number of (arcaded) handles (Mainfort 1996; O'Brien 1994) and vessels that exhibit the Memphis Rim Mode. Extraregional interaction with Mississippian groups to the southeast of the Ohio valley is not as easy to recognize, but it may have occurred. Marine shell objects, such as those found at Slack Farm and Murphy, could have been obtained from Mississippian groups living either to the southwest or the southeast of the lower Ohio valley.

There also is good evidence to suggest that new exchange relationships were established with Oneota tribal societies living to the north of the lower Ohio valley. Objects that reflect this interaction include catlinite disk pipes and pendants; copper snakes and beads; triangular endscrapers; Oneota-like ceramics; and the incorporation of Oneota motifs within Caborn-Welborn decorative designs. Aspiring Caborn-Welborn elites may have developed these new long-distance exchange relations as they searched for ways to validate their positions within Caborn-Welborn society or in an attempt to replace exchange partners lost when nearby chiefdoms collapsed.

## Oneota Potters in Caborn-Welborn Villages

The presence of Oneota vessels in Caborn-Welborn village site ceramic assemblages (i.e., at Slack Farm) can provide further insights into the nature of Caborn-Welborn/Oneota interaction. It is likely that most of the Oneota-like jars from Slack Farm, which are distinguished from Caborn-Welborn Decorated and Mississippi Plain jars by their sharply angled rim/neck juncture, notched rectangular loop handles, and interior lip decoration (Figures 3.17–20), were manufactured by Oneota potters (women), since the manufacture of ceramic vessels often requires the acquisition of motor habits that are usually learned during childhood (Arnold 1985, 1989). Trace element analysis of Caborn-Welborn Decorated and Oneota-like jars recovered from Slack Farm indicates that both were manufactured from local clays (Shergur et al. 2003).

At least two explanations can be offered to account for the presence of the Oneota-like vessels in Caborn-Welborn assemblages. These vessels may have been the product of a migration of several Oneota families into the Caborn-Welborn area, with the Oneota-like vessels being produced by Oneota potters living at Caborn-Welborn communities. If this was the case, one would expect that they would primarily have been recovered from just one portion of Slack Farm. Families that arrived together would have tended to place their houses near each other, and newly arriving families would have tended to settle near the initial Oneota households (see Anthony 1990; Kearney 1980; Lee 1966). These households would have discarded broken vessels in trash disposal areas near where they lived. That the Oneota-like jars were found throughout the site (Pollack and Munson 1996) tends to argue against their association with a migration of families into the region.

An alternative explanation is that the Oneota-like ceramic vessels were manufactured by Oneota women residing at Slack Farm, either as captives who were adopted into Caborn-Welborn society or as Oneota brides (i.e., the practice of bride exchange) whose marriages were arranged to formalize community or aspiring elites' exchange relationships. In order to maintain these relationships, it may have been necessary to have a presence within a trading partner's community to safeguard one's economic interests. This could have been accomplished through the relocation of households, marriages, or the adoption of other types of kinship relationships that bound trading partners to each other. As Galloway has noted among groups that have matrilocal residence patterns, bride exchange would potentially create a "situation in which a child still recognized as having the ethnic identity of his mother (and therefore the allied tribe) would grow up and gain rank within another tribe" (1994:408). At present, it is not known whether Caborn-Welborn residential patterns were matrilocal or patrilocal, nor is there any other evidence from Caborn-Welborn sites that can be used to address this question.

The presence of Oneota potters at Slack Farm is most evident at the beginning of the Caborn-Welborn phase, as the vast majority of the Oneota-like vessels from Slack Farm are assignable to the early Caborn-Welborn subdivision. The absence at later Caborn-Welborn sites of vessels that appear to have been manufactured by Oneota potters suggests that by the middle Caborn-Welborn subdivision, the descendants of these potters had adopted Caborn-Welborn techniques for making ceramic vessels. This change would be expected as their descendants were assimilated into Caborn-Welborn society and learned their techniques for manufacturing ceramic vessels. Continued Oneota influence within the Caborn-Welborn region after A.D. 1450 is reflected by the incorporation of Oneota motifs within the Caborn-Welborn ceramic tradition. However, by this time, Oneota potters were no longer residing in Caborn-Welborn villages. Perhaps by the mid-fifteenth century, mechanisms or rituals that did not require an Oneota presence within Caborn-Welborn communities had been adopted.

It is possible that the Calumet Ceremony (Blakeslee 1981), or something similar to it, also may have been a means by which the Caborn-Welborn population and Oneota tribal societies maintained and sustained economic relationships. This ceremony, which allowed often hostile groups to cease hostilities for a short period of time, is believed to have originated in the Oneota homeland. It had spread south and east of the lower Ohio valley by the period of early European contact (Blakeslee 1981; I. Brown 1989; Hall 1991). The smoking of disk pipes with highly decorated stems was an important component of the Calumet Ceremony (Blakeslee 1981). As such, the presence of catlinite and limestone disk pipes, some with engraved zoomorphic figures, at Slack Farm, Murphy, Blackburn, Hovey Lake, and other Caborn-Welborn sites could reflect Caborn-Welborn participation in this ceremony.

## Contextual Association of Materials that Reflect Extraregional Interaction

Differences have been identified in the contextual associations of ceramic vessels that are indicative of Caborn-Welborn extraregional interaction with groups living to the south and north of the lower Ohio valley, suggesting that these vessels may have served different functions within Caborn-Welborn society. For instance, ceramic jars that reflect interaction with central Mississippi valley groups were often interred with the dead, primarily in the central and western subareas. In contrast, Oneota-like jars were not interred with the dead, nor do Caborn-Welborn Decorated jars that incorporate Oneota-like motifs exhibit a greater tendency to be associated with mortuary than nonmortuary contexts.

Identification of these patterns can be used to suggest that ceramic vessels reflecting extraregional interaction may have been used in different contexts. The association of central Mississippi valley types with mortuary contexts reflects a continuation of Caborn-Welborn participation in pan-regional Mississippian religious and ceremonial life. The presence of these vessels in Caborn-Welborn ceramic assemblages also points to continuation and reaffirmation of Caborn-Welborn social and economic links with Mississippian groups living in the central Mississippi valley. In contrast, the primary association of Oneota-like jars and Caborn-Welborn Decorated jars that incorporate Oneota motifs is within domestic contexts. This points to greater use of these vessels in household activities or perhaps in rituals that involved the maintenance of post–A.D. 1400 exchange relationships with groups living to the north of the Ohio valley.

As with ceramic vessels that reflect interaction with the central Mississippi valley, nonceramic objects Caborn-Welborn groups obtained through long-distance exchange networks were often interred with the dead. Most of these objects were items of personal adornment, such as marine shell beads and gorgets and copper beads. Others, such as the copper snake from Hovey Lake, may have been used in certain religious ceremonies. The inclusion of many of these objects in graves indicates that they were valued items, perhaps reflecting that person's status or position within Caborn-Welborn society (cf. O'Shea 1984).

Because nonlocal prestige goods were recovered from sites throughout the Caborn-Welborn region, it appears that a wide range of individuals had access to these materials. Aspiring Caborn-Welborn elites may have redistributed these items in an attempt to gain prestige and attract followers (Clark and Blake 1994; Hayden 1995). The widespread distribution of these nonlocal prestige goods within the region also may indicate that Caborn-Welborn leaders could not control access to these objects to the same extent as had the earlier Angel elite. This change reflects the decentralization of political power that followed the collapse of the Angel chiefdom. It also may be attributable to the fact that Caborn-Welborn exchange relationships were often with members of more egalitarian tribal societies. In developing exchange relationships with Oneota tribal groups, aspiring Caborn-Welborn leaders may have had to have dealt with lineage heads who also would have been competing for prestige and power within their respective communities. Thus, factionalism within Caborn-Welborn society and within the tribal societies with which they interacted may have hindered attempts by Caborn-Welborn individuals to control and regulate external connections and access to nonlocal goods.

Contacts with Mississippian groups living south of the Ohio valley would have been different than those with the tribal groups. Extraregional interaction with Mississippian societies would have taken place primarily between Caborn-Welborn aspiring elites and regional Mississippian elites. Not only would Mississippian elites have been in a better position to control or regulate access to nonlocal goods, but their positions of power and prestige would have been somewhat more stable than those of Oneota tribal leaders.

However, direct interaction between aspiring Caborn-Welborn elites and Mississippian elites living in the central Mississippi valley or upper Tennessee valley would have required one party to travel to the other's homeland (see Figure 1.3), since at present there is no evidence to suggest that any Mississippian chiefdoms were still active in the intervening areas. Alternatively, nonlocal goods may have made their way into the lower Ohio valley through down-the-line exchange relationships, involving the participation of members of nonhierarchically organized societies. As with Oneota societies, Caborn-Welborn relationships with these societies would have been somewhat unstable, since they were dependant on the power and prestige of local tribal leaders.

Through the establishment and maintenance of extraregional relationships, aspiring Caborn-Welborn elites would have sought to bolster their prestige, solidify their position within Caborn-Welborn society, and gain an advantage over their competitors (see Earle 1991:5; Welch 1991:194). They would have redistributed goods obtained through these long-distance exchange relationships to attract followers (Clark and Blake 1994; Hayden 1995). But as others increased their access to these goods, these items may have lost some of their prestige and mystique (Schortman and Urban 1992). Ultimately, though the value of these items remained high, goods obtained through long-distance exchange relationships may not have afforded aspiring Caborn-Welborn elites the same degree of status and prestige that the earlier Angel elite had derived from their control and regulation of access to nonlocal goods. Following the collapse of the Angel chiefdom, social mechanisms may have developed or resurfaced within Caborn-Welborn society that discouraged individuals from wanting to, or being able to, retain power or that encouraged households to shift their allegiance from those in power to competing factions (Spencer 1993, 1994; Trigger 1990). These changes would have effectively undermined attempts by aspiring elites to gain control over the entire Caborn-Welborn region and centralize power within one community. As such, Caborn-Welborn society may not have experienced the same degree of political centralization as had earlier lower Ohio valley Mississippian societies. This issue is taken up in the next section.

## WAS CABORN-WELBORN A CHIEFDOM OR A CONFEDERACY?

If one accepts the proposition that the bulk of the Caborn-Welborn population is descended from the earlier Angel population (Munson 2000; Pollack 1998; Pollack and Munson 2003), then it is also reasonable to assume that Caborn-Welborn sociopolitical organization retained some elements of the earlier Angel polity. A question arises, however: To what extent did Caborn-Welborn social and political relationships resemble those of the Angel chiefdom or other pre–A.D. 1400 Mississippian polities in the lower Ohio valley? Conversely, one also can ask how Caborn-Welborn sociopolitical organization differed from that of earlier Mississippian chiefdoms in the lower Ohio valley.

In the late fourteenth/early fifteenth centuries, an unstable political landscape existed throughout the Midwest and parts of the Southeast. It was created by the disruption of Mississippian interaction spheres and the collapse of the local Mississippian prestige goods economy, and perhaps by factionalism within these societies as well. In the lower Ohio valley, this situation, coupled perhaps with some degree of environmental degradation, resulted in the collapse of the Angel chiefdom and neighboring polities within an area that has come to be called the Vacant Quarter (see chapter 2) (Williams 1990; see also Cobb and Butler 2002).

Following the collapse of the Angel chiefdom, as in other cycling situations (Anderson 1990, 1994; Halley 1996), aspiring elites would have sought to reestablish a chiefly society similar to that of the Angel polity, this time near the mouth of the Wabash River. It is possible that they were successful and that a new chiefdom was formed, one that was more involved in interregional exchange of goods than had been the earlier Angel chiefdom but one that lacked a clearly identifiable administrative center with one or more platform mounds.

The presence of a settlement hierarchy consisting of farmsteads, hamlets, small villages, and large villages points to some degree of political centralization within the Caborn-Welborn region and could reflect the presence of a post–A.D. 1400 chiefly society centered at the mouth of the Wabash River. Although the Caborn-Welborn settlement system lacked a mound center, Slack Farm can be distinguished from other Caborn-Welborn settlements and could have functioned as an administrative center for a local chiefdom.

Slack Farm is the largest village. It is centrally located within the distribution of Caborn-Welborn settlements; it is the only village that appears to have been occupied for the entire Caborn-Welborn sequence; and its ceramic assemblage is characterized by larger pans and more long-necked bottles and effigy bowls than has been documented at other Caborn-Welborn sites. The types of vessels interred with the dead at this site distinguish it from other Caborn-Welborn sites (with the exception of the nearby Murphy site): at Slack Farm and Murphy, long-necked bottles and effigy bowls are much more common, while elsewhere in the Caborn-Welborn region the dead were interred with plain or decorated jars. Differences in types of vessels, as well as other artifacts buried with the dead, such as marine shell gorgets, catlinite disk pipes, and copper or brass tubes, could reflect the presence of status or wealth differences at Slack Farm and Murphy. (Unfortunately, at Slack Farm, Murphy, and other Caborn-Welborn sites, information is lacking on the contextual association and spatial distribution of grave goods, which hampers efforts to document status differences within Caborn-Welborn cemeteries based on the types and quantities of grave goods associated with specific individuals.)

While the presence of a settlement hierarchy reflects continuity with the preceding Angel chiefdom and points to some degree of political centralization and social inequality within the Caborn-Welborn region, other archaeological correlates of a chiefdom (Earle 1991; Peebles and Kus 1977) do not appear to be present. These include, in addition to the absence of corporate architecture, elite residential zones and cemeteries and identifiable variation in diet that would point to the presence of an elite class. All of the small and large Caborn-Welborn villages lack platform mounds. There is no evidence to suggest that any of these villages had stockades, and there also is nothing about the internal organization of these communities to suggest that they contained a cluster of structures set apart from other houses that might reflect an elite residential area. At Slack Farm, the largest Caborn-Welborn village, there also is little evidence to suggest that individuals interred within one cemetery were treated in a manner different than those interred within other cemeteries. With respect to variation in diet that might reflect the presence of an elite, comparison of nonmetric attributes and dentition among individuals buried in the Slack Farm cemeteries failed to identify any clear differences in the consumption of certain foods that might reflect status differences (Powell et al. 1996; Tench 1996). (It should be noted that little is known about internal variation in the treatment of the dead within these cemeteries or about intracemetery health differences that could reflect status or wealth differences within this community.) The absence of these correlates tends to argue against Caborn-Welborn sociopolitical organization being that of a chiefdom.

In their attempt to reestablish a chiefly society near the mouth of the Wabash River, aspiring Caborn-Welborn elites would have had to have controlled, to some extent, both external and internal Caborn-Welborn social and political relationships (see Feinman 1995; Spencer 1993, 1994). The paucity of nonlocal prestige goods found at the Angel site, coupled with the large number of mounds and other signs of corporate architecture (i.e., a stockade) at Angel, suggests that the Angel elite may have employed a corporate strategy to maintain their political authority (Blanton et al. 1996). According to King (2003:9), such polities are likely to be stable because they limit factionalism by promoting social solidarity and institutionally limiting the ability of individuals to control sources of power. In comparison to the Angel polity, one is tempted to suggest that aspiring Caborn-Welborn elites may have employed a networking strategy to regain political authority over the Caborn-Welborn region. This suggestion is based on data that show an increase in extraregional interaction relative to the earlier Angel chiefdom.

Such a strategy would have fostered a competitive political landscape, one that emphasized external social networks and elite control of prestige goods (King 2003). However, from the preceding discussion about Caborn-Welborn participation in long-distance exchange networks, it appears that at no time during the Caborn-Welborn sequence were aspiring elites able to control or regulate access to nonlocal goods and information. This failure suggests that aspiring Caborn-Welborn elites were unsuccessful at employing a network strategy, and there is no evidence to suggest that they were able to employ a corporate strategy to the same extent as had the earlier Angel elite.

Attempts by aspiring Caborn-Welborn elites to reestablish a chiefdom near the mouth of the Wabash River may have been hindered by the fact that the Caborn-Welborn region was located several hundred kilometers from other regions where Mississippian populations lived in large communities. As Earle has noted, the dynamics of chiefdom evolution can be understood only by "the external relationships involving political competition, long-distance exchange, and international ideologies that act to bind elites to each other" (1991:13). The absence of nearby elites with whom to interact and compete may have hindered attempts by aspiring Caborn-Welborn elites to regulate access to nonlocal goods and information. Such a situation would have limited their ability to control or restrict access to the information and symbols they needed to validate their positions within society.

The size of the Caborn-Welborn region also may have hindered attempts by aspiring elites to control internal relationships. Hally (1993) has suggested that a territory 40 km in size represents the effective limits of a chiefdom, with a 20 km radius around an administrative center being the maximum area that could be effectively served by an elite. The 60 km long Caborn-Welborn region, with its 100 km of river miles, exceeds the territorial limits put forth by Hally. As such, it may not have been a region that could have been effectively administered by the elite of a simple chiefdom.

Based on the data at hand, it is difficult to support a suggestion that aspiring Caborn-Welborn elites were successful in their attempt to reestablish a chiefly society near the mouth of the Wabash River following the collapse of the Angel chiefdom. The size of the Caborn-Welborn region and the inability of aspiring elites to control or regulate external relationships to the same extent as had their earlier Mississippian counterparts indicate that Caborn-Welborn leaders were not able to achieve and sustain the same degree of political centralization within their society as had the earlier Angel elite in theirs. However, while the lack of interelite competition and elite regulation of access to nonlocal goods may have hindered attempts by individuals to achieve and sustain positions of power over the entire Caborn-Welborn region, it may have fostered intraregional competition among village leaders.

The proximity of Caborn-Welborn communities to each other and the association of hamlets and farmsteads with large and small villages points to the presence of village leaders who had influence over households living at nearby farmsteads and hamlets. Within each subarea, the residents of these various settlements undoubtedly were linked by a common ideology, kinship relationships, and political alliances. The presence of plazas/courtyards within Caborn-Welborn villages (e.g., Slack Farm, Hovey Lake, Alzey, and Blackburn) reflects the importance of group ceremonialism and ritual, which may have served to strengthen community ties. Differences in the frequency of occurrence of certain kinds of ceramics at villages versus hamlets and farmsteads suggests that more activities and rituals involved in the serving of food to larger numbers of people were conducted at the former (Welch and Scarry 1995). Aspiring Caborn-Welborn elites may have sponsored these rituals as they competed for power within Caborn-Welborn society.

The existence of a settlement hierarchy within the Caborn-Welborn region not only points to a continuation of some aspects of earlier Angel sociopolitical organization, but it also indicates that village leaders had some measure of control or influence over households residing at nearby farmsteads and hamlets. It also points to the presence of leaders who could mediate disputes both within and between communities, schedule religious ceremonies, coordinate agricultural tasks, and negotiate alliances and exchange relationships with external groups (McGuire and Saitta 1995). As with earlier Mississippian elites, these leaders probably consulted with other members of Caborn-Welborn society when making important decisions (Muller 1997).

If Caborn-Welborn sociopolitical organization was not that of a chiefdom, then what was it? Although available evidence indicates that it was not as complex as earlier lower Ohio valley Mississippian chiefdoms, Caborn-Welborn sociopolitical organization probably was more hierarchically organized than that of contemporary Oneota tribal groups (Green 1995) located north of the Ohio valley or the late Madisonville horizon Fort Ancient Big Man societies (Pollack and Henderson 1992a, 2000) located upstream in the middle Ohio valley. Both of these regions lack a clearly defined settlement hierarchy or a concentration of settlements comparable to that of the Caborn-Welborn area (Benn 1989; Henderson 1992). Within both Oneota and Fort Ancient societies, each village appears to have been economically and politically autonomous, and there is no evidence to suggest that village leaders ever achieved power beyond their own communities.

Knight (1990) has suggested that because the structure of the social system that typified many Historic Southeastern tribes—that of exogamous ranked clans—was hierarchical by nature, their sociopolitical organization could move from a tribe to a chiefdom and back again without requiring a major restructuring of social relationships. If the Angel chiefdom's social structure did resemble that of ranked clans, then it is quite possible that the development of Caborn-Welborn sociopolitical organization did not result in a major reconfiguration of social relationships but rather only changes in the power and prestige of the members of highest ranked clan(s).

After the collapse of the Angel chiefdom, not only was there a decline in the power and prestige of societal leaders, but by A.D. 1450, there is some evidence to suggest that, in addition to the former Angel population, segments of other earlier lower Ohio valley chiefdoms had moved into the region. Intraregional cultural differences reflected in the spatial distribution of Caborn-Welborn Decorated jar shoulder design, cemetery location, and the types of jars interred with the dead point to an east-west cultural division within the Caborn-Welborn region. It is possible that the identified patterns reflect the presence of at least two different groups, the eastern group derived from the Angel population and the western group primarily derived from segments of a Mississippian polity or polities that had been located downstream from the mouth of the Saline River.

If this was the case, then Caborn-Welborn political organization could have been similar to that of Historic Indian confederacies, such as the Creek and Choctaw (Galloway 1994; Knight 1994; Swanton 1911, 1946). Both of these confederacies consisted of remnants of former chiefdoms that had banded together for political and economic reasons. Historically, this kind of political organization often brought together spatially distinct societies in response to external threats (Bradley 1987; Trigger 1981).

It is this characteristic, the bringing together of different groups (Blitz 1999:587–588), that makes the concept of a Caborn-Welborn confederacy so appealing. Caborn-Welborn society may have consisted of segments of more than one earlier Mississippian chiefdom that banded together for a common good and to continue their Mississippian lifestyle. Active participation in intersocietal exchange and interaction networks appears to have been an important component of this confederacy. The use of this term, however, is not meant to imply that a Caborn-Welborn confederacy was anywhere near the size or scale of many of the Historic Indian confederacies. Nor is its use intended to suggest that Caborn-Welborn settlement patterns and sociopolitical organization developed in response to external threats.

Contact period confederacies of the Southeast have been described as having a "scaled hierarchy of potentially impermanent aggregations that developed on a contingent basis in response to crises of greater or lesser importance" (Knight 1994:389). Thus, leadership roles within these confederacies are more heterarchical (Crumley 1987) and situational (Sahlins 1968) than hierarchical. Possessing the potential for being ranked in a number of different ways (Crumley 1987:158; Dillehay 1992:386–387), depending on economic, social, and political circumstances and under certain conditions, aspiring elites within these confederacies may have temporarily acquired power over the entire territory. However, none appears to have been able to consolidate and hold on to these positions of power for an extended period of time in order for a chiefdom to develop.

In a similar vein, McGuire and Saitta (1995; see also Hayden 1995; Levy 1995; Petersen 1993; Plog 1995) have suggested that societies can be both egalitarian and hierarchical. They argue that although late-fourteenth-century Western Pueblo society was for the most part egalitarian, under certain circumstances and for short periods of time an elite was needed to take control of social and political affairs. These individuals occupied positions of power until a particular crisis had passed. As with the Creek and Choctaw confederacies, these shifts in power relationships are suggestive of more heterarchical than hierarchical political relationships. The ease with which some societies appear to have been able to switch from a decentralized to a centralized political structure suggests that the establishment of more permanent elites is tied to the ability to hold on to these positions of power for an extended period of time and to pass this acquired power to one's descendants.

Considered as a confederacy, all of the residents of the Caborn-Welborn region would have shared a common body of ideological and social beliefs at one level, but at another they would have retained an ethnic identity that would have distinguished members of one group from another. The east-west division previously discussed reflects such cultural or ethnic differences. For example, in the eastern subarea, the dead were primarily interred within villages, which represents a continuation of the earlier Angel mortuary program. In contrast, the dead in the western subarea were primarily interred within cemeteries on the bluffs overlooking the Ohio River floodplain and Caborn-Welborn settlements, a continuation of the early Mississippian mortuary program of groups living in other portions of the lower Ohio valley (Clay 1997; Muller 1986). Other differences parallel that of the contrasting mortuary programs, including differences in the kinds of decorated jars used as grave goods and variation in the use of lines and punctations to fill triangular areas on Caborn-Welborn Decorated jars.

Within each subarea, hamlets and farmsteads tend to cluster near large or small villages, forming settlement clusters. Settlement clusters have an average length of about 20 km. Thus, as noted in chapter 4, no Caborn-Welborn farmstead or hamlet is situated more than 20 km from a small or large village. In addition, all of the villages are located within 20 km of the centrally located Slack Farm site. The clustering of Caborn-Welborn settlements within the three subareas and the diversity of domestic habitation sites in the Caborn-Welborn region suggests that political as well as social and economic interaction and interconnectedness existed between the smaller settlements and nearby villages as well as between villages.

Each settlement cluster may have acted somewhat independently with respect to internal matters. Neighboring settlement clusters may have cooperated with each other to meet subsistence needs, to arrange marriages, and to conduct ceremonial events. These intercommunity relationships would have been driven, in large part, by kinship relations. Within each settlement cluster, Caborn-Welborn leaders may have sought to develop, maintain, and regulate extraregional exchange relationships as a way to attain and sustain positions of authority within their society.

Competition among aspiring leaders may have taken place within each subarea. The successful leader, upon consolidating his position of power within his subregion, would have been in a position to compete with other leaders for control over the entire Caborn-Welborn region. This scenario allows for competition and cooperation among aspiring leaders at different levels (heterarchy) while at the same time accounting for the cultural differences documented archaeologically within the Caborn-Welborn region.

At times, political and economic situations may have arisen that required the leaders of the different cultural or ethnic groups comprising the Caborn-Welborn confederacy to work together for a common good. This need would have created situations where some individuals acquired power over the entire Caborn-Welborn region. They may have occupied these positions until a crisis passed or was resolved. If this was the case, then Caborn-Welborn society must have been structured in such a way as to inhibit individuals from holding on to power for extended periods of time (see Spencer 1993, 1994; Trigger 1990). That is, aspects of Caborn-Welborn sociopolitical organization would have discouraged individuals from retaining power or encouraged households to shift their allegiance from those in power to competing factions, effectively undermining attempts by aspiring elites to centralize power. The widespread occurrence of nonlocal goods throughout the Caborn-Welborn region also indicates that aspiring Caborn-Welborn elites were not able to maintain control over extraregional exchange relationships and did not have the same degree of power as had the earlier Angel elite. In general, the decentralization of political power that appears to typify Caborn-Welborn social and political relationships suggests that the leveling mechanisms inherent in small-scale societies, which had been overcome to some degree by Mississippian elites, reemerged during the Caborn-Welborn phase.

## CONCLUSIONS

As in many regions of the eastern United States where the collapse of chiefdom-level societies occurred, the demise of the Angel chiefdom ca. A.D. 1400 led to the abandonment of the regional center (the Angel site) and its associated villages, hamlets, and farmsteads. In the Ohio-Wabash River confluence region, Angel's collapse was followed by a reconfiguration of social, political, and economic relationships during the subsequent Caborn-Welborn phase (A.D. 1400–1700). This response of the regional population to collapse differs from that of most other post-collapse responses in that households did not relocate to another region or become more inward-looking, as reflected by a reduction in extraregional interaction. Instead, the Caborn-Welborn population simply shifted their settlements a short distance downstream and expanded their participation in extraregional exchange and interaction networks, which led to increased access to and availability of nonlocal goods throughout the Caborn-Welborn region.

Identifying the Caborn-Welborn population's economic response is fairly straightforward. Continued participation in a prestige goods economy is reflected by the presence of marine shell objects (and, later, objects manufactured from European materials) as grave goods. Intersocietal exchange relationships with other Mississippian groups also continued, reflected in the presence of central Mississippi valley ceramic types in Caborn-Welborn ceramic collections. An expansion of long-distance exchange relationships to include tribal societies situated to the north of the lower Ohio valley is reflected by the presence of Oneota-like ceramics, triangular endscrapers, and catlinite disk pipes.

How the Caborn-Welborn population (descendants of Angel and segments of other former lower Ohio valley chiefdoms) reconstructed social and political relationships is not as easy to discern, however. As in other situations of collapse, the transition from Angel to Caborn-Welborn is marked by a decentralization of political power and the formation of a less complex society. The absence of clearly identifiable chiefdom characteristics (regional center with monumental architecture, elite residential or mortuary areas, and subsistence differences that reflect differential access to resources) argues against the formation of a Caborn-Welborn chiefdom, similar to the earlier Angel polity. However, the presence of a settlement hierarchy (farmsteads, hamlets, small villages, and large villages) clearly illustrates a continuation of some type of formalized social inequality. Group ceremonialism and ritual, as reflected by the presence of plazas/courtyards at villages and intersettlement differences in the use of ceramic vessel forms, continued to be important within Caborn-Welborn society, with these activities primarily conducted at small and large villages.

The continuation of a settlement hierarchy and the clustering of settlements within each of three Caborn-Welborn subareas point to the presence of leaders who had some degree of power and influence beyond their own village. As with leaders of other farming societies, aspiring Caborn-Welborn elites would have been responsible for mediating disputes both within and between communities, scheduling religious ceremonies, coordinating agricultural tasks, and negotiating alliances and exchange relationships with external groups. But the absence of a clearly identifiable regional administrative center suggests that Caborn-Welborn leadership roles may not have been as centralized as those of the earlier Angel chiefdom.

Throughout the 300 years of the Caborn-Welborn sequence, leaders may have competed and cooperated with each other to gain control of the entire region, in an attempt to centralize political control under their leadership (i.e., to create an Angel-like chiefdom). Expansion of extraregional exchange relationships may have provided households greater access to nonlocal goods, hindering attempts by aspiring Caborn-Welborn elites to control and regulate access to these materials and to legitimize their positions of power within Caborn-Welborn society. The size of the Caborn-Welborn region and the lack of neighboring elites with whom to compete also may have hindered attempts by aspiring Caborn-Welborn elites to centralize power under their authority. The 60 km long Caborn-Welborn region, with its 100 km of river miles, is much larger than the 40 km limit that has been suggested by some archaeologists as the maximum size of Mississippian chiefdoms. The nearest Mississippian populations that were still living in large villages after A.D. 1400 were located several hundred kilometers from the Caborn-Welborn region. That there is no evidence of a centralization of power within the Caborn-Welborn area indicates that the leveling mechanisms inherent in small-scale societies, which had been overcome to some degree by the Angel elite, reemerged after the collapse of Angel.

Caborn-Welborn sociopolitical organization, however, clearly was more hierarchically structured than contemporary tribal societies. These groups lacked a clearly defined settlement hierarchy or a concentration of settlements within a restricted region comparable to that of the Caborn-Welborn area.

Instead, each village apparently was economically and politically autonomous, and village leaders within these societies never achieved power beyond their own communities.

Though Caborn-Welborn sociopolitical organization does not exhibit the same level of political centralization as the earlier Angel chiefdom, it was more hierarchically organized than contemporary tribal societies. Therefore, it is suggested that it resembled a confederacy, similar to those of the southeastern Indian confederacies of the Contact period, though on a much smaller scale. Those societies consisted of the segments of earlier Mississippian chiefdoms that banded together to achieve common political and economic goals. If Caborn-Welborn sociopolitical organization resembled those confederacies, then at times some members of Caborn-Welborn society may have attained positions of power that transcended the entire Caborn-Welborn region. However, the absence of a clearly identifiable regional administrative center suggests that they were not able to hold on to this power for an extended period of time.

Support for characterizing Caborn-Welborn sociopolitical organization as a confederacy comes from the intraregional differences identified in ceramic designs (use of lines vs. punctations as fill), location of cemeteries (within village vs. blufftop), and types of decorated jars placed with the dead (Caborn-Welborn Decorated vs. central Mississippi valley types) that point to the presence of more than one ethnic group within the Caborn-Welborn region. If this was the case, the former Angel population may have lived primarily upstream from the mouth of the Wabash River, while the area downstream from the mouth of the Wabash River may have been settled by households that relocated to this area following the demise of chiefdoms situated downstream from the mouth of the Saline River.

An examination of the spatial distribution of Caborn-Welborn ceramics and settlements and the identification of extraregional interaction networks, intraregional cultural differences, and a settlement hierarchy has provided information on how one society reconstructed social, political, and economic relationships following the demise of a complex society. Most studies that deal with the emergence of social inequality focus on how power becomes centralized in the hands of an elite class. The results of this study indicate that in this region, populations that had experienced centralized political power did not do so again to the same extent. As such, throughout its 300-year history, Caborn-Welborn society can be characterized as less centralized and more egalitarian relative to the earlier Angel chiefdom.

This study has contributed to our understanding of how regional populations respond to the collapse of Mississippian chiefdoms. It has shown that the collapse of these societies need not always lead to a dispersal of the local population, a decrease in population density, and a reduction in extraregional interaction. In some instances, as the local populations reconfigured the social boundaries that served to distinguish the elite from the rest of society, household resistance to elite authority and the leveling tendencies of small-scale societies reasserted themselves. This appears to have been the case with the Caborn-Welborn population living along the Ohio River near the mouth the Wabash River.

# References Cited

Adams, William R.

1949 *Archaeological Notes on Posey County, Indiana.* Indiana Historical Bureau, Indianapolis.

Ahler, Steven, Jon Muller, and Joel Rabinowitz

1980 *Archaeological Testing for the Smithland Pool, Illinois.* Research Paper No. 13. Center for Archaeological Investigations, Southern Illinois University, Carbondale.

Allen, Kathleen Mae Sydoriak

1988 *Ceramic Style and Social Continuity in an Iroquoian Tribe.* Unpublished Ph.D. dissertation, Department of Anthropology, State University of New York at Buffalo.

Anderson, David G.

1990 Stability and Change in Chiefdom Level Societies: An Examination of Mississippian Political Evolution on the South Atlantic Slope. In *Lamar Archaeology: Mississippian Chiefdoms in the Deep South,* edited by Mark Williams and Gary Shapiro, pp. 187–213. University of Alabama Press, Tuscaloosa.

1994 *The Savannah River Chiefdoms: Political Change in the Late Prehistoric Southeast.* University of Alabama Press, Tuscaloosa.

Anthony, David W.

1990 Migration in Archeology: The Baby and the Bathwater. *American Anthropologist* 92(4):895–914.

Arnold, Dean E.

1985 *Ceramic Theory and Cultural Process.* New Studies in Archaeology. Cambridge University Press, Cambridge.

1989 Patterns of Learning, Residence, and Descent Among Potters in Ticul, Yucatan, Mexico. In *Archaeological Approaches to Cultural Identity,* edited by Stephen J. Shennan, pp. 174–184. Unwin Hyman Ltd., London.

Bareis, Charles J., and James W. Porter

1984 *American Bottom Archaeology: A Summary of the FAI-270 Project Contribution to the Culture History of the Mississippi River Valley.* University of Illinois Press, Urbana.

Barker, Alex W., and Timothy R. Pauketat

1992 Introduction: Social Inequality and the Native Elites of Southeastern North America. In *Lords of the Southeast: Social Inequality and the Native Elites of Southeastern North America,* edited by Alan W. Barker and Timothy R.

Pauketat, pp. 1–10. Archaeological Papers No. 3. American Anthropological Association, Washington, D.C.

Benn, David W.

1989 Hawks, Serpents, and Bird-Men: Emergence of the Oneota Mode of Production. *Plains Anthropologist* 34(125):233–260.

Black, Glenn A.

1967 *Angel Site: An Archaeological, Historical, and Ethnological Study.* 2 vols. Indiana Historical Society, Indianapolis.

Blakeslee, Donald J.

1981 The Origin and Spread of the Calumet Ceremony. *American Antiquity* 46:759–768.

Blanton, Richard, Gary M. Feinman, Stephen A. Kowalewski, and Peter N. Peregrine

1996 A Dual Processual Theory for the Evolution of Mesoamerican Civilization. *Current Anthropology* 37(1):15–32.

Blitz, John H.

1993a *Ancient Chiefdoms of the Tombigbee.* University of Alabama Press, Tuscaloosa.

1993b Big Pots for Big Shots: Feasting and Storage in a Mississippian Community. *American Antiquity* 58:80–95.

1999 Mississippian Chiefdoms and the Fission-Fusion Process. *American Antiquity* 64(4):577–592.

Bluhm, Elaine A., and Gloria J. Fenner

1961 The Angker Site. In Chicago Area Archaeology, edited by Elaine A. Bluhm. *Illinois Archaeological Survey Bulletin* 3:138–161.

Bluhm, Elaine A., and Allen Liss

1961 The Oak Forest Site. In Chicago Area Archaeology, edited by Elaine A. Bluhm. *Illinois Archaeological Survey Bulletin* 3:89–137.

Boszhardt, Robert F.

1994 Oneota Group Continuity at LaCrosse: The Brice Prairie, Pammel Creek, and Valley View Phases. *Wisconsin Archaeologist* 75:173–236.

Bradley, James W.

1987 *Evolution of the Onondaga Iroquois: Accommodating Change, 1500–1655.* Syracuse University Press, Syracuse, New York.

Brown, Ian W.

1981 A Study of Stone Box Graves in Eastern North America. *Tennessee Anthropologist* 6(1):1–26.

1989 The Calumet Ceremony in the Southeast and Its Archaeological Manifestations. *American Antiquity* 54:311–331.

Brown, James A.

1989 On Style Divisions of the Southeastern Ceremonial Complex: A Revisionist Perspective. In *The Southeastern Ceremonial Complex: Artifacts and Analysis,* edited by Patricia Galloway, pp. 183–204. University of Nebraska Press, Lincoln.

Brown, James A., and Patricia J. O'Brien
1990 *At the Edge of Prehistory: Huber Phase Archaeology in the Chicago Area.* Center for American Archaeology, Kampsville, Illinois.

Brown, James A., Richard A. Kerber, and Howard D. Winters
1990 Trade and the Evolution of Exchange Relations at the Beginning of the Mississippi Period. In *The Mississippian Emergence,* edited by Bruce D. Smith, pp. 251–280. Smithsonian Institution Press, Washington, D.C.

Brumfiel, Elizabeth M.
1994 Factional Competition and Political Development in the New World: An Introduction. In *Factional Competition and Political Development in the New World,* edited by Elizabeth M. Brumfiel and John W. Fox, pp. 3–14. New Directions in Archaeology Series. Cambridge University Press, Cambridge.

Butler, Brian M.
1977 *Mississippian Settlement in the Black Bottom, Pope and Massac Counties, Illinois.* Unpublished Ph.D. dissertation, Department of Anthropology, Southern Illinois University, Carbondale.
1991 Kincaid Revisited: The Mississippian Sequence in the Lower Ohio Valley. In *Cahokia and the Hinterlands: Middle Mississippian Cultures of the Midwest,* edited by Thomas E. Emerson and R. Barry Lewis, pp. 264–273. University of Illinois Press, Urbana.

Butler, Brian M., and Charles R. Cobb
1996 A Tale of Two Villages: Mississippian Life in Upland Southern Illinois. Paper presented at the 53rd Southeastern Archaeological Conference, Birmingham, Alabama.

Butler, Brian M., Glen P. Harrell, and Mary C. Hamilton
1979 *An Archaeological Reconnaissance of the Illinois Portions of the Smithland Pool of the Ohio River.* Research Paper No. 5. Center for Archaeological Investigations, Southern Illinois University, Carbondale.

Chapman, Carl H., and L. O. Anderson
1955 The Campbell Site: A Late Mississippi Town Site and Cemetery in Southeast Missouri. *The Missouri Archaeologist* 17.

Clark, John E., and Michael Blake
1994 The Power of Prestige: Competitive Generosity and the Emergence of Rank Societies in Lowland Mesoamerica. In *Factional Competition and Political Development in the New World,* edited by Elizabeth M. Brumfiel and John W. Fox, pp. 17–30. New Directions in Archaeology Series. Cambridge University Press, Cambridge.

Clay, R. Berle
1963a *Ceramic Complexes of the Tennessee-Cumberland Region in Western Kentucky.* Unpublished Master's thesis, Department of Anthropology, University of Kentucky, Lexington.
1963b The Tinsley Hill Mound. Manuscript on file, William S. Webb Museum of Anthropology, University of Kentucky, Lexington.

1979 A Mississippian Ceramic Sequence for Western Kentucky. *Tennessee Anthropologist* 4(2):111–128.

1997 Mississippian Succession on the Lower Ohio. *Southeastern Archaeology* 16(1):16–32.

Cobb, Charles R., and Brian M. Butler

2002 The Vacant Quarter Revisited: Late Mississippian Abandonment of the Lower Ohio Valley. *American Antiquity* 67(4):625–642.

Cole, Fay-Cooper, Robert Bell, John Bennett, Joseph Caldwell, Norman Emerson, Richard MacNeish, Kenneth Orr, and Roger Willis

1951 *Kincaid: A Prehistoric Illinois Metropolis.* University of Chicago Press, Chicago.

Converse, Henry T., and Frank H. Cox, Jr.

1967 *Soil Survey of Henderson County, Kentucky.* United States Department of Agriculture, Soil Conservation Service, Washington, D.C.

*Courier-Journal* (Louisville, Kentucky)

1968 Article about a site being looted in Union County, Kentucky. On file, Office of State Archaeology, University of Kentucky, Lexington.

Cowgill, George L.

1979 Teotihuacan, Internal Militaristic Competition, and the Fall of the Classic Maya. In *Maya Archaeology and Ethnohistory,* edited by Norman Hammond and Gordon R. Willey, pp. 51–62. University of Texas Press, Austin.

Crumley, Carole L.

1987 A Dialectical Critique of Hierarchy. In *Power Relations and State Formation,* edited by T. C. Patterson and C. W. Gailey, pp. 155–169. American Anthropological Association, Washington, D.C.

Curry, Hilda J.

1950 *Negative Painted Pottery of Angel Mounds Site and Its Distribution in the New World.* Unpublished Master's thesis, Department of Anthropology, Indiana University, Bloomington.

DeBoer, Warren R., and J. A. Moore

1982 The Measurement and Meaning of Stylistic Diversity. *Naupa Pacha* 20:147–162.

DiBlasi, Philip J., and Bobbie K. Sudhoff

1978 *An Archaeological Reconnaissance of the Kentucky Side of the Smithland Pool Project on the Ohio River.* Archaeological Survey, University of Louisville, Louisville.

Dillehay, Tom D.

1992 Keeping Outsiders Out: Public Ceremony, Resource Rights, and Hierarchy in Historic and Contemporary Mapuche Society. In *Wealth and Hierarchy in the Intermediate Area,* edited by Frederick W. Lange, pp. 379–422. Dumbarton Oaks Research Library and Collection, Washington D.C.

Dobyns, Henry F.

1983 *Their Number Become Thinned.* University of Tennessee Press, Knoxville.

Drennan, Robert D., and Carlos A. Uribe (editors)
1987 *Chiefdoms in the Americas.* University Press of America, Lanham, Maryland.
Drooker, Penelope Ballard
1992 *Mississippian Village Textiles at Wickliffe.* University of Alabama Press, Tuscaloosa.
1997 *The View from Madisonville: Protohistoric Western Fort Ancient Interaction Patterns.* Memoir No. 31. University of Michigan, Museum of Anthropology, Ann Arbor.
Earle, Timothy (editor)
1991 *Chiefdoms: Power, Economy, and Ideology.* Cambridge University Press, Cambridge.
Edging, Richard B.
1995 *Living in a Cornfield: The Variation and Ecology of Late Prehistoric Agriculture in the Western Kentucky Confluence Region.* Unpublished Ph.D. dissertation, Department of Anthropology, University of Illinois, Urbana-Champaign.
Eisenstadt, Shmuel N.
1995 Beyond Collapse. In *The Collapse of Ancient States and Civilizations,* edited by Norman Yoffee and George L. Cowgill, pp. 236–243. University of Arizona Press, Tucson.
Faulkner, Charles H.
1972 *The Late Prehistoric Occupation of Northwestern Indiana: A Study of the Upper Mississippi Cultures of the Kankakee Valley.* Indiana Historical Society, Prehistory Research Series V, Indianapolis.
Feinman, Gary M.
1995 The Emergence of Inequality: A Focus on Strategies and Processes. In *Foundations of Social Inequality,* edited by T. Douglas Price and Gary M. Feinman, pp. 255–279. Plenum Press, New York.
Fidlar, Marion M.
1942 *Physiography of the Lower Wabash Valley.* Unpublished Ph.D. dissertation, Indiana University, Bloomington.
Flannery, Kent V.
1976 Evolution of Complex Settlement Systems. In *Early Mesoamerican Village,* edited by Kent V. Flannery, pp. 162–172. Academic Press, New York.
Frankenstein, Susan, and Michael J. Rowlands
1978 The Internal Structure and Regional Context of Early Iron Age Society in Southwestern Germany. *University of London Institute of Archaeology Bulletin* 15:73–112.
Galloway, Patricia
1994 Confederacy as a Solution to Chiefdom Dissolution: Historical Evidence in the Choctaw Case. In *The Forgotten Centuries: Indians and Europeans in the American South 1521–1704,* edited by Charles Hudson and Carmen Chaves Tesser, pp. 393–420. University of Georgia Press, Athens.
Garmiewicz, Rexford C.
2000 Appendix III: Analysis of Faunal Remains from the Murphy and Hovey

Lake Sites, Posey County, Indiana: Preliminary Results. In *Archaeological Survey and Testing at Protohistoric Mississippian Sites in Southwestern Indiana,* by Cheryl Ann Munson. Department of Anthropology, Indiana University, Bloomington.

Gersch, Holly Kae-Brangwyn, J. David Robertson, A. Gwynn Henderson, David Pollack, and Cheryl Ann Munson

1998 PIXE Analysis of Prehistoric and Protohistoric Caborn-Welborn Phase Copper Artifacts from the Lower Ohio River Valley. *Journal of Radioanalytical and Nuclear Chemistry* 234(1–2):85–90.

Gibbon, Guy E.

1973 *The Sheffield Site: An Oneota Site on the St. Croix River.* Minnesota Prehistoric Archaeology Series No. 10. Minnesota Historical Society, Minneapolis.

Green, Thomas J.

1977 *Economic Relationships Underlying Mississippian Settlement Patterns in Southwestern Indiana and North-Central Kentucky.* Unpublished Ph.D. dissertation, Department of Anthropology, Indiana University, Bloomington.

Green, Thomas J., and Cheryl Ann Munson

1978 Mississippian Settlement Patterns in Southwestern Indiana. In *Mississippian Settlement Patterns,* edited by Bruce D. Smith, pp. 292–330. Academic Press, New York.

Green, William (editor)

1995 *Oneota Archaeology: Past, Present, and Future.* Office of the State Archaeologist, University of Iowa, Iowa City.

Griffin, James B.

1978 Late Prehistory of the Ohio Valley. In *Northeast,* edited by Bruce G. Trigger, pp. 547–559. Handbook of North American Indians, vol. 15, William G. Sturtevant, general editor. Smithsonian Institution, Washington, D.C.

Guernsey, E. Y.

1939 Relationships Among Various Clark County Sites. *Proceedings of the Indiana Academy of Science* 48:27–32.

Gunderson, James

1994 Source Areas of Caborn-Welborn and Fort Ancient Redstone Pipes. Report on file, Kentucky Heritage Council, Frankfort.

Hall, Robert

1962 *The Archaeology of Carcajou Point.* University of Wisconsin Press, Madison.

1991 Cahokia Identity and Interaction Models of Cahokia Mississippian. In *Cahokia and the Hinterlands: Middle Mississippian Cultures of the Midwest,* edited by Thomas E. Emerson and R. Barry Lewis, pp. 3–34. University of Illinois Press, Urbana.

Hally, David J.

1986 The Identification of Vessel Function: A Case Study from Northwest Georgia. *American Antiquity* 51:267–295.

1993 The Territorial Size of Mississippian Chiefdoms. In *Archaeology of Eastern North America: Papers in Honor of Stephen Williams,* edited by James

Stoltman, pp. 143–168. Mississippi Department of Archives and History, Jackson.

1996 Platform-Mound Construction and the Instability of Mississippian Chiefdoms. In *Political Structure and Change in the Prehistoric Southeastern United States,* edited by John F. Scarry, pp. 92–127. University Press of Florida, Gainesville.

Hayden, Brian

1995 Pathways to Power: Principles for Creating Socioeconomic Inequalities. In *Foundations of Social Inequality,* edited by T. Douglas Price and Gary M. Feinman, pp. 15–86. Plenum Press, New York.

Helms, Mary W.

1979 *Ancient Panama: Chiefs in Search of Power.* University of Texas Press, Austin.

Henderson, A. Gwynn

1999 Caborn-Welborn Decorated Textiles from Impressions on Pans. Paper presented at the 64th annual meeting of the Society for American Archaeology, Chicago.

2003 Appendix III: Textile Structures in the Fabric-Impressed and Net-Impressed Ceramic Assemblage from the Bone Bank Site (12Po4). In Bone Bank: Archaeological Rescue Investigations at a Late Mississippian Site, Posey County, Indiana. Report on file at the Department of Anthropology, Indiana University, Bloomington.

Henderson, A. Gwynn (editor)

1992 *Fort Ancient Cultural Dynamics in the Middle Ohio Valley,* Monographs in World Archaeology No. 8. Prehistory Press, Madison, Wisconsin.

Henderson, A. Gwynn, David Pollack, and Christopher A. Turnbow

1992 Chronology and Cultural Patterns. In *Fort Ancient Cultural Dynamics in the Middle Ohio Valley,* edited by A. Gwynn Henderson, pp. 253–279. Monographs in World Archaeology No. 8. Prehistory Press, Madison, Wisconsin.

Henderson, A. Gwynn, Laura Turner, David Pollack, and Cheryl Ann Munson

1996 Lower Ohio Valley Caborn-Welborn Phase Mississippian Textiles: Impressions and Patterns. Poster presented at the 61st annual meeting of the Society for American Archaeology Meeting, New Orleans.

Henn, Robert

1971 A Preliminary Report on the Leonard Site. *Proceedings of the Indiana Academy of Sciences* 80:67–73.

Henrickson, Elizabeth F., and Mary M. A. McDonald

1983 Ceramic Form and Function: An Ethnographic Search and An Archaeological Application. *American Anthropologist* 85(3):630–643.

Herold, Elaine Bluhm, Patricia J. O'Brien, and David J. Wenner, Jr.

1990 Hoxie Farm and Huber: Two Upper Mississippian Archaeological Sites in Cook County, Illinois. In *At the Edge of Prehistory: Huber Phase Archaeology in the Chicago Area,* edited by James A. Brown and Patricia J. O'Brien, pp. 1–119. Center for American Archaeology, Kampsville, Illinois.

Hilgeman, Sherri L.

1991 Angel Negative Painted Design Structure. *Midcontinental Journal of Archaeology* 16:3–33.

1992 *Pottery and Chronology of the Angel Site, a Middle Mississippian Center in the Lower Ohio Valley.* Unpublished Ph.D. dissertation, Department of Anthropology, Indiana University, Bloomington.

2000 *Pottery and Chronology at Angel.* University of Alabama Press, Tuscaloosa.

Hodder, Ian

1978 Social Organization and Human Interaction: The Development of Some Tentative Hypotheses in Terms of Material Culture. In *The Spatial Organization of Culture,* edited by Ian Hodder, pp. 199–269. University of Pittsburgh Press, Pittsburgh.

Hoffman, Michael A.

1966 Archaeological Surveys of the Newburgh and Uniontown Lock and Dam Areas on the Kentucky side of the Ohio River. Manuscript on file, Office of State Archaeology, University of Kentucky, Lexington.

House, John H.

1991 *Monitoring Mississippian Dynamics: Time, Settlement and Ceramic Variation in the Kent Phase, Eastern Arkansas.* Unpublished Ph.D. dissertation, Department of Anthropology, Southern Illinois University, Carbondale.

1993 Dating the Kent Phase. *Southeastern Archaeology* 12:21–32.

Jacobs, Eullas H.

1981 *Soil Survey of Union and Webster Counties, Kentucky.* United States Department of Agriculture, Soil Conservation Service, Washington, D.C.

Johnson, Allen W., and Timothy Earle

1987 *The Evolution of Human Societies from Foraging Group to Agrarian State.* Stanford University Press, Stanford.

Justice, Noel D.

1987 *Stone Age Spear and Arrow Points of the Midcontinental and Eastern United States: A Modern Survey and Reference.* Indiana University Press, Bloomington.

Kearney, Michael

1980 From the Invisible Hand to the Visible Feet: Anthropological Studies of Migration and Development. *Annual Review of Anthropology* 15:331–361.

Kellar, James H.

1967 Material Remains. In *Angel Site: An Archaeological, Historical, and Ethnological Study,* by Glenn A. Black, vol. 2, pp. 431–487. Indiana Historical Society, Indianapolis.

Kelly, John E.

1991 Cahokia and Its Role as a Gateway Center in Interregional Exchange. In *Cahokia and the Hinterlands: Middle Mississippian Cultures of the Midwest,* edited by Thomas E. Emerson and R. Barry Lewis, pp. 221–226. University of Illinois Press, Urbana.

King, Adam

2003 *Etowah: The Political History of a Chiefdom Capital.* University of Alabama Press, Tuscaloosa.

Kintigh, Keith W.

1985 Social Structure, the Structure of Style, and Stylistic Patterns in Cibola Pottery. In *Decoding Prehistoric Ceramics,* edited by Ben A. Nelson, pp. 35–74. Southern Illinois University Press, Carbondale.

Knight, Vernon J., Jr.

1986 The Institutional Organization of Mississippian Religion. *American Antiquity* 51(4):675–687.

1990 Social Organization and the Evolution of Hierarchy in Southeastern Chiefdoms. *Journal of Anthropological Research* 46(1):1–23.

1994 The Formation of the Creeks. In *The Forgotten Centuries: Indians and Europeans in the American South 1521–1704,* edited by Charles Hudson and Carmen Chaves Tesser, pp. 373–392. University of Georgia Press, Athens.

Kreisa, Paul P.

1988 *Second-Order Communities in Western Kentucky: Site Survey and Excavations at Late Woodland and Mississippian Period Sites.* Western Kentucky Project Report No. 7. Department of Anthropology, University of Illinois, Urbana.

1990 *Organizational Aspects of Mississippian Settlement Systems in Western Kentucky.* Unpublished Ph.D. dissertation, Department of Anthropology, University of Illinois, Urbana.

1995 Mississippian Secondary Centers Along the Lower Ohio River Valley: An Overview of Some Sociopolitical Implications. In *Current Research in Kentucky,* vol. 3, edited by John F. Doershuk, Christopher A. Bergman, and David Pollack, pp. 161–178. Kentucky Heritage Council, Frankfort.

Lane, Leon

1993 *A Bioarchaeological Analysis of the Human Skeletal Population from Tinsley Hill (15Ly18a&b).* Unpublished Master's thesis, Department of Anthropology, University of Kentucky, Lexington.

1998 Skeletal and Mortuary Analyses. In *Mississippian Adaptations along the Barren River in South Central Kentucky,* by William Lowthert, Carl Shields, and David Pollack, pp. 118–131. Research Report No. 1. Kentucky Archaeological Survey, Lexington.

Lawrence, William L., and Robert C. Mainfort, Jr.

1995 Otto Sharp: A Protohistoric Site in the Reelfoot Basin, Lake County, Tennessee. In *Current Research in Kentucky,* vol. 3, edited by John F. Doershuk, Christopher A. Bergman, and David Pollack, pp. 265–278. Kentucky Heritage Council, Frankfort.

Lawton, Sherman P.

1964 Test Excavations in Owl Cave. *Bulletin of the Oklahoma Anthropological Society* 12:87–102.

Lee, Everett S.

1966 A Theory of Migration. *Demography* 3(1):47–57.

Levy, Janet E.

1995 Heterarchy in Bronze Age Denmark: Settlement Pattern, Gender, and Ritual. In *Heterarchy and the Analysis of Complex Societies,* edited by Robert M. Ehrenreich, Carole L. Crumley, and Janet E. Levy, pp. 41–54. Archaeological Papers No. 3. American Anthropological Association, Washington, D.C.

Lewis, R. Barry

1990 Mississippi Period. In *The Archaeology of Kentucky: Past Accomplishments and Future Directions,* edited by David Pollack, pp. 375–466. Comprehensive Plan Report No. 1. Kentucky Heritage Council, Frankfort.

Lewis, R. Barry (editor)

1986 *Mississippian Towns of the Western Kentucky Border: The Adams, Wickliffe, and Sassafras Ridge Sites.* Kentucky Heritage Council, Frankfort.

Loughridge, Robert H.

1883 *Report on the Geological and Economic Features of the Jackson Purchase Region.* Kentucky Geological Survey, Lexington.

Lyon, Sidney S.

1871 Report of an Exploration of Ancient Mounds in Union County, Kentucky (Made by the Request and at the Expense of the Smithsonian Institution). *Annual Report of the Board of Regents of the Smithsonian Institution for 1870,* pp. 392–405. Washington, D.C.

Mainfort, Robert C.

1996 Late Period Chronology in the Central Mississippi Valley: A Western Tennessee Perspective. *Southeastern Archaeology* 15(2):172–180.

Matternas, Hugh B.

1995 Mound C and the Mississippian Decline: A View of Culture Preserved in Wickliffe's Mortality Data. In *Current Research in Kentucky,* vol. 3, edited by John F. Doershuk, Christopher A. Bergman, and David Pollack, pp. 179–204. Kentucky Heritage Council, Frankfort.

McGuire, Randall H.

1989 The Greater Southwest as a Periphery of Mesoamerica. In *Centre and Periphery: Comparative Studies in Archaeology,* edited by Timothy C. Champion, pp. 40–66. Unwin Hyman Ltd., Cambridge.

McGuire Randall H., and Dean J. Saitta

1995 Although They Have Petty Captains, They Obey Them Badly: The Dialectics of Prehispanic Western Pueblo Social Organization. *American Antiquity* 61(2):197–216.

McNutt, Charles H. (editor)

1996 *Prehistory of the Central Mississippi Valley.* University of Alabama Press, Tuscaloosa.

McWilliams, Kendall M.

1979 *Soil Survey of Posey County, Indiana.* United States Department of Agriculture, Soil Conservation Service, Washington, D.C.

Michalik, Laura, and James A. Brown

1990 (Ceramic Artifacts). The Oak Forest Site. In *At the Edge of Prehistory: Huber Phase Archaeology in the Chicago Area,* edited by James A. Brown and Patricia

J. O'Brien, pp. 199–217. Center for American Archaeology, Kampsville, Illinois.

Milner, George R.

1990 The Late Prehistoric Cahokia Cultural System of the Mississippi River Valley: Foundations, Florescence, and Fragmentation. *Journal of World Prehistory* 4(1):1–43.

Moorehead, Warren K.

1906 Explorations at the Mouth of the Wabash. *Phillips Academy Bulletin* 3:62–86.

Morse, Dan F., and Phyllis A. Morse

1983 *Archaeology of the Central Mississippi Valley.* Academic Press, New York.

Muller, Jon

1978 The Kincaid System: Mississippian Settlement in the Environs of a Large Site. In *Mississippian Settlement Patterns,* edited by Bruce D. Smith, pp. 269–292. Academic Press, New York.

1986 *Archaeology of the Lower Ohio River Valley.* Academic Press, New York.

1997 *Mississippian Political Economy.* Interdisciplinary Contributions to Archaeology. Plenum Press, New York.

Muller, Jon, and Jeanette E. Stephens

1991 Mississippian Sociocultural Adaptations. In *Cahokia and the Hinterlands: Middle Mississippian Cultures of the Midwest,* edited by Thomas E. Emerson and R. Barry Lewis, pp. 297–310. University of Illinois Press, Urbana.

Munson, Cheryl Ann

1980 Air Photo Interpretation of the Hovey Lake Site: A Retrodictive and Predictive Study. Paper presented at the Ohio Valley Archaeological Conference, Knoxville, Tennessee.

1983 Variation in Regional Settlement Organization and Community Behaviors: A Comparison of the Mississippian Angel and Caborn-Welborn Phases. Paper presented at the 48th Annual Meeting of the Society for American Archaeology, Pittsburgh.

1984 Preliminary Description of Caborn-Welborn Decorated. Paducah Ceramics Conference, Paducah, Kentucky.

1994 *Archaeological Investigations at the Southwind Site, a Mississippian Community in Posey County, Indiana.* Department of Anthropology, Indiana University, Bloomington.

1995 An Archaeological Survey of Caborn-Welborn Phase Mississippian Settlement in the Vicinity of the Caborn Site, Posey County, Indiana. Report on file, Department of Anthropology, Indiana University, Bloomington.

1997 Archaeological Survey and Testing of Mississippian Caborn-Welborn Phase Sites in Posey County, Indiana, 1996–1997: Investigations at the Hovey Lake and Murphy Sites and Environs. Report on file, Department of Anthropology, Indiana University, Bloomington.

2000 Archaeological Survey and Testing at Protohistoric Mississippian Sites in Southwestern Indiana. Report on file at the Department of Anthropology, Indiana University, Bloomington.

Munson, Cheryl Ann, and Della Collins Cook
2001 Residential Mortuary Practices and Skeletal Biology at the Late Mississippian Hovey Lake Site, Posey County, Indiana. *Midcontinental Journal of Archaeology* 26(1):1–52.

Munson, Cheryl Ann, and Thomas J. Green
1973 The Caborn-Welborn Complex of Southwestern Indiana. Paper presented at the Central States Anthropological Society Annual Meeting, St. Louis, Missouri.

Munson, Cheryl Ann, and Marjorie Melvin Jones
1991 Radiocarbon and Artifact Chronology of the Protohistoric Caborn Site (12Po32), Posey County, Indiana (abstract). In *Current Research in Indiana Archaeology and Prehistory: 1990*. Research Reports 12:10–12. Glenn A. Black Laboratory of Archaeology, Indiana University, Bloomington.

Munson, Cheryl Ann, Bruce Eisterhold, and Marjorie Jones
1987 An Archaeological Survey of the Caborn Site (12Po32), Posey County, Indiana (abstract). In *Current Research in Indiana Archaeology and Prehistory: 1986*. Research Reports 7:8–10. Glenn A. Black Laboratory of Archaeology, Indiana University, Bloomington.

Munson, Cheryl Ann, Marjorie Melvin Jones, and Bret J. Ruby
1989 The 1988 Archaeological Test Excavations at the Caborn Site, a Protohistoric Mississippian Village in Posey County, Indiana (abstract). In *Current Research in Indiana Archaeology and Prehistory: 1987 and 1988*. Research Reports 10:41–42. Glenn A. Black Laboratory of Archaeology, Indiana University, Bloomington.

Niquette, Charles M. (editor)
1991 *Excavations at the Andalex Village (15Hk22), Hopkins County, Kentucky*. Contract Publication Series 91-03. Cultural Resource Analysts, Inc., Lexington.

O'Brien, Michael J.
1994 *Cat Monsters and Head Pots: The Archaeology of Missouri's Pemiscot Bayou*. University of Missouri Press, Columbia.

O'Brien, Michael J., and Gregory L. Fox
1994 Sorting Artifacts in Space and Time. In *Cat Monsters and Head Pots: The Archaeology of Missouri's Pemiscot Bayou*, by Michael J. O'Brien, pp. 25–60. University of Missouri Press, Columbia.

O'Shea, John
1984 *Mortuary Variability: An Archaeological Investigation*. Academic Press, New York.

Parsons, Jeffrey R.
1971 *Prehistoric Settlement Patterns in the Texcoco Region, Mexico*. Museum of Anthropology, Memoirs No. 3. University of Michigan, Ann Arbor.

Pauketat, Timothy R., and Thomas E. Emerson
1991 The Ideology of Authority and the Power of the Pot. *American Anthropologist* 93(4):919–941.

Peebles, Christopher S., and Susan M. Kus
1977 Some Archaeological Correlates of Ranked Societies. *American Antiquity* 42:421–448.

Peregrine, Peter
1992 *Mississippian Evolution: A World-System Perspective.* Prehistory Press, Madison, Wisconsin.

Petersen, Glenn
1993 Kanengamah and Pohnpei's Politics of Concealment. *American Anthropologist* 95:334–352.

Phillips, Philip
1970 *Archaeological Survey of the Lower Yazoo Basin, Mississippi, 1947–1955.* 2 vols. Peabody Museum of Archaeology and Ethnology Paper No. 60. Harvard University, Cambridge.

Phillips, Philip, James A. Ford, and James B. Griffin
1951 *Archaeological Survey in the Lower Mississippi Valley, 1940–1947.* Papers of the Peabody Museum of Archaeology and Ethnology No. 25. Harvard University, Cambridge.

Plog, Stephen
1995 Equality and Hierarchy: Holistic Approaches to Understanding Social Dynamics in the Pueblo Southwest. In *Foundations of Social Inequality,* edited by T. Douglas Price and Gary M. Feinman, pp. 189–206. Plenum Press, New York.

Pollack, David
1998 *Intraregional and Intersocietal Relationships of the Late Mississippian Caborn-Welborn Phase of the Lower Ohio River Valley.* Unpublished Ph.D. dissertation, Department of Anthropology, University of Kentucky, Lexington.

Pollack, David, and A. Gwynn Henderson
1992a Toward a Model of Fort Ancient Society. In *Fort Ancient Cultural Dynamics in the Middle Ohio Valley,* edited by A. Gwynn Henderson, pp. 281–294. Monographs in World Archaeology No. 8. Prehistory Press, Madison, Wisconsin.
1992b The Possible Role of Salt Production in Fort Ancient Cultural Development from A.D. 1200 to 1550. In *Long-Term Subsistence Change in Prehistoric North America,* edited by D. R. Croes, Rebecca A. Hawkins, and Barry L. Isaac, pp. 77–79. Research in Economic Anthropology, Supplement 6. JAI Press, Greenwich, Connecticut.
2000 Insights into Fort Ancient Culture Change: A View From South of the River. In *Cultures Before Contact: The Late Prehistory of Ohio and Surrounding Regions,* edited by Robert A. Genheimer, pp. 194–227. Ohio Archaeological Council, Cincinnati.

Pollack, David, and Cheryl Ann Munson
1989 Slack Farm, Union County, Kentucky: The Looting of a Late Mississippian Site. Prepared for the National Park Service. On file, Kentucky Heritage Council, Frankfort.

1996 Caborn-Welborn Ceramics from Slack Farm, Hovey Lake, and Caborn. Manuscript on file, University of Kentucky, Department of Anthropology, Lexington.

1998 Caborn-Welborn Ceramics: Intersite Comparisons and Extraregional Interaction. In *Current Archaeological Research in Kentucky,* vol. 5, edited by Charles D. Hockensmith, Kenneth C. Carstens, Charles Stout, and Sara J. Rivers, pp. 163–202. Kentucky Heritage Council, Frankfort.

2003 The Angel to Caborn-Welborn Transition in Southwestern Indiana, Northwestern Kentucky, and Southeastern Illinois. In *Facing the Final Millennium: Studies in the Late Prehistory of Indiana,* A.D. *700–1700,* edited by Brian Redmond and James R. Jones III, pp. 255–286. Indiana Department of Natural Resources, Division of Historic Preservation and Archaeology, Indianapolis.

Pollack, David, and Jimmy A. Railey

1987 *Chambers (15ML109): An Upland Mississippian Village in Western Kentucky.* Kentucky Heritage Council, Frankfort.

Pollack, David, A. Gwynn Henderson, and Christopher Begley

2002 Fort Ancient/Mississippian Interaction on the Northeastern Periphery. *Southeastern Archaeology* 21(2):206–220.

Powell, Mary Lucas, Mark R. Schurr, Wayna Roach, and Jeff Irwin

1996 The Bioarchaeology of Slack Farm: Demography, Diet, Skeletal Metrics, and Skeletal Pathology. Manuscript on file, University of Kentucky, Department of Anthropology, Lexington.

Railey, Jimmy A.

1992 Chipped Stone Artifacts. In *Fort Ancient Cultural Dynamics in the Middle Ohio Valley,* edited by A. Gwynn Henderson, pp. 137–169. Monographs in World Archaeology No. 8. Prehistory Press, Madison, Wisconsin.

Ramenofsky, Ann F.

1987 *Vectors of Death: The Archaeology of European Contact.* University of New Mexico Press, Albuquerque.

Rautman, Alison E.

1993 Resource Variability, Risk, and the Structure of Social Networks: An Example from the Prehistoric Southwest. *American Antiquity* 58(3):403–424.

Ray, Louis

1965 *Geomorphology and Quaternary Geology of the Owensboro Quadrangle, Indiana and Kentucky.* Professional Paper No. 488. U.S. Geological Survey, Washington, D.C.

Renfrew, Colin A.

1974 Beyond a Subsistence Economy: The Evolution of Social Organization in Prehistoric Europe. In *Reconstructing Complex Societies,* edited by C. B. Moore, pp. 69–85. American School of Oriental Research, Cambridge, Massachusetts.

Rindos, David, and Sissel Johannessen

1991 Human-Plant Interactions and Cultural Change. In *Cahokia and the Hinter-*

*lands: Middle Mississippian Cultures of the Midwest,* edited by Thomas E. Emerson and R. Barry Lewis, pp. 35–45. University of Illinois Press, Urbana.

Roach, Wayna

1995 The Application of Fluorine Dating at the Slack Farm Site, Union County, Kentucky. Paper presented at the 12th Annual Kentucky Heritage Council Archaeology Conference, Richmond, Kentucky.

Robinson, Kenneth W.

1982 *A Cultural Resource Assessment of the Tri-State Synfuels Project Areas.* Environmental Consultants, Inc., Lexington, Kentucky.

Rossen, Jack

1994 The Archaeobotanical Record of the Late Mississippian Caborn-Welborn Culture. Paper presented at the 54th Annual Meeting of the Southeastern Archaeological Conference, Lexington, Kentucky.

1995 The Archaeobotanical Record of the Late Mississippian Caborn-Welborn Culture: The Slack Farm, Caborn, and Hovey Lake Sites. Manuscript on file, University of Kentucky, Department of Anthropology, Lexington.

Sahlins, Marshall D.

1968 *Tribesmen.* Prentice-Hall, Englewood Cliffs, New Jersey.

Schortman, Edward M.

1989 Interregional Interaction in Prehistory: The Need for a New Perspective. *American Antiquity* 54(1):52–65.

Schortman, Edward M., and Patricia A. Urban

1992 Current Trends in Interaction Research. In *Resources, Power, and Interregional Interaction,* edited by Edward M. Schortman and Patricia A. Urban, pp. 235–255. Plenum Press, New York.

Schroeder, Sissel

2003 Inferences and Evidence: A Reconsideration of the Occupation History of Jonathan Creek. Paper presented at the 68th Annual Meeting of the Society for American Archaeology, Milwaukee.

Schurr, Mark R.

1992 Isotopic and Mortuary Variability in a Middle Mississippian Population. *American Antiquity* 57:300–320.

1994 Assessing the Maize Consumption of Fort Ancient and Middle Mississippian Populations of the Ohio Valley: New Stable Isotope Evidence. Paper presented at the 54th Annual Meeting of the Southeastern Archaeological Conference, Lexington, Kentucky.

Schwartz, Douglas W.

1961 *The Tinsley Hill Site: A Late Prehistoric Stone Grave Cemetery in Lyon County, Kentucky.* Studies in Anthropology No. 1. University Press of Kentucky, Lexington.

Seeman, Mark F., and Cheryl A. Munson

1980 Determining the Cultural Affiliation of Terminal Late Woodland-Mississippian Hunting Stations: A Lower Ohio Valley Example. *North American Archaeologist* 2(1):53–65.

Shennan, Stephen J.

1989 Introduction: Archaeological Approaches to Cultural Identity. In *Archaeological Approaches to Cultural Identity,* edited by Stephen J. Shennan, pp. 1–32. Unwin Hyman, London.

Shergur, Jason, Rachel S. Popelka, J. David Robertson, and David Pollack

2003 Distinct Chemical Patterns in Late Mississippian Caborn-Welborn Phase Ceramics of the Lower Ohio River Valley. *North American Archaeologist,* in press.

Sinopoli, Carla M.

1991 *Approaches to Archaeological Ceramics.* Plenum Press, New York.

Smith, Bruce D.

1978 Variation in Mississippian Settlement Patterns. In *Mississippian Settlement Patterns,* edited by Bruce D. Smith, pp. 479–502. Academic Press, New York.

1986 The Archaeology of the Southeastern United States: From Dalton to DeSoto, 10,500–500 B.P. In *Advances in World Archaeology,* vol. 5, edited by Fred Wendorf and A. E. Close, pp. 1–92. Academic Press, Orlando.

Smith, Bruce D. (editor)

1990 *The Mississippian Emergence.* Smithsonian Institution Press, Washington, D.C.

Smith, Gerald

1990 The Walls Phase and Its Neighbors. In *Towns and Temples Along the Mississippi,* edited by David H. Dye and Cheryl A. Cox, pp. 135–169. University of Alabama Press, Tuscaloosa.

Smith, Marvin T.

1987 *Archaeology of Aboriginal Culture Change in the Interior Southeast: Depopulation During the Early Historic Period.* Ripley P. Bullen Monographs in Anthropology and History, No. 6. University Press of Florida, Gainesville.

Spencer, Charles S.

1993 Human Agency, Biased Transmission, and the Cultural Evolution of Chiefly Authority. *Journal of Anthropological Archaeology* 12:41–74.

1994 Factional Ascendance, Dimensions of Leadership, and the Development of Centralized Authority. In *Factional Competition and Political Development in the New World,* edited by Elizabeth M. Brumfiel and John W. Fox, pp. 31–43. New Directions in Archaeology Series, Cambridge University Press, Cambridge.

Steponaitis, Vincas P.

1978 Location Theory and Complex Chiefdoms: A Mississippian Example. In *Mississippian Settlement Patterns,* edited by Bruce D. Smith, pp. 417–454. Academic Press, New York.

1983 *Ceramics, Chronology, and Community Patterns: An Archaeological Study at Moundville.* Academic Press, New York.

1986 Prehistoric Archaeology in the Southeastern United States, 1970–1985. *Annual Review of Anthropology* 15:363–404.

1991 Contrasting Patterns of Mississippian Development. In *Chiefdoms: Power,*

*Economy, and Ideology,* edited by Timothy Earle, pp. 193–228. Cambridge University Press, Cambridge.

Stuiver, M., and Pearson, G. W.
1993 High-precision Bidecadal Calibration of the Radiocarbon Time Scale, A.D. 1950–500 B.C. and 2500–6000 B.C. *Radiocarbon* 35:1–23.

Swanton, John R.
1911 *Indian Tribes of the Lower Mississippi Valley and Adjacent Coast of the Gulf of Mexico.* Bulletin 43. Bureau of American Ethnology, Washington, D.C.
1946 *The Indians of the Southeastern United States.* Bulletin 137. Bureau of American Ethnology, Washington, D.C.

Tainter, Joseph A.
1988 *The Collapse of Complex Societies.* New Studies in Archaeology Series. Cambridge University Press, Cambridge.

Tench, Pat
1996 Intrasample Homogeneity at Slack Farm: A Between-Cluster Anlaysis of Nonmetric Cranial and Postcranial Skeletal Traits. Manuscript on file, University of Kentucky, Department of Anthropology, Lexington.

Trigger, Bruce G.
1981 Prehistoric Social and Political Organization: An Iroquoian Case Study. In *Foundations of Northeast Archaeology,* edited by Dean R. Snow, pp. 1–50. Studies in Archaeology. Academic Press, New York.
1990 Maintaining Economic Equality in Opposition to Complexity: An Iroquoian Case Study. In *The Evolution of Political Systems: Sociopolitics in Small-Scale Sedentary Societies,* edited by Steadman Upham, pp. 119–145. Cambridge University Press, Cambridge.

Turnbow, Christopher A., and A. Gwynn Henderson
1992 Ceramic Analysis. In *Fort Ancient Cultural Dynamics in the Middle Ohio Valley,* edited by A. Gwynn Henderson, pp. 113–135. Monographs in World Archaeology No. 8. Prehistory Press, Madison, Wisconsin.

Wallace, Donald L., and J. B. Fehrenbacher
1969 *Soil Survey of Gallatin County, Illinois.* United States Department of Agriculture, Soil Conservation Service, Washington, D.C.

Walthall, John A.
1980 *Prehistoric Indians of the Southeast: Archaeology of Alabama and the Middle South.* University of Alabama Press, University, Alabama.

Waring, Antonio J., Jr., and Preston Holder
1945 A Prehistoric Ceremonial Complex in the Southeastern United States. *American Anthropologist* 47:1–34.

Webb, William S.
1952 *The Jonathan Creek Village.* Reports in Anthropology and Archaeology 8(1). University of Kentucky, Lexington.

Webb, William S., and William D. Funkhouser
1931 *The Tolu Site in Crittendon County.* Reports in Archaeology and Anthropology, 1(5). University of Kentucky, Lexington.

1932 *Archaeological Survey of Kentucky.* Reports in Archaeology and Anthropology 2. University of Kentucky, Lexington.

Welch, Paul D.

1991 *Moundville's Economy.* University of Alabama Press, Tuscaloosa.

Welch, Paul D., and C. Margaret Scarry

1995 Status-Related Variation in Foodways in the Moundville Chiefdom. *American Antiquity* 58:397–419.

Wesler, Kit W.

1992 Chronological and Spatial Perspectives on Ceramic Vessel Form at Wickliffe Mounds (15Ba4). In *Current Research in Kentucky,* vol. 2, edited by David Pollack and A. Gwynn Henderson, pp. 119–138. Kentucky Heritage Council, Frankfort.

1994 Historical Archaeology and Prehistory: Experimenting With Dating Formulas for Mississippi Period Ceramics. *Midcontinental Journal of Archaeology* 19(2):260–290.

2001 *Excavations at Wickliffe Mounds.* University of Alabama Press, Tuscaloosa.

Williams, Bill

1978 *A Sampler on Sampling.* John Wiley & Sons, New York.

Williams, Stephen

1990 The Vacant Quarter and Other Late Events in the Lower Valley. In *Towns and Temples Along the Mississippi,* edited by David H. Dye and Cheryl A. Cox, pp. 170–180. University of Alabama Press, Tuscaloosa.

Wobst, Martin

1977 Stylistic Behavior and Information Exchange. In *For the Director: Essays in Honor of James B. Griffin,* edited by Charles Cleland, pp. 317–342. Anthropological Papers No. 61. University of Michigan, Ann Arbor.

Work Projects Administration

1941 *Union County: Past and Present.* Schuhmann Printing Company, Louisville, Kentucky.

Wright, Henry T.

1984 Prestate Political Formations. In *On the Evolution of Complex Societies: Essays in Honor of Harry Holjer,* edited by Timothy Earle, pp. 41–78. Undena Publications, Malibu, California.

Yoffee, Norman, and George L. Cowgill (editors)

1995 *The Collapse of Ancient States and Civilizations.* University of Arizona Press, Tucson.

# Index